EVE OF DESTRUCTION

Somewhere in Europe, a brilliant man is working behind the scenes to gain a position of absolute power over the emerging New World Order.

Who is this Antichrist? Will he appear in our lifetime? What is the mysterious Mark of the Beast? Why is the number 666 so significant in the rise of the Antichrist? Does the Bible offer any hope of escape from the coming Great Tribulation? Is this the generation that will witness these incredible events? How should we respond in light of these prophecies being fulfilled in our day?

In this book we will examine hundreds of ancient biblical prophecies that reveal the answers to these questions and many others. We will explore the astonishing predictions concerning the Antichrist's dramatic rise to become dictator of the coming world government. These threats to our freedom and warnings of impending catastrophe demand our attention.

D0826807

Books by Grant R. Jeffrey

Armageddon: Appointment with Destiny
Heaven: The Last Frontier
*Messiah: War in the Middle East and the Road to
Armageddon*
Apocalypse: The Coming Judgment of the Nations

PRINCE OF DARKNESS

Antichrist
and the
New World Order

Grant R. Jeffrey

BANTAM BOOKS
New York • Toronto • London • Sydney • Auckland

PRINCE OF DARKNESS

A Bantam Book / published by arrangement
with Frontier Research Publications

PUBLISHING HISTORY
Frontier Research Publications edition published February 1994
Bantam edition / June 1995

Scripture quotations are from the New King James Version of the
Holy Bible, Copyrighted 1979, 1980, 1982 by Thomas Nelson,
Inc. Also quoted is (KJV), Authorized King James Version.

ISBN 0-553-56223-1

Published simultaneously in the United States and Canada

Bantam Books are published by Bantam Books, a division of Bantam Doubleday Dell Publishing Group, Inc. Its trademark, consist-
ing of the words "Bantam Books" and the portrayal of a rooster,
is Registered in U.S. Patent and Trademark Office and in other
countries. Marca Registrada. Bantam Books, 1540 Broadway, New
York, New York 10036.

PRINTED IN THE UNITED STATES OF AMERICA

RAD   0 9 8 7 6 5 4

Acknowledgment

Prince of Darkness is the result of thirty years of intense research and Bible study on the prophecies of the Bible. Over the last two thousand years many scholars have written about the mysterious individual known as the Antichrist. A number of writers that provided significant insights into the role of Satan's Prince of Darkness are listed in the select bibliography. However, the inspired Word of God has been my major source throughout these studies. My hope is that my research will help you understand the secret agenda of those who wish to replace our form of government with a one world government that will set the stage for the dictator of the coming New World Order. The prophecies should awaken us to the profound choices facing every human in the final decade of this century.

I dedicate *Prince of Darkness* to my wife Kaye and thank her for her inspiration and assistance in completing this book. Her commitment to Christ is demonstrated in every aspect of our publications, television programs and teaching ministry. I am grateful for the spiritual legacy of my parents, Lyle and Florence Jeffrey, that included a tremendous love for the Word of God and a longing for the return of Jesus Christ.

I trust *Prince of Darkness* will encourage you to study the prophecies of the Second Coming of Christ for yourself. You will discover the promises of Christ's triumphant victory over the forces of evil and the establishment of His righteous Kingdom.

Table of Contents

PRINCE OF DARKNESS
Antichrist and the New World Order

Introduction: Prince of Darkness 1

1. The Struggle for Planet Earth.............................13
2. The Battle Between Christ and Antichrist.................25
3. Ancient Writings About the Prince of Darkness 40

The Coming New World Order

4. Plans for a New World Order................................58
5. The Globalist Agenda for World Government.........75
6. The Assault on Your Freedoms 92
7. The Financial Road to World Government............105

The Rise of Satan's Prince

8. The Rise of the European Super State 115
9. Israel—The Key to World Government................129
10. America and the Coming Economic Crash 152
11. The Great Russian Deception.............................168
12. The Coming Russian Invasion
    of the Middle East..192
13. Will the Church Face the Antichrist?..................206

The Kingdom of the Antichrist

14. The Rise of the Prince of Darkness......................225
15. The Great Tribulation and the Wrath of God.....247
16. The Final Witnesses to the Coming Messiah.......261
17. The False Prophet and the Prince of Darkness....281
18. The Technology of the Mark of the Beast..........292
19. The Coming Inquisition...300
20. Antichrist in the Temple of God..........................309

Final Conflict - Final Victory

21. Is This the Generation of Christ's Return?..........320
22. The Battle of Armageddon....................................333
23. The Ultimate Victory of the Messiah...................344

Selected Bibliography...354

Introduction

Prince of Darkness

Somewhere in Europe, a brilliant man is working behind the scenes to gain a position of absolute power over the emerging New World Order. Someday this man will sell his soul to Satan to "receive the kingdoms of this world." The ancient prophecies of the Bible call the coming world dictator the "Antichrist." He is destined to lead the world during the terrible period of time the prophets call the Great Tribulation. The actions of this individual will profoundly alter the lives of every man and woman on the earth during the coming years, culminating in the Battle of Armageddon. It is our destiny to live in the generation the ancient sages called the "birth pangs of the Messiah."

Who is this Antichrist? Will he appear in our lifetime? What is his origin? Where does he receive his supernatural power? What is the purpose of the mysterious Mark of the Beast? These questions have aroused the interest of students of prophecy for thousands of years. In this book we will examine hundreds of biblical prophecies that reveal the answers to these questions and many others. We will analyze the predictions of the Antichrist's dramatic rise to become dictator of the New World Order during a future political crisis. We will explore the writings of ancient Jewish and Christian scholars to reveal their penetrating insights into the astonishing events leading to the rise and fall of the Antichrist. *Prince of Darkness* will identify the incredible Bible prophecies about this awesome personality who will rule the planet. We will focus on developments in the political, military and intelligence fields that will enable this man to establish his reign of terror. Initially the Antichrist will succeed in establishing a totalitarian one-world government to dominate the earth. However, his evil career will be shattered at the Battle of Armageddon. There he will meet his ultimate destruction when Jesus Christ, the King of kings, returns in glory to establish His kingdom on earth.

The prophecies of the Bible enable us to understand the rapidly unfolding events in our generation. They indicate that we are entering the time the ancient sages called the "footsteps of the Messiah." The incredible fulfillment of biblical prophecies in our day demands more of a response than mere intellectual curiosity. This book will challenge you to consider the evidence that convinces many that we are living in the "last days" described by the prophets of the Bible. I challenge you to examine the Bible's prophecies referred to in the following pages. Compare them with recent history and the current unfolding events in our world. It is impossible that these historical events precisely have followed the prophecies of the Bible by chance alone. The odds against these prophecies being fulfilled by chance are simply astronomical. Examine the evidence and come to your own conclusion. If the Bible is wrong in its predictions, then it is simply the writing of religious men and you can safely ignore it. However, if the Bible's prophecies are truly being fulfilled, then it must be the inspired Word of God. These warnings of impending catastrophe cannot be ignored.

We need to consider the words of Jesus Christ: "He who believes in the Son has everlasting life: and he who does not believe the Son shall not see life, but the wrath of God abides on him" (John 3:36). Jesus asked His disciples a vital question, "Who do you say that I am? And Simon Peter answered and said, 'You are the Christ, the Son of the living God' " (Matthew 16:15,16). Each of us must answer that question about Christ for ourselves. What does Christ mean to you? If the Bible is truly the Word of God, as the prophetic evidence proves, our answer to that question will determine our eternal destiny. We cannot evade it. After we examine the hundreds of fascinating prophecies about the Antichrist and the coming Messiah throughout this book, we will return to this pivotal question about our attitude to Christ.

The Scriptures declare that the only hope for man lies in abandoning our sinful rebellion and returning to a loving relationship with God. Those who believe the truth of the Bible are called to be "witnesses" of Christ's message to our world. Our role as a Christian witness demands an active, not passive, involvement in the lives of our fellowmen. It requires a willingness to pay the price of a personal commitment to our coming Messiah. Our belief in the imminent Second Coming of Christ should motivate each of us to a renewed love of Christ and a willingness to witness to our brothers about His salvation. This hope will also purify our walk before the Lord, as John said, "And everyone who has this hope in Him purifies himself, just as He is pure" (1 John 3:3).

Sir Isaac Newton, one of the greatest scientists in history, was fascinated by prophecy. In his brilliant study *Observations on Daniel and the Revelation* he wrote about the fundamental importance of prophecy for Christians. "The giving ear to the Prophets is a fundamental character of the true Church. For God has so ordered the Prophecies, that in the latter days the wise may understand, but the wicked shall do wickedly, and none of the wicked shall understand. . . . The authority of the Prophets is divine, and comprehends the sum of religion. . . . Their writings contain the covenant between God and His people, with instructions for keeping this covenant, instances of God's judgments upon them that break it: and predictions of things to come."

For a thousand years the ancient Roman empire strode across the world as an iron colossus crushing all opposition beneath its iron legs. Its emperors ruled their conquered lands with absolute dictatorial power. The Bible foretold a miraculous revival of the Roman Empire in the last days that will be led by the final world dictator. The identity and character of this man was revealed through a series of prophetic titles including "the prince," the "man of sin" and the "son of perdition." He will rule the earth during its final crisis just before the return of Jesus Christ as the true Messiah. Hundreds of prophecies about this terrible personality are found throughout the Old and New Testaments. Both Jewish and Christian prophetic literature contain fascinating analysis and commentary about this satanically inspired leader. In addition we will examine many secular prophecies from various cultures that predict the earth will undergo a terrible period of persecution under a satanic leader before the arrival of the Messiah.

The man known as the Antichrist will dominate the political, military and religious events of the last days. It is vital that we understand the Bible's revelations about the Antichrist. The people who live under his rule will face a terrible choice when he claims to be "god on earth." He will demand that everyone worship him and receive the Mark of the Beast. The Scriptures declare that anyone who receives his Mark will be damned forever to hell. The martyrs who reject the Antichrist's claims and worship Jesus Christ will receive the gift of eternal life in heaven. If we are to have a clear understanding of the amazing times we live in, we need to examine the prophecies about the revival of the Roman Empire and its coming dictator—the Antichrist.

For thousands of years Bible students contemplated the ancient prophecies about the Antichrist and the coming apocalypse. It was difficult to visualize how biblical prophecies such as attacks from the air, the poisoning of one-third of the planet, and the deaths of billions could actually be fulfilled. Should the prophecies be interpreted literally as referring to actual future events? Were the prophecies only spiritual symbols of the ultimate war between good and evil? However, our generation has witnessed the horrible reality of the Holocaust, thermonuclear weapons, biological warfare and decades of totalitarian control over half of the human race. For the first time in history we possess the technologies and weapons that can destroy life on this planet. These incredible innovations have changed history forever. Some scientists fear that these "doomsday" technologies will put an end to human history. Every lethal weapon system developed to date, no matter its horror, has been used in war. The collapse of the Soviet Union has opened a Pandora's box of forty-five thousand nuclear weapons falling into the hands of unknown individuals in potentially irresponsible countries. The awful potential of chemical, biological and nuclear weapons in the hands of terrorists and unstable regimes such as Libya and Iraq has produced nightmare scenarios for the intelligence agencies of the West. This situation must give any serious observer grave concern that we stand in danger of disasters and plagues far worse than the Black Plague of the fourteenth century. There is still no antidote to the bubonic plague that devastated Europe six hundred years ago. Bubonic plague, anthrax and many other deadly plagues are now in the weapons laboratories of over 40 countries, including Syria, Iran, Iraq and Libya.

In addition to Scriptural prophecies, many non-biblical predictions appeared during the last few decades that point to the approaching crisis for the human race. A secular magazine, *Omni*, devoted its entire January, 1992, issue to predictions about the year 2000. People as diverse as social scientists, military strategists and physicists have begun to "think about the unthinkable." *Omni* magazine reported Dr. Michael Grosso's comments about the change in people's perceptions of the possibility of Armageddon. "There is something different about 2000, however. Since 1945 it began to be technologically feasible to end life on this planet." A University of Connecticut psychologist, Kenneth Ring, stated in the article, "Apocalyptic thinking is in the air. As we approach that subjective date, 2000, images stored in the collective unconscious begin to populate our dreams and visions."

We are rapidly approaching the greatest crisis in human history. The choices facing mankind are truly awesome in their magnitude and terrible consequences. The world is drifting toward a whirlpool of unimaginable destruction. This apocalyptic disaster could mean the end of human life; perhaps the end of history itself. Rampant nationalism and ethnic hatreds, combined with the devastating power of nuclear and biological weapons, could easily lead to horrors that would eclipse the worst excesses of World War II. On the other hand, the New World Order could easily become a vehicle for a totalitarian government that would extinguish all hope of human freedom forever. Lord Acton said, "Absolute power corrupts absolutely." A strong case can be made for the argument that human freedom can only exist for a long period of time in a political system that divides power among different groups to create natural checks and balances between competing interests. However, current trends are leading us inexorably toward a New World Order in which all power on the planet will be possessed in one supranational institution led by one supreme leader.

Even if the first few leaders of the world government are benevolent, eventually an evil individual will arise who will use this absolute power to create a world-wide totalitarian dictatorship. Can you imagine what life would have been like if Adolph Hitler had succeeded in establishing a worldwide Third Reich? The history of this century suggests that there is no shortage of candidates with dictatorial tendencies. Once this individual seizes power there will be no opposing nation states left to resist such a totalitarian world government. Where would the suffering citizens of such a worldwide dictatorial government turn for relief from the long dark night of slavery? The world would descend into a black abyss of totalitarian power beyond our darkest nightmares. The awesome weapons and the overwhelming surveillance powers of such a "Big Brother" government would leave people without hope or the possibility of escape. This desperate nightmare will become real if the proponents of this "Brave New World" succeed in achieving their goal of a one-world government.

The Scriptures indicate that man is approaching a profound crisis beyond anything ever experienced by humans. Only God can save the planet from the approaching disaster. The prophets promise that this crisis will be resolved by the miraculous intervention of the Messiah who will save mankind from destruction and establish the Kingdom of God on earth. The Great Tribulation will end in a cataclysmic battle between the worldwide dictatorship of the Antichrist and the coming Messiah. Christ's victory over Satan's Prince of Darkness will bring about the realization of all our hopes and dreams of "a paradise regained" under the rule of the Messiah-King.

THE IMPORTANCE OF BIBLE PROPHECY

Throughout history men have wondered what tomorrow will hold. Hopes and fears for tomorrow have inspired men to speculate about the future of life on earth. The libraries are filled with philosophical and religious speculations including future utopias and doomsday scenarios. However, for millennia, only one book has claimed to exclusively and accurately predict man's ultimate destiny. That book of course is the Bible, the Word of God. Any serious seeker of truth must confront this basic question: Is the Bible true? Is the Bible truly the Word of God? Does it contain the authentic revelation of God about our spiritual destiny and the future of man? In the course of this study we will explore many of the Bible's prophecies that have already been fulfilled with absolute precision. These perfectly fulfilled prophecies are the strongest credentials that the Bible is precisely what it claims to be—the inspired Word of God. These precisely fulfilled prophecies should motivate us to carefully examine those predictions that relate to our immediate future.

From Genesis to Revelation the Word of God unfolds a prophetic program revealing the past, present and future. From the first prediction of the Messiah's virgin birth in Genesis 3:15 to the closing prophecies of the book of Revelation the central role of Jesus Christ is revealed through the unfailingly accurate predictions of the ancient prophets. The prophet Isaiah declared that God alone knows the future: "Behold, the former things have come to pass, and new things I declare; before they spring forth I tell you of them" (Isaiah 42:9). No other religious book contains detailed predictions of future events, because no one but God can predict the future accurately. Satan, himself, cannot prophesy accurately. If the devil could predict the future with precision he would inspire his New Age followers to do so to impress mankind. A detailed examination of prophecies outside the Bible will prove that these predictions are almost always both vague and incorrect. The study, *The Shattered Crystal Ball*, discussed in my book *Armageddon—Appointment with Destiny* examined the track record of the predictions made by these modern secular prophets and psychics. The three-year study revealed that an average of 98 percent of these secular prophecies were wrong! Only the Bible contains accurate predictions because only God can prophesy the future.

As Isaiah declared, "Thus says the Lord, the King of Israel, and his Redeemer, the Lord of hosts: 'I am the First and I am the Last; besides Me there is no God. And who can proclaim as I do? Then let him declare it and set it in order for Me, since I appointed the ancient people. And the things that are coming and shall come, let them show these to them' " (Isaiah 44:6–7). Jesus Christ was also a prophet. He offered the evidence of the fulfillment of His predictions as proof of His claim to be the promised Messiah. "Now I have told you before it comes, that when it does come to pass, you may believe" (John 14:29). For thousands of years the prophecies of the Bible have foretold the rise and fall of nations and empires. Without exception, the Bible's revelations have proven true. Therefore, as we witness the fulfillment of these biblical prophecies in our generation, we need to seriously consider its warnings about the coming crisis. The great challenge for Christians today is not just to understand the prophecies about Israel and the nations; but rather to do those things that our Lord requires of us.

The prophets revealed God's plan to redeem mankind through the death, resurrection and ultimate victory of Jesus Christ. The Bible itself attests to the critical nature of prophecy. "We also have the prophetic word made more sure, which you do well to heed as a light that shines in a dark place, until the day dawns and the morning star rises in your hearts" (2 Peter 1:19). The purpose of Bible prophecy is to illuminate God's continuing plan of redemption for mankind through His Son Jesus the Messiah.

The Holy Spirit declared that "all Scripture is given by inspiration and is profitable for reproof, for correction, for instruction in righteousness" (2 Timothy 3:16). The word "inspired" in the original language means "God-breathed." This reveals that these prophecies were supernaturally given to the biblical writer by the divine will of God. Since one-quarter of the Bible is prophecy this is a vital part of God's message to mankind. Therefore, if we want to understand our role in this generation we need to become familiar with the prophetic message of the coming Kingdom of God. Christ commands us to "study to show thyself approved unto God, a workman that needeth not to be ashamed, rightly dividing the word of truth" (2 Timothy 2:15 KJV). The Apostle Peter points out that "prophecy never came by the will of man, but holy men of God spoke as they were moved by the Holy Spirit" (2 Peter 1:21). In one passage the Apostle Paul indicated that the Jews tragically rejected Jesus Christ as their Messiah because they failed to understand the prophecies. "For those who dwell in Jerusalem, and their rulers, because they did not know Him, nor even the voices of the Prophets which are read every Sabbath, have fulfilled them in condemning Him" (Acts 13:27).

Tragically, many religious leaders today are as unconcerned about prophecy as rulers in Jerusalem were two thousand years ago. Despite clear warnings in the Bible to heed the warnings of prophecy, many remain uninterested. The study of Bible prophecy has been my passion for many years. When I was fourteen my father took me to a prophecy conference in Ottawa, Canada. My parents love the Lord and the Word of God. My mother and father gave me a precious spiritual legacy, their love of prophecy. I began to purchase specialized commentaries and old books on prophecy, history and archeology. After almost thirty years of study and the accumulation of some five thousand volumes from around the world I still have the same passion for prophecy imparted to me so long ago. Several years ago I was given the opportunity to share my love to prophecy with a group of Bible college students. I fell in love with teaching. Over the years I learned many things from the great Bible teachers whose works I studied. One of the key concepts was this: whoever teaches the Word of God honestly should not think of himself as a scholar; he should always remain a student sharing with other students. It is my hope that I will be able to share with you as a fellow student my gleanings and discoveries concerning the prophecies of the coming Antichrist and the glorious return of our Messiah.

The precise fulfillment of prophecy provides unshakeable proof that the Bible is the inspired Word of God. Fulfilled prophecy is the signature of God on the pages of Scripture proving that the Bible is His inspired revelation to mankind. Prophecy reveals God's purposes from creation to eternity enabling us to understand our role in His unfolding plan. It introduces us to the Bible's great themes including the coming redemption of the earth from the curse of sin. Far from being a narrow area of study, prophecy sets the stage for the study of every other area of theology. *Prince of Darkness* will examine the prophecies relating to the Antichrist, his rise and fall and the coming of the Messiah to establish His Kingdom on earth.

PRINCIPLES OF PROPHETIC INTERPRETATION

There are a number of key principles that are vital for us to keep in mind if we are to understand the ancient prophecies. These principles of interpretation, known as hermeneutics, have stood the test of time over many centuries. The Christian writers of the first centuries of our era, including the New Testament writers, interpreted the Old Testament prophecies according to these principles. Some of the most vital principles are: (1) Take Scripture literally—except where the context makes it clear that the statement or vision is symbolic. (2) The symbols used by the prophets can be interpreted correctly by referring to the Bible's own usage of that symbol in related passages. When symbols are used, they point to something that is literal. (3) When figurative language is used, the inspired writer used the best language available to describe the spiritual vision he received. (4) When the plain sense of the prophecy makes common sense, we should take the words at face value in their ordinary and literal meaning. We should remember that the Bible was written and intended to be read by ordinary men and women—not just scholars. (5) Humility is required. Dogmatism should be avoided. The nature of Bible prophecy is such that some predictions will only be understood when they have been fulfilled.

Many in the Church view prophecy pessimistically

believing it is only concerned with "doom and gloom."
However, I look at prophecy with great hope and opti-
mism because it contains God's greatest promise to man.
The Lord has promised to send His Messiah to establish
the Kingdom of God on earth. After the terrible crisis
known as the Great Tribulation is finished, God promised
that man will finally enjoy the peace, justice and joy that
has eluded man since the Garden of Eden. Finally, when
the Messiah reigns, the torture chambers will be destroyed; the world will never again experience war, violence or starvation. The guns will be silenced forever. Men
and women will finally experience the love, beauty and
peace we lost so long ago. Christ's victory over Satan's
Prince of Darkness will establish true justice and righteousness forever. The ancient prophecy of the coming
Messiah will finally be fulfilled. "But with righteousness
He shall judge the poor, and decide with equity for the
meek of the earth . . . The wolf also shall dwell with the
lamb, the leopard shall lie down with the young goat,
the calf and the young lion and the fatling together; and
a little child shall lead them . . . They shall not hurt nor
destroy in all My holy mountain, for the earth shall be
full of the knowledge of the Lord as the waters cover the
sea" (Isaiah 11:4,6,9).

In *Prince of Darkness* we will investigate the secret
agenda of the New World Order and its goals of a totalitarian world government. The roles of America, Russia
and the European Community will be analyzed together
with the prophetic outline of events setting the stage for
the final crisis of history. Powerful financial, military, and
political groups have marshalled their forces to achieve
the goals of this New World Order. The growing technological and legal attacks on our privacy and financial independence will be analyzed in light of Bible prophecy.
The prophetic role of the Antichrist and his seven-year
treaty with Israel are vital keys to understand the timing
of the approaching crisis. These issues will profoundly affect the life of every person on earth in the coming years.

How can people survive the coming Kingdom of the
Antichrist? What is the Mark of the Beast? Why is the
number 666 so significant in the rise of the Antichrist?
Does the Bible offer any hope of escape from the coming

Great Tribulation? Is this the generation that will witness these incredible events? What should you or I do in light of these prophecies being fulfilled in our day? These questions and others will be examined in depth in this fascinating study.

Finally, *Prince of Darkness* will analyze the tremendous prophecies that reveal the incredible future millennial kingdom awaiting us when the Antichrist and the forces of evil are defeated. The Bible assures us that the coming Messiah will defeat Satan's plan to destroy mankind. The prophecies point to a future reality beyond our finest dreams when Christ will finally establish His Messianic Kingdom on earth. The ancient prophet received a vision of the coming triumph of the Messiah. "Of the increase of His government and peace there will be no end, upon the throne of David and over His kingdom, to order it and establish it with judgment and justice from that time forward, even forever" (Isaiah 9:6,7).

1

The Struggle for Planet Earth

It is fascinating that the first prophecy in the Bible foretells both the coming of the Messiah and His ultimate victory over the Antichrist. "And I will put enmity between you and the woman, and between your seed and her seed; He shall bruise your head, and you shall bruise His heel" (Genesis 3:15). From the first prophecy in Genesis to the last book of the Bible, Revelation, there is a curious parallel in the series of predictions about the coming Messiah and the future Antichrist. The opening and closing chapters of the Scriptures focus on the career and final destruction of Satan's *Prince of Darkness*. Unless we study these prophecies about Christ and Antichrist we will not understand God's prophetic program to redeem the earth.

While historical events appear to occur by chance, the Scriptures reveal that history is unfolding according to the precise plan of God outlined thousands of years ago. A curious statement in Genesis 15:16 tells us that the length of Israel's exile in Egypt was determined in relation to the "iniquity of the Amorites" not yet being complete. This wicked race of Amorites opposed Israel and God. However, God delayed Israel's exodus from Egypt and the conquest of Canaan until the Amorites completed their sinful rebellion and their hour of judgment arrived. The Lord told Abraham that the Jews would remain slaves in Egypt because of their sins until He would return them to the Promised Land after four hundred years. "But in the fourth generation they [Israel] shall return here, for the iniquity of the Amorites is not yet complete" (Genesis 15:16). When the sins of the Amorites were full, God delivered the order for their judgment and extermination. Our evil generation will not reach the moment of its prophesied judgment until its transgressions and sins have also come to the full. When will this occur? The Bible tells us that the sins of this generation will come to the full in the last days. During the Great Tribulation the majority of men will not only reject Jesus Christ as God's promised Messiah, but they will knowingly accept Satan's Antichrist in the place of Christ. Scripture indicates that the final apostasy will be the most blatant and open sinful rebellion against the will of God.

For the first time in history, man has developed doomsday weapons capable of devastating vast areas of our planet. Since God gave man the stewardship of this Paradise we have polluted our planet's environment, poisoned the precious water, and eroded the fertile topsoil. In the last few decades we have burned the irreplaceable Amazon rain forest and turned northern Africa into a desert. Most of these depredations of the earth have occurred due to our sinful pride and greed. Rather than tend our treasured earth as good stewards, we have selfishly despoiled our planet in our short-sighted grasp for profit and gain. The sinful rebellion during the Great Tribulation will produce the most appalling evil, violence, debauchery, blasphemy and persecution in human history. The "mystery of iniquity" that has worked in secret for thousands of years will finally, in the last days, openly manifest its spirit of lawlessness in the evil blasphemy of the "man of sin," the coming Antichrist.

THE FIRST PROPHECY ABOUT THE ANTICHRIST

The first prediction about the Antichrist appears in Genesis 3:15: "And I will put enmity between you and the woman, and between your seed and her seed; He shall bruise your head, and you shall bruise His heel." In this remarkable prophecy we also find the first promise of the virgin birth of Jesus in the unusual expression "her seed." The word seed normally occurs in Scripture in connection with "the seed of the father." This is the only place in the Hebrew Scriptures that the phrase "her seed" occurs. This unusual phrase predicts the unique virgin birth of Jesus; that He would be the Seed of the woman, not the natural seed of a father. The verse also reveals the future conflict between the coming Antichrist, the "seed" of Satan and Jesus Christ, "her Seed." Just as Jesus, the son of Mary, was uniquely the "seed" of the woman, the Antichrist will in some mysterious way be the "seed" of Satan. The vision foresaw the crucifixion of Jesus when Satan was able to "bruise his heel." Finally, Jesus Christ's ultimate defeat of Satan was prefigured in the expression "her seed . . . shall bruise your head." The first messianic prophecy illustrates the age-long conflict between Satan and Jesus Christ. It also predicts the long struggle between Satan and Israel, represented by the woman. Genesis 3:15 may also imply that the Antichrist will present himself as a counterfeit messiah as indicated more clearly by other prophecies.

SATAN ATTEMPTS TO RULE THE EARTH AS "GOD"

One of the most fascinating prophecies in the Bible is found in Ezekiel 28. It details the astonishing career of Satan from his creation in heaven, his rebellion, his possession of the soul of Antichrist and his ultimate doom. Though some cults believe that Satan is an evil god, this prophecy clearly tells us that Satan is not an eternal being or a god. Jesus Christ created Satan in the dateless past as an angel. In Ezekiel's prophecy Satan appears under the prophetic title of the "Prince of Tyre." However the description clearly reveals that the subject is Satan, not an earthly prince. "Son of man, say to the prince of Tyre, 'Thus says the Lord God: "Because your heart is lifted up, and you say, 'I am a god, I sit in the seat of gods, in the midst of the seas,' yet you are a man, and not a god, though you set your heart as the heart of a god . . . You were the seal of perfection, full of wisdom and perfect in beauty. You were in Eden, the garden of god . . . The workmanship of your timbrels and pipes was prepared for you on the day you were created . . . You were the anointed cherub who covers; I established you; you were on the holy mountain of God; you walked back and forth in the midst of fiery stones. You were perfect in your ways from the day you were created, till iniquity was found in you" ' " (Ezekiel 28:2,12,13–15).

This passage reveals Satan's creation as an "anointed cherub" who was "perfect in your ways" until his sinful pride led him to rebel against God. He may once have guarded the throne of God with the other cherubim described in the book of Revelation. Unlike the ugly depictions of Satan found in mediaeval art he was created as "the seal of perfection, full of wisdom and perfect in beauty." The Scriptures tell us that he succeeded in taking a third of the angels of heaven with him when he rebelled in his fall from grace. Satan attempted to take the place of God in the universe when he claimed, "I am a god, I sit in the seat of gods." This began his fateful war that was destined to drag all of mankind into thousands of years of sinful rebellion against our Creator.

The prophet Isaiah tells us about the fall of Satan. "How you are fallen from heaven, O Lucifer, son of the morning! How you are cut down to the ground, you who weakened the nations! For you have said in your heart: 'I will ascend into heaven, I will exalt my throne above the stars of God; I will also sit on the mount of the congregation on the farthest sides of the north" (Isaiah 14:12–13). He was created as a "son of the morning" or "morning star" without sin. However, because of his pride in his beauty and wisdom, Satan rose in rebellion against God. Certainly, he was present with the other "sons of God" at the moment of this world's creation. God asked Job, "Where were you when I laid the foundations of the earth . . . When the morning stars sang together, and all the sons of God shouted for joy?" (Job 38:4,7).

The Bible calls Satan "the prince of the power of the air" (Ephesians 2:2) because he had great power over the earth since the fall of Adam and Eve. Jesus referred to Satan as a king of an evil kingdom in Matthew 12:24–30. Daniel 10:13 refers to demonic fallen angels that are associated with particular kingdoms on this planet. "But the prince of the kingdom of Persia withstood me twenty-one days; and behold, Michael, one of the chief princes, came to help me, for I had been left alone there with the kings of Persia." This verse suggests the extent of the continuing spiritual warfare in the heavens that will ultimately culminate in the Battle of Armageddon. Ephesians 6:12 warns Christians: "For we do not wrestle against flesh and blood, but against principalities, against powers, against the rulers of the darkness of this age, against spiritual hosts of wickedness in the heavenly places."

Since his fall, Satan has retained access to some part of the heavenlies and also the earth. He does not rule in hell as mediaeval mythology suggested. The devil will not descend to hell until Jesus casts him into the Lake of Fire after his final rebellion at the end of the Millennium. Satan's access to the heavenlies will end half-way through the seven-year treaty when he and his angels are cast out of heaven by Michael, the archangel. John prophesied that when "war broke out in heaven: Michael and his angels fought against the dragon; and the dragon and his angels fought, but they did not prevail, nor was a place found for them in heaven any longer" (Revelation 12:7). When Satan is thrown from heaven to the earth he will totally possess the soul of the wicked dictator who will take over the revived Roman Empire. At that point this man will become the Antichrist, Satan incarnate. From that moment he will force men to worship him as god.

The book of Job tells us that Satan appeared with the other angels, before God's throne to accuse Job to the Lord. "Now there was a day when the sons of God came to present themselves before the Lord, and Satan also came among them" (Job 1:6). We are also told in the New Testament that the devil accuses us to God daily and will continue until he is cast out of heaven. When that occurs the angels will rejoice. As the prophet John recorded in his vision, "Then I heard a loud voice saying in heaven, 'Now salvation, and strength, and the kingdom of our God, and the power of His Christ have come, for the accuser of our brethren, who accused them before our God day and night, has been cast down' " (Revelation 12:10).

In my book *Heaven—The Last Frontier* I examined the biblical account of the great Flood. Satan tried to demonically corrupt all "the daughters of men" through impregnating them by fallen angels. His evil purpose was to eliminate the possibility of the Messiah's birth by defiling every family on earth through demonic relations. If he had succeeded, not a single pure woman would remain to give birth to the promised Seed, the Messiah. Noah and his family was the last family on earth that was not demonically corrupted. The Bible declares that Noah was "perfect in his generations." In mercy God sent the Flood to destroy the wicked generation. The Lord supernaturally preserved Noah's pure family on the ark to allow the future Messiah to be born to redeem mankind. Later, after the Flood, Satan again tried to corrupt the races living in Canaan, as Genesis records "There were giants on the earth in those days, and also afterward, when the sons of God came in to the daughters of men and they bore children to them. Those were the mighty men who were of old, men of renown" (Genesis 6:4). This demonic invasion explains the great battles of the Israelites against the giant races when Israel entered the Promised Land. Joshua records, "There we saw the giants (the descendants of Anak came from the giants); and we were like grasshoppers in our own sight, and so we were in their sight" (Numbers 13:33). The Lord miraculously delivered Israel from the superior military power of their huge enemies so they could inhabit the Promised Land in fulfillment of God's covenant with Abraham.

Satan tempted many of Israel's kings and religious leaders to rebel against God. However, the Lord established His unshakable covenant and revelation through His inspired Word written by His great prophets during a period spanning sixteen centuries. The Bible, containing God's promise of a Messiah-Redeemer and thousands of prophecies of His ultimate victory over evil, became the greatest treasure of mankind. The Word of God has been a dominant influence on men, nations and historical events over the last three and a half thousand years. It is impossible to fully appreciate or understand Western culture and history without considering the tremendous role played by the Holy Scriptures. Satan, over the centuries, has tried to destroy the Bible in a multitude of ways including burning, banning, discounting and academic criticism. However, despite these continuing attacks by Satan, the Bible remains the most widely read and most influential book in the history of man.

SATAN BATTLES CHRIST AT THE CROSS

Satan thought he had defeated God's plan to redeem mankind when Christ was crucified. The devil, though "wiser than Daniel" was unable to realize that the Cross, which appeared to represent Christ's defeat, ultimately won salvation for all who would trust in Jesus. The Lord used "the foolishness of the cross" to confound the wise and defeat Satan's plan to ensnare men's souls. On Good Friday it appeared that Satan had won. Jesus was dead, his followers dispersed. But Resurrection Sunday came. The grave was opened and all could see the evidence of Christ's victory over death and sin. As I indicated in my book *MESSIAH*, the historical evidence proving the death and resurrection of Jesus is overwhelming for any honest student who will fairly examine the records. The truth of Christ's resurrection is fundamental to God's plan to redeem mankind from the curse of sin and death.

The Church was transformed by the resurrection of Jesus. It immediately began to fulfill the Great Commission of Christ, "Go therefore and make disciples of all the nations, baptizing them in the name of the Father and of the Son and of the Holy Spirit" (Matthew 28:19). Initially, Satan used the emperors and his pagan followers in Rome to oppress and persecute the Christians. Millions of Christians were tortured and killed for their faith in ten succeeding waves of persecutions under the demonically inspired Roman emperors. The brave deaths of these martyrs forced the world to examine what inspired these men and women to such profound faith and conviction. As a result of their faithful witness during the first three hundred years of pagan persecution, almost half of the Roman Empire became followers of Jesus of Nazareth.

After Emperor Constantine became a follower of Christ in A.D. 300, he transformed the legal position of the church from an outlaw organization to the officially sanctioned state church. Satan then tried to subvert the Church from within by infiltrating the newly legalized Christian church. In the final analysis this subtle attack was a far greater threat to the true Church than the former open attacks by the pagan emperors. Previously, under severe persecution, only true believers joined the church. However, once the church was officially sanctioned by the state, thousands of unrepentant pagans joined in their desire for potential social, financial, and political advantage. Over the centuries the Roman state church adopted many Babylonian mystical religious features to appeal to these new pagan "converts." False pagan practices were introduced over the centuries including veneration of images, false miracles, elevation of the clergy above the worshipers and rampant corruption. The religious transformation was so profound that a believer from the first century would not have recognized the official state church of the tenth century as Christian. Many believers who held to the true faith were forced to go underground.

SATAN'S WAR AGAINST THE MEDIAEVAL CHURCH

Corruption and pagan practices entered the official church at all levels during the Mediaeval period. Satan almost smothered the burning embers of truth that survived from the early faith of the first century Christians. Evil church officials amassed political and financial powers in an unholy alliance with secular leaders, including kings and officials. Laws were passed forbidding any Christian layman to possess the Scriptures or to worship as the New Testament commanded. The Western world spiritually entered "the Dark Ages" for many centuries. Despite these centuries of satanic attacks on the truth, millions of Christians in Europe and Africa resisted the inquisition and religious corruption. The Waldenses, the Albigenses, the Cathari and many other groups of Bible-believing Christians held to the apostolic faith despite centuries of trials, torture and death. They secretly copied manuscripts of the Bible and smuggled the Scriptures from city to city to share with the underground church. The act of reading the Bible was illegal according to official church law. In fact, it remained illegal for a layman to possess a Bible in Italy until 1870.

The ancient Waldenses were Christians that had continued in the faith since separating from the increasingly corrupt official state church in the seventh century. They lived in the high mountain valleys in inaccessible areas of northern Italy where they could worship Christ as the New Testament commanded. The Waldenses and their fellow believers were pre-reformation Protestants long before Martin Luther posted his Ninety-Five Theses on the church door at Wittenberg in A.D. 1520. Luther proclaimed the recovery of these first century truths creating the Protestant Reformation. However, he acknowledged that he was simply carrying on the true faith of earlier underground Christian groups, such as the Waldenses.

The Waldenses possessed a manuscript dated A.D. 1120 called "A Treatise concerning Antichrist" containing their understanding of Bible prophecy. Their interpretations were obviously conditioned by their terrible experiences of torture and murder under the Inquisition. They thought the Antichrist and the Great Whore of Babylon from the book of Revelation were identical, though we understand them to be two different things. "Antichrist is a falsehood, or deceit varnished over with the semblance of truth, and of the righteousness of Christ and of His spouse, yet in opposition to the way of truth, righteousness, faith, hope, charity, as well as to moral life . . . it is a system of falsehood. The system of iniquity . . . taken together, comprises what is called Antichrist or Babylon, the fourth beast, the whore, the man of sin, the son of perdition . . . He is termed Antichrist, because being disguised under the names of Christ and of His church and faithful members, he opposes the salvation which Christ wrought out." This short passage indicates they did not develop a detailed analysis of the fulfillment of prophecies. The Waldenses focused on the larger issues dealing with Satan's attack on the true church and connected the biblical prophecies of the Antichrist and Babylon with the great evils they were facing during their struggle for religious freedom.

In Provence, France, toward the end of the thirteenth century, the mediaeval Catholic Church launched a crusade against the Albigenses. They beheaded over fifty thousand Albigensian Christians during one twenty-four hour period because they would not renounce the true faith. The history of that tragic period reveals that over a million Christians were savagely tortured and killed in southern France alone (Jones' *History of the Christian Church* - 1826). Only heaven will reveal the total record of the courageous faith of these believers who stood without flinching against all the attacks of Satan. Throughout Europe millions of underground believers held on to the true faith in the gospel of Jesus Christ during the centuries of persecution.

SATAN'S FUTURE ATTACK DURING THE TRIBULATION PERIOD

In Ezekiel 28, God addressed Satan as "the prince of Tyre." This prophecy confirms the Genesis account that the serpent (Satan) was in the Garden of Eden. However, Ezekiel assures us that, despite Satan's wisdom and power, he will finally be defeated by Christ when he makes his great attack against God using the Antichrist. "Therefore thus says the Lord God: 'Because you have set your heart as the heart of a god, behold, therefore, I will bring strangers against you, the most terrible of the nations; and they shall draw their swords against the beauty of your wisdom, and defile your splendor. They shall throw you down into the Pit, and you shall die the death of the slain in the midst of the seas' " (Ezekiel 28:6–9).

When God created man in the Garden of Eden all of creation, including man was "good." However, because the Lord valued our freedom so highly He allowed Satan to tempt man to rebel against God. This temptation was the same one that had ensnared Satan—to become as god. Satan offered Eve that chance to "know good and evil" as god if she would sinfully rebel against God's expressed command. The tragic result of man's rebellion was the loss of innocence and the promised blessing that God had intended for a holy people. The gates of Eden were closed to man. Fortunately, God's love would not abandon man. The Lord prophesied that he would send His Messiah to defeat Satan and restore man's relationship with God.

THE COMING ANTICHRIST

In later chapters of this book we will examine many biblical prophecies that warn of the coming Antichrist and the reign of terror in the last days before the return of the Messiah. "And it was granted to him to make war with the saints and to overcome them. And authority was given him over every tribe, tongue, and nation . . . He was granted power to give breath to the image of the beast, that the image of the beast should both speak and cause as many as would not worship the image of the beast to be killed" (Revelation 13:7,15). Christ promised that the war for the planet earth will end with His total victory over evil when He returns to establish His kingdom. However, the prophets warn that the Antichrist and Satan will unleash unprecedented spiritual warfare against the tribulation saints during the Great Tribulation.

THE PRINCE OF THIS WORLD

Scripture tells us that at the very moment of Christ's apparent defeat on the cross He won the battle for the earth and the souls of men. "Now is the judgment of this world; now the ruler [Prince] of this world will be cast out. And I, if I am lifted up from the earth, will draw all peoples to Myself" (John 12:31,32). The final judgment of this world and the defeat of Satan, the prince of this world, was made certain when Jesus uttered the words, "It is finished." The subsequent spiritual battles over the following two thousand years will culminate in the dramatic victory of Jesus Christ at the Battle of Armageddon. However, from the standpoint of eternity, the victory over

Satan was won by Christ two thousand years ago at Calvary. When Christ rose from the grave, triumphing openly over Satan, He defeated death. Jesus resurrected a great company of Old Testament saints to prove His divine victory over death and sin (Matthew 27:52,53).

THE ANTICHRIST—SATAN'S "PRINCE OF DARKNESS"

Man joined in Satan's rebellion against God when Adam and Eve sinned in the Garden of Eden. God entrusted the stewardship of the planet to man. In a sense, man's sinful rebellion had the effect of mortgaging the "dominion" of earth to Satan. This transfer of dominion allowed Satan to become the prince of this world and the king of this evil kingdom. From that moment man has been living in enemy-occupied territory awaiting the triumphant return of our Messiah-King. The Old Testament law provided for a kinsman-redeemer to repurchase a relative's property that had been forfeited to a lender. This principle is illustrated in the Bible when Boaz, an ancestor of Jesus, redeemed Ruth. As Boaz fulfilled the role of kinsman-redeemer, Jesus Christ will return in the last days to redeem the earth from its curse and bondage under the control of Satan.

The Bible contrasts the roles of Jesus as the "light of the world" with the spiritual "darkness" that represents our sinful rebellion against God. John says that Jesus was, "the true Light which gives light to every man who comes into the world" (John 1:9). In explaining the continuing conflict with Satan, he declares, "And this is the condemnation, that the light has come into the world, and men loved darkness rather than light, because their deeds were evil" (John 3:19).

As we approach the climactic events of the Great Tribulation the Bible warns that Satan will soon offer the world his counterfeit messiah, the Antichrist, his *Prince of Darkness*. The greatest conflict in history will end with his spectacular defeat at the hands of Christ. In the following chapters we will investigate the prophecies of the rise and fall of this Antichrist and his New World Order.

2

The Battle Between Christ and Antichrist

From the moment of Satan's fall from grace at the beginning of time, an ongoing spiritual warfare has affected every life on this planet. Though we are often unaware of this battle, the Bible assures us that "we do not wrestle against flesh and blood, but against principalities, against powers, against the rulers of the darkness of this age, against spiritual hosts of wickedness in the heavenly places" (Ephesians 6:12). Behind every battle and war on earth there occurred a spiritual battle against "the rulers of the darkness of this age." This "ruler of the darkness" is Satan. In the last great conflict of the age he will ultimately do battle with Christ in the guise of a satanically possessed man known as Antichrist, the *Prince of Darkness*.

THE CONTRAST BETWEEN CHRIST AND ANTICHRIST

The origin, nature and purpose of Christ and Antichrist are fundamentally opposed. This list of titles and characteristics reveals the vast gulf between the careers and destinies of Jesus and the one who will soon imitate Him in his attempt to deceive the world.

THE CHARACTERISTICS OF CHRIST AND ANTICHRIST

Christ	Antichrist
The Truth	The Lie
The Holy One	The Lawless One
The Man of Sorrows	The Man of Sin
The Son of God	The Son of Perdition
The Mystery of Godliness	The Mystery of Iniquity

These opposing biblical names show the opposing and contrasting natures of Christ and Antichrist. Every characteristic and title of Christ is derived from His holy nature as our righteous Lord. The Antichrist's character and titles are derived from his origin as the "seed" of Satan, the "father of lies." While Jesus represents the truth of God, the Antichrist will deceive the earth through his lies. Every action of Christ illustrated His holiness while the man of sin will despise God's holy laws. Jesus was known as the man of sorrows bearing the weight of our sins to the Cross while the title, the man of sin, reflects Antichrist's rebellious career. The Antichrist is known as the son of perdition because his career will be marked by destruction of his enemies. Jesus, the Son of God, came to do the will of His heavenly Father. Jesus represents the mystery of godliness demonstrating the Father's infinite mercy for mankind. The Antichrist is the mystery of iniquity. There is a mystery involved in why God allows Satan to continue when He could destroy him at any time. However, Jesus Christ will finally destroy Satan's Prince of Darkness "by the brightness of His coming." The contrast between the two is summed up in these opposing descriptions.

THE CONTRAST BETWEEN CHRIST AND ANTICHRIST

Feature:	Christ	Antichrist
Origin	Heaven	The Bottomless Pit
Nature	The Good Shepherd	The Idol Shepherd
Destiny	To Be Exalted on High	To Be Cast Down to Hell
Goal	To Do His Father's Will	To Do His Own Will
Purpose	To Save the Lost	To Destroy the Holy people
Authority	His Father's Name	His Own Name
Attitude	Humbled Himself	Exalts himself
Fruit	The True Vine	The Vine of the earth
Response	Despised	Admired

The Antichrist will attempt to counterfeit the biblical prophecies about the coming Messiah in his attempt to deceive Israel and the nations about his true identity. However, he will ultimately fail. In every single area, Jesus Christ and the Antichrist are fundamentally opposed. While it is worthwhile to note the differences between their divergent roles in prophecy, it is also helpful to consider our own spiritual life and goals in light of the "spirit of antichrist" that prevails in our world. Are we seeking to exalt ourselves or are we modelling our life after Christ in humbling ourselves? Are we seeking to do the will of our heavenly Father as Jesus did, or are we trying to accomplish our own will? The spirit of this age is self-exaltation. The musical tune containing the lyrics "I did it my way" is illustrative of the self-indulgent attitude of our generation. This spirit of selfishness, lawlessness and anarchy is truly the spirit of antichrist manifesting itself in our generation. Jesus Christ came to serve mankind, to help others and to save the lost. His servant spirit stands in stark contrast to the proud and boastful attitudes so common in our day. A recent psychological study of graduates of "assertiveness training" courses indicated that the majority were very unhappy as individuals. In contrast, the message of Christ is that service to others leads to the greatest happiness.

TWO OPPOSING TRINITIES

The mystery of God's nature is presented to us throughout the Bible as a Trinity. While the Scriptures declare "Behold O Israel, the Lord your God is One" both the Old and New Testaments affirm repeatedly that God manifests Himself in the form of three persons, the Father, the Son and the Holy Spirit. The Bible also reveals that Satan, the great enemy of God, will present himself in a triune manner in the last great conflict of this age. Opposing the Father, Son and Holy Spirit we find a satanic trinity composed of Satan, Antichrist and the False Prophet. The Bible declares that Jesus Christ, though He is truly God, came to "do the will of His Father." The Antichrist will be a man totally possessed by Satan's power as Daniel 8:24 declares: "His power shall be mighty, but not by his own power." His purpose will be to serve his father Satan. Just as the Holy Spirit directs men to worship the Father through Jesus Christ, the False Prophet will force men living during the Great Tribulation to worship Satan through the person of the Antichrist. In Revelation 13:12 the prophet John tells us that the False Prophet, "causes the earth and those who dwell in it to worship the first beast, whose deadly wound was healed."

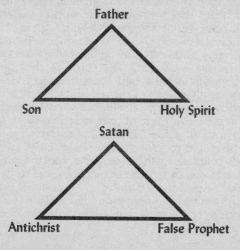

OLD TESTAMENT TITLES OF
THE ANTICHRIST

Throughout the Old Testament the prophets foretold the
ultimate conflict between God's Chosen People and Satan's world dictator. From Genesis to Malachi the prophets described this enemy of God under a variety of names
and titles that indicate his rise, his career and his ultimate
defeat at the hands of the coming Messiah. An examination of these prophetic titles will reveal the nature and
character of the Antichrist.

SATAN'S SEED

"And I will put enmity between you and the woman, and
between your seed and her Seed; He shall bruise your
head, and you shall bruise His heel" (Genesis. 3:15). The
first prophecy in the Bible was made by God to Satan (the
serpent) in the presence of Adam and Eve. The Lord
prophesied about the Antichrist under the title "your
seed" because he will attempt to do the will of his father,
Satan, the "father of all lies." It describes the eternal
hatred between Christ and Satan's seed. There is also a
suggestion in this prophecy that there is something
supernatural and satanic about the birth of this evil
man.

THE KING OF BABYLON

"Take up this proverb against the king of Babylon, and
say: 'How the oppressor has ceased, the golden city
ceased!' " (Isaiah 14:4). Isaiah addresses the Antichrist
by the title, the "king of Babylon," because he will make
the rebuilt city of Babylon one of his capitals during his
brief reign. Both Isaiah and Revelation reveal that the
city of Babylon will be rebuilt and finally destroyed by
fire from heaven from God during the Great Day of the
Lord. To date, the Iraqi government of President Saddam
Hussein has spent more than $800 million in rebuilding
the city. The wicked city of Babylon will be burned at the

same time the Antichrist is destroyed by Christ at His return.

PRINCE OF TYRE

"Son of man, say to the prince of Tyre, 'Thus says the Lord God: "Because your heart is lifted up, and you say, 'I am a god, I sit in the seat of gods, in the midst of the seas,' yet you are a man, and not a god, though you set your heart as the heart of a god" ' " (Ezekiel 28:2). The prophet Ezekiel called the Antichrist the "prince of Tyre" in his prophecy declaring that though he will be possessed by Satan "yet you are a man, and not a god." He will oppose and exalt himself to be worshiped as God exactly as Satan originally attempted to rebel and be worshiped by the fallen angels as god.

THE LITTLE HORN

"I was considering the horns, and there was another horn, a little one, coming up among them, before whom three of the first horns were plucked out by the roots. And there, in this horn, were eyes like the eyes of a man, and a mouth speaking pompous words" (Daniel 7:8). The prophet Daniel calls him "a little horn" in contrast to the ten horns that represent ten nations arising out of the boundaries of the ancient Roman Empire. Though endowed by Satan with supernatural powers he will be a man. He will be a great and powerful speaker, impressing people with his brilliant speech.

A KING OF FIERCE COUNTENANCE

"And in the latter time of their kingdom, when the transgressors have reached their fullness, a king shall arise, having fierce features, who understands sinister schemes" (Daniel 8:23). The Antichrist will be a "king" (or prince) with "fierce features." This prophecy indicates that he will have a striking appearance and will possess great personal power. The phrase, "when the transgressors have reached their fullness" reminds us that the fulfillment of these prophecies will not occur until man's sinful rebellion reaches the breaking point. There is a final point where the Lord draws the line and He will not allow man to go any farther without receiving the judgment of God. As Genesis 6:3: "My Spirit shall not strive with man forever." Mankind's final appointment with destiny is quickly approaching.

THE PRINCE WHO IS TO COME

"And after the sixty-two weeks Messiah shall be cut off, but not for Himself; and the people of the prince who is to come shall destroy the city and the sanctuary. The end of it shall be with a flood, And till the end of the war desolations are determined" (Daniel 9:26). The unusual grammar in this verse reveals that the Antichrist will be a "prince" who will lead the revived Roman Empire. Daniel's prophecy of the "people . . . who . . . shall destroy the city and the sanctuary" was fulfilled precisely in A.D. 70 when the Roman (people) armies burnt the Temple and Jerusalem. Since "the prince that shall come" will come out of the Roman people, scholars conclude that the Antichrist will arise and take over the ten nations of the revived Roman Empire.

THE WILLFUL KING

"Then the king shall do according to his own will: he shall exalt and magnify himself above every god, shall speak blasphemies against the God of gods, and shall prosper till the wrath has been accomplished; for what has been determined shall be done" (Daniel 11:36). In total contrast to Jesus who came to "do His Father's will" the Antichrist will "do according to his own will." The coming *Prince of Darkness* will be a true child of this age of assertiveness, self-promotion and self-will. He will exalt his own sinful desires against all opposition until he is defeated by Christ.

THE ASSYRIAN

"Therefore thus says the Lord God of hosts: 'O My people, who dwell in Zion, do not be afraid of the Assyrian. He shall strike you with a rod and lift up his staff against you, in the manner of Egypt' " (Isaiah 10:24). While the prophets clearly identify the Antichrist as a Jew who will rule the Roman Empire, we are also told of his future connection with the Middle East and the rebuilt capital city of Babylon. Ancient Assyria, the enemy of Israel, occupied the same geographic area as Babylon until its defeat in 608 B.C. Possibly the prophet identified the Antichrist as "the Assyrian" because the world dictator will be the enemy of Israel just as Assyria was in the ancient past.

THE IDOL SHEPHERD

"For, lo, I will raise up a shepherd in the land, which shall not visit those that be cut off, neither shall seek the young one, nor heal that that is broken, nor feed that that standeth still: but he shall eat the flesh of the fat, and tear their claws in pieces. Woe to the idol shepherd that leaveth the flock! the sword shall be upon his arm, and upon his right eye: his arm shall be clean dried up, and his right eye shall be utterly darkened" (Zechariah 11:16,17, KJV).

In contrast to Jesus Christ, the Good Shepherd, who gives His life for His sheep, the Antichrist is called the "idol shepherd." His purpose, as an evil shepherd, will be to use and destroy the sheep for his own benefit. Zechariah may call him the idol shepherd because the False Prophet will set up an idol or statue of the Antichrist in the rebuilt Temple to be worshiped by men (Revelation 13:14,15). It is possible that Zechariah was indicating that the Antichrist will be wounded in the arm and right eye by a sword wound. Revelation 13:3 tells us that someone will kill the Antichrist with a "wound to death." John also reveals that this wound will be made with a sword (Revelation 13:14). The prophet declares, "his deadly wound was healed. And all the world marveled and followed the beast" (Revelation 13:3).

SPOILER AND EXTORTIONER

"Let My outcasts dwell with you, O Moab; be a shelter to them from the face of the spoiler. For the extortioner is at an end, devastation ceases, the oppressors are consumed out of the land" (Isaiah 16:4). The prophet Isaiah describes the Antichrist as "the spoiler" and "the extortioner" because he will attempt to destroy all who resist his claims to be "god" while using extortion to gain great riches. In Isaiah's prophecy we see a parallel with Revelation chapter 12 where the "woman" (Israel) flees for three and a half years to a place of divine safety in the wilderness of Moab (Jordan) to escape the Antichrist after he defiles the rebuilt Temple.

THE WICKED

"With righteousness He shall judge the poor, and decide with equity for the meek of the earth; He shall strike the earth with the rod of His mouth, and with the breath of His lips He shall slay the wicked" (Isaiah 11:4). Paul also calls the Antichrist by this name. "And then shall that Wicked be revealed, whom the Lord shall consume with the spirit of his mouth, and shall destroy with the brightness of his coming" (2 Thessalonians 2:8, KJV). Both Isaiah and the Apostle Paul describe the Antichrist as the "wicked" because he will give himself entirely to Satan's evil designs to destroy God's people and laws. Despite Satan's initial success, the prophets declare that Jesus Christ will "destroy with the brightness of his coming." In Revelation John reveals that "the beast was captured and with him the false prophet . . . These two were cast alive into the lake of fire burning with brimstone" (Revelation 19:20).

NEW TESTAMENT TITLES OF ANTICHRIST

The New Testament prophets from Matthew to Revelation warn about the last great enemy of God who will oppress the tribulation believers during the last days. While some of the New Testament prophets, like the Apostles Paul and John, use the same titles as the Old Testament prophets, many of the names applied to the Antichrist are new. The names and descriptions in these New Testament prophecies tell us more about the Antichrist's rise to power and warn of his worldwide reign of terror.

THE MAN OF SIN

"Let no one deceive you by any means; for that Day will not come unless the falling away comes first, and the man of sin is revealed, the son of perdition" (2 Thessalonians 2:3). Paul promises us that the Great Day of the Lord will not come until the "falling away comes first." Other prophecies also warn about the religious apostasy of the last days. The Antichrist will only be revealed at the appropriate time after God removes His restraining power, the Holy Spirit.

THE SON OF PERDITION

"For that Day will not come unless the falling away comes first, and the man of sin is revealed, the son of perdition," (2 Thessalonians 2:3). He is called the "son of perdition" because Antichrist, as the seed of Satan, is destined to destroy and to be destroyed by God. He is the personification of lawlessness. He will be sent to perdition in hell, because of his sinful rebellion, just as Judas Iscariot, the other "son of perdition." The Apostle Paul called the Antichrist the "son of perdition" in contrast to Jesus "the son of God."

ANTICHRIST

"Little children, it is the last hour; and as you have heard that the Antichrist is coming, even now many antichrists have come, by which we know that it is the last hour" (1 John 2:18). "Who is a liar but he who denies that Jesus is the Christ? He is antichrist who denies the Father and the Son" (1 John 2:22). The name "antichrist" is the most commonly used title to describe the last great enemy of mankind. The name suggests both his total opposition to Christ and his wicked attempt to counterfeit Christ. The Bible indicates that he will imitate and emulate the true Messiah to deceive men about his true identity. He will try to fulfill the Old Testament prophecies regarding Jewish expectations of the coming Messiah. Remember that Jesus Himself warned that "many will come in My name saying 'I am the Christ.' " The False Prophet "makes fire come down from heaven" (Revelation 13:13) in his attempt to fulfill the role of the expected prophet Elijah as the forerunner of the Messiah.

THE FIRST HORSEMAN—THE RIDER ON THE WHITE HORSE

"And I looked, and behold, a white horse. And he who sat on it had a bow; and a crown was given to him, and he went out conquering and to conquer" (Revelation 6:2). John's vision in the Apocalypse reveals that the Antichrist will initially present himself as the great peacemaker. He will deceive many people with a false peace. The first horseman on the white horse is a symbol of the Antichrist coming in false peace. Notice that he holds a bow with no arrow representing disarmament and peace. Yet he "went out conquering and to conquer" just as the prophets warned. In the same deceitful manner of Adolph Hitler earlier in this century, he will use peace treaties and agreements to disarm his enemies. The white horseman of false peace will be followed immediately by the Red Horseman of war who will "take peace from the earth."

THE FIRST BEAST

"Then I stood on the sand of the sea. And I saw a beast rising up out of the sea, having seven heads and ten horns, and on his horns ten crowns, and on his heads a blasphemous name" (Revelation 13:1). He is identified as the first "beast" and is seen rising "out of the sea" representing the world of politics and, possibly, the Mediterranean Sea. The "beast" is a symbol of the Antichrist in some passages. In other verses the symbol of the "beast" stands for the ten-nation kingdom with its leader.

THE NUMBER OF THE BEAST

"Here is wisdom. Let him who has understanding calculate the number of the beast, for it is the number of a man: His number is 666" (Revelation 13:18). This passage indicates that the Mark of the Beast, which will be used as a totalitarian control device to enforce the worship of the man of sin, will be connected with the name of the Antichrist. The numerical value of his name in the Greek or Hebrew language will be connected with 666. This will be discussed in detail in a later chapter.

ANTICHRIST WILL COME IN HIS OWN NAME

"I have come in My Father's name, and you do not receive Me; if another comes in his own name, him you will receive" (John 5:43). Hundreds of specific prophecies point to Jesus of Nazareth as the promised Messiah of the Jews. He fulfilled the prophecies to the letter, spoke "with authority," performed countless miracles including raising people from the dead. Yet, despite this overwhelming evidence, many in Israel and other nations rejected the claims of Jesus as the Messiah-King. The tragic rejection of Christ's message by both the Jews and the Gentiles led directly to the Cross. This postponed the promise of the kingdom for Israel. Two thousand years of exile from the Promised Land followed. Christ warned Israel that although they rejected Him who came in the name of His Father, the Jews would one day accept for a time the false claims of the Antichrist as their promised Messiah. He warned, "if another comes in his own name, him you will receive." The false messiah and his False Prophet will launch the worst period of persecution in the history of the world, known as the "time of Jacob's trouble."

Since the prophecies tell us that the Antichrist will present himself to Israel as the Messiah many scholars have concluded that he must be Jewish. Certainly no religious Jew would dream of accepting a Gentile as the Messiah of Israel. Jesus Himself continually warned of the false messiah in the last days. As the following chapters indicate, the False Prophet will certainly present himself as the prophet Elijah and seek to counterfeit his miracle of "bringing fire down from heaven." Obviously, the False Prophet must be a Jew to imitate Elijah.

The Nature of Antichrist

The Antichrist is a liar because his father is Satan, the "father of lies" (John 8:44). His whole career from beginning to end will be marked by deceit and lies. Yet the people will accept his lies because they love darkness rather than light. The Apostle John describes the nature of the spirit of Antichrist. He declares, "Who is a liar but he who denies that Jesus is the Christ? He is antichrist who denies the Father and the Son" (1 John 2:22). The Bible declares that anyone who denies that Jesus is the Messiah is denying the Father and the Son and has adopted the spirit of Antichrist.

The Antichrist Spirit of this Age

John also tells us that "every spirit that does not confess that Jesus Christ has come in the flesh is not of God. And this is the spirit of the Antichrist, which you have heard was coming, and is now already in the world" (1 John

4:3). This passage confirms the other Scriptures that tell us that the Spirit of God reveals the truth to us as it did to the Apostle Peter. If someone refuses to accept that Jesus came "in the flesh" he is rejecting the Word of God. The Antichrist spirit that denies that Christ came in the flesh two thousand years ago is the same spirit of unbelief that denies that Christ will literally come again in the flesh. Today there are many both within and outside the Church who deny the doctrine of the literal return of Jesus Christ. Some wish to "spiritualize" the prophecies and interpret them as allegories. They often ridicule those who believe that there are still prophecies to be fulfilled as literally as those fulfilled in the past. John warned that the "spirit of Antichrist" had already entered the world in his day. The widespread denial and ridicule of Christ's return is another sign that the spirit of Antichrist is being manifested today.

One of the most curious of the prophecies about the man of sin was written by the prophet Daniel. He warned: "He shall regard neither the God of his fathers nor the desire of women, nor regard any god; for he shall magnify himself above them all" (Daniel 11:37). This vision has puzzled many people but it would seem to confirm that the Antichrist will be a Jew since it declares he won't have "regard" for "the God of his Fathers." That expression is used in the Bible only in connection with Jews. If he was a pagan, God would not point out his rejection of the pagan faith of his fathers as a point of condemnation. Furthermore, this verse tells us he will not "regard . . . the desire of women." Some have suggested that this means he will be a eunuch or a homosexual. While that is possible, it is more probable in the context that Daniel is referring to the fact that he will have no "regard" for the "desire of [Jewish] women" to bear the Messiah as their son. Since the time of Moses, devout Jewish women have prayed for the privilege of bearing the promised redeemer, the Messiah-King. The whole context of this prophecy is religious and this appears to be the preferred interpretation.

This continuing struggle between Christ and Antichrist will reach its final conclusion after the concluding three-and-a-half years of "hell on earth" known as the Great Tribulation. In the balance of this book we will examine the Bible's prophecies of the incredible events that will transform life on this planet in the momentous years just ahead of us.

3

Ancient Writings About the Prince of Darkness

The Scriptures contain thousands of specific prophecies that God will send His Messiah to redeem mankind and establish His kingdom of righteousness at the end of this age. Yet, the Bible also warns that a False Messiah will arise in the last days to plunge the world into a cataclysmic crisis. Throughout history hundreds of prophecies have been precisely fulfilled, especially in this century. The Lord declared that these fulfilled prophecies are the unquestionable proof that He is in control of the future. "I have declared the former things from the beginning; they went forth from My mouth, and I caused them to hear it. Suddenly I did them, and they came to pass" (Isaiah 48:3). The focus of many of the Bible prophecies is the approaching age of the Messiah.

Through centuries of bitter exile the Jews longed for their coming Messiah who would redeem the earth from the curse of sin and suffering. The rabbis and sages wrote about their hopes and fears for this awesome period that became known as the *Ikveta de Meshicha*, the "birthpangs of the Messiah." Just as a woman endures pain and danger to give birth to her child, the years preceding the Messiah's appearance will be like the "birthpangs" of a woman. Today, after the miraculous return of the exiles to the Promised Land, we are entering the most exciting and dangerous period in history. The fulfillment of the dreams of forty generations of Jewish exiles is at hand. The prophecies of a coming Messiah have comforted millions of Jews and Christians that God will finally redeem the earth from the curse of sin and suffering. This chapter will explore the prophetic hopes and fears of both Jews and Christians about the "birthpangs of the Messiah."

MOSES MAIMONIDES' FAITH IN THE COMING MESSIAH

The belief in the Messiah and the ultimate redemption of Israel is one of the most basic of Jewish religious beliefs. The Jewish people comforted themselves during their centuries of exile by remembering the prophecies of the coming Messiah who will return the captives to their homeland and re-establish the throne of David. This fervent expectation was codified in A.D. 1200 by the great Jewish scholar Moses Maimonides in his *Thirteen Principles of Faith*. One of those principles is as follows: "I believe with perfect faith in the coming of the Messiah. Even if he delays I will wait every day for him to come."

Rabbi Moses Maimonides claimed that anyone who did not believe in the Messiah or long for His coming actually denied the Torah, the law of Moses. This messianic vision is the great inspiration that motivated and instilled hope in the heart of Jews for thousands of years. Tragically, this messianic expectation will one day lead many in Israel to initially accept the Antichrist's and False Prophet's messianic claims. Later, when Antichrist defiles the rebuilt Temple, Israel will recognize him as an evil imposter. Many Jews will form part of the "remnant" during the Tribulation period who will flee into the wilderness to escape the Antichrist. In this chapter we will examine the writings of a number of ancient Jewish and Christian writers to further our understanding of how they interpreted the prophecies about the Man of Sin.

THE BOOK OF ZERUBBABEL

This apocalyptic book of late Jewish origin refers to the false messiah by the name "Armillus." He is also known as "Romulus" which revealed his connection to Rome. The Jewish sages say he will be the head of idolatry, the tenth king of Rome. They believe Armillus will go to Jerusalem after the War of Magog and slay the first Jewish messiah, Messiah the son of Joseph. This writer expects the second messiah, Messiah the son of David, will come to destroy Armillus. The Targums, ancient Jewish paraphrases of the Bible, also identified Daniel's "prince who is to come" (9:26) as a leader of the Roman Empire. Many rabbis believe the last great enemy of Israel will arise from Rome. The Emperor Hadrian destroyed over a million and a half Jews on the ninth day of Av, A.D. 135 in his savage defeat of the Bar Kochba Rebellion. Several rabbis speak of the "spirit of Hadrian" rising in the last days to attack Israel until the Messiah defeats him.

THE MESSIAH AND THE REBUILDING OF THE TEMPLE

The ancient rabbis believed that Zechariah and Ezekiel predicted that the Messiah would restore the *Bet Hamikdash*, the Holy Temple, in the last days. After predicting the miraculous return of the exiles to the Promised Land, Ezekiel prophesied: "Moreover I will make a covenant of peace with them, and it shall be an everlasting covenant with them; I will establish them and multiply them, and I will set My sanctuary in their midst forevermore" (Ezekiel 37:26).

Moses Maimonides also wrote about Jewish messianic expectations in connection with the building of the Third Temple. In his fourteenth volume of the Mishneh Torah he declared, "In the future the King Messiah will arise and renew the Davidic dynasty, restoring it to its initial sovereignty. He will rebuild the Temple and gather the dispersed remnant of Israel" (Halachah 11:1). The majority of Jewish commentators interpreted the prophecies to teach that the Messiah would build the Third Temple himself. Zechariah 6:12 declares, "Thus says the Lord of hosts, saying: 'Behold, the Man whose name is the Branch! From His place He shall branch out, and He shall build the temple of the Lord.' "

However, a number of other sources take the position that the Temple will be built by the Jewish people or by God just before the coming of the Messiah. These sources include the *Zohar* 1:28a, 183b and the *Rosh Hashanah* 30a. Several Jewish commentators tried to reconcile these two apparently contradictory positions. Of course Christians understand that the Bible teaches that both positions are correct and can be reconciled. The prophecies teach that the Jewish people, inspired by God, will rebuild the Third Temple in Jerusalem on the Temple Mount. Then, after the defilement of the Temple by the Antichrist, the Messiah will defeat him in battle during the Great Day of the Lord. Then the Messiah will cleanse and sanctify the Third Temple. When He establishes the Kingdom He will build the fourth Temple north of Jerusalem as described in detail by Zechariah 6:12 and Ezekiel chapters 40 to 48. The Millennial Temple is predicted to have walls over a mile in length. This vast size would not fit in the whole of Jerusalem, let alone on the Temple Mount. Ezekiel indicates that it will be located in the section of land known as the prince's portion (Ezekiel 45:7) about twenty-five miles north of Jerusalem in a new Millennial city of the Messiah (Ezekiel 40 to 48).

This Jewish expectation that the Messiah will rebuild the Temple may explain why many in Israel will accept the Antichrist as Messiah. If this false Messiah actually enables Israel to rebuild the third Temple many Jews would accept this as the Antichrist's credentials to be accepted as their true Messiah. The ninety-year-old Lubavitcher Rabbi Menachem Schneerson, whose followers have declared that he is the Messiah, also points to the rebuilding of the Temple as the supreme sign of the coming Messiah. In his recent book on the Messiah, *I Await His Coming Every Day*, Rabbi Schneerson discussed the growing hopes of Jews for their coming Messiah.

Elijah the Prophet

The Jewish sages expect Elijah the Prophet to appear as a forerunner of the Messiah as detailed by the prophet Malachi. "Behold, I will send you Elijah the prophet before the coming of the great and dreadful day of the Lord. And he will turn the hearts of the fathers to the children, and the hearts of the children to their fathers, lest I come and strike the earth with a curse" (Malachi 4:5,6). The sages believe that the prophecies of the rebuilding of the Temple and the division of the land (Ezekiel 40 to 48) cannot be fulfilled unless someone identifies every Jew's proper tribal lineage (*Arachin* 32b and *Hilchot Shemitah Veyovel* 10:8,9). They interpreted Malachi's prophecy that Elijah "will sit as a refiner and a purifier" (3:3) to indicate that Elijah will return from heaven to supernaturally determine the tribal identities and lineage of all the Jews worldwide. . . . They also believe he will identify who is qualified to be Kohanim (priests) or proper Leviyim (Levites) in the resumed Temple worship.

When the Jews returned from their captivity in Babylon, Nehemiah determined the true lineage of each Jewish family based on witnesses. Without the genealogical records that were lost when the Temple was burned, they could not determine who truly belonged to the priesthood "till a priest could consult with the Urim and Thummim" (Ezra 2:63). The sages believe that, in the age of the Messiah, a priest will stand up "with the Urim and Thummim." They hope this will occur when Elijah returns with the breastplate of the High Priest. The Urim and Thummim was lost in the destruction of Solomon's Temple by the Babylonians in 587 B.C. The device was connected with the Breastplate of the High Priest and supernaturally revealed the will of God for Israel. The book of Revelation declares that God will choose twelve thousand Jews from each of the twelve tribes as His special 144,000 witnesses. The prophet Ezekiel tells us that God will divide the Promised Land between the twelve tribes in the Millennium (Ezekiel 47 and 48). How will the Jews learn their proper tribal identity? Today the only Jews who can definitely determine their tribal origin are those named Levi or Cohen, indicating they belong to the Levites or

Kohanim, the "sons of Aaron." It is possible that God will use Elijah as one of the two witnesses to miraculously determine the proper tribal identities to facilitate this choosing of the 144,000 Jewish witnesses during the tribulation period.

THE TALMUD

In the New Testament Jesus Christ described the prophetic events just before His return as "the beginnings of sorrows." The Jewish sages call this time of trouble the "Ikvot Meshicha"—"the Time just before the Messiah." The Talmud is a group of writings composed by the rabbis during their exile from Jerusalem. From 100 B.C. to A.D. 400 the great rabbis in Babylon and in Tiberias on the shores of Lake Galilee codified Jewish beliefs and interpretations of the Law. The Jews believed that Moses transmitted these instructions orally through a series of some fifty "receivers" who faithfully preserved the instructions of God given to Moses on Mount Sinai. During the leadership of Rabbi Judah this oral tradition was finally recorded in writing known as the "Talmud." Throughout the Talmud the great sages interpreted the Bible's prophecies about the last days and the time of the coming of the Messiah.

The Talmud lists the prophetic signs that will point to the coming of the Messiah: an increase in oppression, rampant inflation, pride, irresponsible government, wars, widespread poverty, despising of wisdom, lack of respect for elders and righteous men, and the breakup of families. Additionally, they speak of other problems as final signs: famine, epidemics and plagues, blasphemy, international warfare, unspeakable suffering, hatred and betrayal, evil government, hatred of scholarship and religion. The sages called these terrible events the "birthpangs of the Messiah." The fear of these "birthpangs of the Messiah" led some Jewish rabbis to say, "Let the Mashiach [Messiah] come, but let him come at a time when I will not see him." Though they long for the Messiah's deliverance of the Chosen People, their fear of the terrible events leading to His coming caused some rabbis to pray that he comes after they have safely "gone to their fathers."

The rabbinic authorities do not see all the signs of the birthpangs of the Messiah in negative terms. Some of the prophetic signs are positive, including: rising prosperity in some places, growth in Torah study, great scientific advances, a time of miracles. The Talmud contains many prophetic speculations about the nature and career of the future Messiah. Tragically these expectations will prepare some in Israel to initially accept the false messiah, the Antichrist before they finally see their true Messiah face-to-face. Most rabbis believe that the Messiah will be a normal human, born of a mother and father, who will live a righteous life of religious study. Based on their interpretations of the Old Testament passages, the rabbis often connected the Messiah with King David and Moses. In other words, they are looking for a man with a divine mission like Moses, rather than God incarnating in a body as Jesus Christ did two thousand years ago.

For centuries rabbis and sages debated about the timing of the Messiah's appearance. They also discussed the necessity for Israel to repent before God would send their Redeemer. Some believed that God would not send the Messiah until all of Israel repented in one generation. Others felt that God would finally send the Messiah whether or not all of Israel repented at one time. "All the predestined dates have passed and the matter [of Messiah's coming] depends only on repentance and good deeds ... Rabbi Joshua said: If they do not repent, will they not be redeemed? But the Holy One blessed be He, will set up a king over them, whose decrees shall be as cruel as Haman's whereby Israel shall engage in repentance, and he will then bring them back to the right path" (Sanhedrin 97a).

This incredible statement in the Talmud suggests that God will allow the Antichrist, an evil tyrant "as cruel as Haman," to rule over Israel for a time to bring the Jews to repentance so the Messiah can appear. This rabbinic understanding that God "will set up a king over them" parallels the Christian interpretation of Daniel's prophecies of the coming Antichrist. Both expect that God will allow this evil Prince of Darkness to establish his tyranical rule over Israel for a period of time to cause them to repent and return to God. Rabbi Joshua thought this "king" would be "as cruel as Haman," their ancient enemy who tried to destroy all of the Jews in the Persian Empire.

EARLY CHRISTIAN BELIEFS ABOUT THE ANTICHRIST

The rise and fall of the Antichrist was of tremendous interest to the first-century Church. Jesus Christ warned His disciples about the coming Antichrist's "abomination of desolation." The words of Jesus were: "Therefore when you see the 'abomination of desolation,' spoken of by Daniel the prophet, standing in the holy place (whoever reads, let him understand), then let those who are in Judea flee to the mountains" (Matthew 24:15,16). He reminded His hearers that the prophet Daniel declared that the Antichrist, the "prince who will come," will defile the "holy place" in the rebuilt Temple. These Gospel accounts were discussed widely in the first-century Church. The prophecies gave believers a clear understanding of the future prophetic crisis involving the Antichrist and his reign of terror in the last days.

Each of the major prophets received visions of the coming Antichrist, the Battle of Armageddon and the ultimate victory of the Messiah. Paul prophesied about the career and final destruction of the Antichrist in 2 Thessalonians 2:3–12. The book of Revelation describes the career of the Antichrist in great detail in chapters 4 to 19. Many writings by Christians in the first three centuries contain quotations from Daniel, Paul's Epistles and Revelation about the Antichrist, the "man of sin." Several examples from this period will illustrate their beliefs about the last days. Many Bible predictions have already been fulfilled and they were fulfilled precisely to the day as foretold by the prophets of God. Logic dictates that the prophecies yet to be accomplished will also be fulfilled with an equal precision. Throughout this book we will explore these various prophecies together with their startling political, economic and military fulfillments in our generation.

THE APOCALYPSE OF PETER

The *Apocalypse of Peter* is a commentary on the Mount of Olives Discourse recorded in Matthew 24 and Luke 21 that was composed by an unknown writer around A.D. 140. However, the *Apocalypse* gives us a valuable insight into the views of the early Church about prophecy and the Antichrist. "And when they shall see with wickedness of their deeds (even of the false christs), they shall turn away after them and deny him to whom our fathers gave praise, the first Christ whom they crucified and thereby sinned exceedingly. But this deceiver is not the Christ. And when they reject him, he will kill with the sword and there shall be many martyrs. Then shall the boughs of the fig tree, the house of Israel, sprout, and there shall be many martyrs by his hand: they shall be killed and become martyrs."

The *Apocalypse of Peter* reveals the early Christians understood that a series of false christs would be followed by a final Antichrist, but "this deceiver is not the Christ." His words "this is the deceiver who must come into the world" suggests that he is quoting John's prophecy from memory. "For many deceivers have gone out into the world who do not confess Jesus Christ is come in the flesh. This is a deceiver and an antichrist" (2 John 7). The statement in the *Apocalypse of Peter* that, "he will kill with the sword" reveals the writer's familiarity with the book of Revelation. Several modern scholars deny that the symbol of the fig tree mentioned in Matthew 24 represents Israel. However, it is significant that this commentary, written only a century after Christ, declares clearly that the fig tree is the "house of Israel."

THE DIDACHE

The *Didache* is a fascinating manual of church regulations from the early days of the Christian era. It is one of the earliest of church writings that survived. Most scholars believe it was written during the first decade of the second century (A.D. 100 to 110). The writer clearly believed in an imminent rapture of Christians as indicated by his command to "Be ready" for the Lord's return at any moment. If the Rapture can occur without warning at any moment then it logically follows that it will occur before the prophetic events of the Tribulation.

The *Didache* (section 16) declares:

1. Be ye watchful for your life! Let not your lamps be extinguished nor your loins ungirded, but be ye ready! For ye know not the hour in which your Lord cometh ...
4. For as lawlessness increases, they shall hate one another and shall persecute and betray, and then the world-deceiver shall appear as a son of God, and shall work signs and wonders, and the earth shall be delivered into his hands, and he shall commit crimes such as have never been seen since the world began.
5. Then shall created mankind come to the fire of testing, and many shall be offended and perish, but those who have endured in the faith shall be saved by the (Christ).
6. And then shall the signs of the truth appear, first, the sign of a rift in heaven, then the sign of the sound of a trumpet, and thirdly, a resurrection of the dead.
7. But not of all, but as it was said, "The Lord will come and all his saints with him."
8. Then shall the world see the Lord coming on the clouds of heaven.

It is obvious that the writer is quoting from Matthew 24 to a great extent. He believes clearly in the coming of a personal Antichrist (the world-deceiver) as the persecutor, betrayer of truth and a man of lawlessness. The author declares that "the world-deceiver shall appear as a son of God, and shall work signs and wonders." This Antichrist will possess miraculous powers, derived from Satan, and will use "signs and wonders" to deceive the world about his true nature. He will "appear as a son of God" attempting to deceive the world, especially Israel, about his identity. The *Didache* describes his temporary success as follows, "the earth shall be delivered into his hands." The Apostle Paul describes him as the "son of perdition" and the *Didache* says, "he shall commit crimes such as have never been seen since the world began."

THE ASCENSION OF ISAIAH

The *Ascension of Isaiah* is an interesting Christian apocalypse from the second century after Christ. The first part is a Martyrdom of Isaiah and the second part contains apocalyptic material related to the coming of Christ. This non-canonical writing provides additional insight into the early Christian's understanding of the Antichrist and the Second Coming. The apocryphal *Ascension of Isaiah* refers to the future Antichrist under the name "Beliar." It says, "Many in Jerusalem and in Judah will he cause to depart from the true faith. Beliar will dwell in Manasseh." This speculation about the Antichrist dwelling in Manasseh (Samaria—Israel's West Bank) is fascinating in light of other verses connecting him to the Romans "of the race of Augustus."

> *The Ascension of Isaiah* (Section 4) declares:
> These are the days of the completion of the world. And after it has come to its consummation, Beliar, the great prince, the king of this world who has ruled it since it came into being, shall descend; he will come down from his firmament in the form of a man, a lawless king, a slayer of his mother . . . This ruler will thus come in the likeness of that king and there will come with him all the powers of this world and they will hearken to him in all that he desires . . . All that he desires he will do in the world; he will act and speak in the name of the Beloved and say, "I am God and before me there has been none else." And all the people in the world will believe in him, and will sacrifice to him and serve him saying, 'This is God and beside him there is none other' . . . and the power of his miracles will be

manifest in every city and region and he will set up his image before him in every city ... The Lord will come with his angels and with the hosts of the saints from the seventh heaven with the glory of the seventh heaven, and will drag Beliar with his hosts into Gehenna and He will bring rest to the pious who shall be found alive in the body in this world and to all who through faith in him have cursed Beliar and his kings. But the saints will come with the Lord in their garments which are stored on high in the seventh heaven.

The *Ascension* identifies the future Antichrist as a man possessed by Satan, "the king of this world," who will assume the position of a "great prince" and "lawless king." The writer declares that he "will come with all the powers of this world" in confirmation of Revelation 13:13–14, "He performs great signs, so that he even makes fire come down from heaven on the earth in the sight of men. And he deceives those who dwell on the earth by those signs which he was granted to do in the sight of the beast, those who dwell on the earth to make an image to the beast who was wounded by the sword and lived."

The phrase in the *Ascension of Isaiah* that "he will act and speak in the name of the Beloved and say 'I am God' " exactly parallels the warnings of Jesus: "I have come in My Father's name, and you do not receive Me; if another comes in his own name, him you will receive" (John 5:43). The statement in the Ascension that the Antichrist "will set up his image before him in every city" reveals the writer's familiarity with Revelation's (13:14) declaration that Satan will deceive "those who dwell on the earth to make an image, to the beast wounded by the sword and lived."

THE PSEUDO-TITUS EPISTLE

The Pseudo-Titus Epistle is an early Church manuscript that confirms their understanding that Daniel 9:24–27 prophesied a final seven-year tribulation period under the

Antichrist at the end of this age. Some recent critics of the premillennial and pretribulation rapture position have falsely described the concept of a future Antichrist and this seven-year treaty period as a new theory invented in 1820 by John Darby. The truth is that a large number of Christian writers from the early centuries, including the *Pseudo-Titus Epistles*, clearly taught about these matters. While this manuscript carries the name Titus, virtually no scholars believe that Paul's associate Titus wrote it. A Christian writer in the following centuries likely wrote this scroll and affixed the name Titus to it in honor of the apostle.

He writes about the future Antichrist under the prophetic title of "Nebuchadnezzar" as he sees a parallel in their shared satanic hatred of the Jews. "In the end you also will be delivered up to the wicked king of Nebuchadnezzar, as he says, i.e. to the devil who will fall upon you. And as they [the Jews], after they had spent seventy years in anguish, returned to their own place of abode, so a period of seven years is [now] appointed under Antichrist. But the pain of the seven years prevents eternal anguish." The writer refers to the duration of the future Antichrist's power over the Jewish tribulation saints as exactly "a period of seven years." He is obviously referring to the prophecy of Daniel, "And he shall confirm a covenant with many for one week" (Daniel 9:27).

IRENAEUS

Irenaeus, was a Christian writer whose life spanned most of the second century after Christ (A.D. 120 to 202). He studied the Gospels under Polycarp, who was a disciple of the Apostle John. Irenaeus witnessed a series of persecutions of the Church, knew the men taught by the apostles, and became a martyr to Christ after leading his church through a very turbulent period. Irenaeus' work, *Against Heresies*, is one of the most important writings of the early Church. In this book he discusses at length the career of the Antichrist in its relation to Christ's Second Coming. Irenaeus wrote, "For he [Antichrist] being endued with all the power of the devil, shall come, not as a righteous king, nor as a legitimate king, [one] in subjection to God, but an impious, unjust, and lawless one; as an apostate, iniquitous and murderous; as a robber, concentrating in himself [all] satanic apostasy, and setting aside idols to persuade [men] that he himself is God, raising up himself as the only idol, having in himself the multifarious errors of the other idols."

Irenaeus also refers to this Antichrist sitting in a rebuilt "Temple in Jerusalem." He says, "in which [Temple] the enemy shall sit, endeavoring to show himself as Christ, as the Lord also declares" quoting Matthew 24:15. Discussing Daniel's prophecies of the coming Antichrist he wrote, "For when he [Antichrist] is come, and of his own accord concentrates in his own person the apostasy, and accomplishes whatever he shall do according to his own will and choice, sitting also in the temple of God, so that his dupes may adore him as the Christ; wherefore also shall he deservedly 'be cast into the lake of fire.' . . . Daniel too, looking forward to the end of the last kingdom, i.e., the ten last kings, amongst whom the kingdom of those men shall be partitioned, and upon whom the son of perdition shall come, declares that ten horns shall spring from the beast, and that another little horn shall arise in the midst of them, and that three of the former shall be rooted up before his face."

Irenaeus clearly identified the kingdom of the Antichrist with the future revival of the Roman Empire, the fourth beast of Daniel 7. He believed Satan's prince will violently overthrow three of the ten nations forming the revived Roman Empire. Referring to Daniel 9:24–27 he says, "He points out the time that his tyranny shall last, during which the saints shall be put to flight, they who offer a pure sacrifice unto God: 'And in the midst of the week,' he says, 'the sacrifice and the libation shall be taken away, and the abomination of desolation [shall be brought] into the temple: even unto the consummation of the time shall the desolation be complete.' Now three-years-and-six months constitute the half-week." This fascinating passage by Irenaeus clearly proves that the early Church understood Daniel's prophecy of the Seventy Weeks as we do today. They expected the final Seventieth

Week to be fulfilled at the end of this age by a seven-year treaty leading to the return of Christ.

In his *Against Heresies* Irenaeus reveals that the early Church knew that the prophecies of Revelation would be fulfilled in the last days leading to the Second Coming of Christ. Recently Kingdom Now and Dominion Theology scholars have revived the old Preterist Theory which claims Revelation's prophecies were written about A.D. 66 and were completely fulfilled in the destruction of Jerusalem. However, this theory is clearly repudiated by the writings of Irenaeus, as a disciple of Polycarp, who was taught personally by John. Irenaeus knew that John's tremendous prophecies were not fulfilled in the burning of Jerusalem and the Temple by the Romans in A.D. 70. He says, "In a still clearer light has John, in the Apocalypse, indicated to the Lord's disciples what shall happen in the last times, and concerning the ten kings who shall then arise, among whom the empire which now rules [the earth] shall be partitioned . . . It is manifest, therefore that of these [potentates], he who is to come shall slay three, and subject the remainder to his power, and that he shall be himself the eighth among them." Irenaeus obviously anticipated the fulfillment of this prophecy at some point in the future because the Roman army destroyed the city of Jerusalem more than eighty-five years before he wrote his book *Against Heresies*.

JEROME AND HIPPOLYTUS

Jerome was one of the most important of the early Church writers. His commentary on the book of Daniel outlines the views of many Christian scholars of the first few centuries following Christ. Writing on Daniel's prophecy (9:24–27) about the Antichrist, Jerome quotes Hippolytus, the most brilliant of these scholars. "Moreover Hippolytus places the final week at the end of the world and divides it into the period of Elias [Elijah] and the period of Antichrist, so that during the first three and a half years of the last week the knowledge of God is established. And as for the statement, 'He shall establish a compact with many for a week' (Daniel 9:27), during the

other three years under the Antichrist the sacrifice and offering shall cease. But when Christ shall come and shall
slay the wicked one by the breath of His mouth, desolation shall hold sway till the end." Jerome confirms the
widespread early Church belief in a future Antichrist, the
Great Tribulation and the premillennial return of Christ
to set up His Kingdom.

LATER CHRISTIAN VIEWS OF THE ANTICHRIST

Although prophecy was not a major focus during the Medieval period a number of manuscripts from that period
spoke of the future role of the Antichrist in the last days.
During the period leading up to the First Crusade, Pope
Urban made a speech encouraging the Christians of Europe to recover the Holy Land. "According to Daniel and
Jerome, the interpreter of Daniel, he [the Antichrist] is to
fix his tents on the Mount of Olive . . . and he will first
kill the Kings of Egypt, Africa and Ethiopia . . . Behold
the Gospel cries out, 'Jerusalem shall be trodden down by
the Gentiles until the times of the Gentiles be fulfilled' . . .
These times will now be fulfilled . . . With the end of the
world already near . . . it shall please God to send . . . Antichrist, the head of all evil, who is to occupy there [Jeru-
salem] the throne of the kingdom" (*The First Crusade*,
August Krey, 1921, Princeton). Although there were many
theological distortions during the medieval ages the
knowledge of a future tyrant known as the Antichrist was
not totally lost.

MARTIN LUTHER

The great reformer Martin Luther clearly saw Christ's
coming as the key to the defeat of a future Antichrist at
the end of this age. "Our Lord Jesus Christ yet liveth and
reigneth, who, I firmly trust, will shortly come and slay
with the spirit of His mouth, and destroy with the brightness of His Coming, that man of sin" (D'Aubigne, *Historical Reformation*, Vol. 2, p. 166). It is intriguing to note

that Luther also concluded from his study of Psalm 90 that the Lord would return to establish his kingdom at the end of six thousand years from Adam's creation.

Bishop Newton

Bishop Newton wrote a fascinating treatise, On The Prophecies, in the year A.D. 1800. After a detailed analysis of the precision of fulfilled biblical prophecy, Bishop Newton declared,

> History is the great interpreter of prophecy ... Prophecy is, as I may say, history anticipated and contracted; history is prophecy accomplished and dilated, and the prophecies contain the fate of the most considerable nations, and the substance of the most memorable transactions in the world, from the earliest to the latest times.

His evaluation of the importance of prophecy remains as true today as when he penned these words two hundred years ago. In his On the Prophecies, Dissertation 22, Bishop Newton wrote that 2 Thessalonians 2:8 "is partly taken from Isaiah 11:4, 'and with the breath of His lips shall He slay the wicked one.' " He notes that the Jewish commentaries placed an emphasis on "the wicked one" as the Chaldee passage describes it, "He shall destroy the wicked Roman." In fact, the Chaldee paraphrase actually translates the verse as, "And by the Word of His lips He shall slay the wicked Armillus." Of course, the name "Armillus" occurs throughout ancient Jewish writing as "the last great enemy of their people" who would appear after the War of Gog and Magog and would be finally slain by the Messiah ben David at the end of the age. The ancient Jews had a clear notion of the defeat of an "anti-Messiah" figure by the true Messiah before their ultimate deliverance into the promised Kingdom of God.

W. B. YEATS

Even secular writers and poets have contemplated the ancient prophecies that warn of a great crisis that will grip civilization as we approach the new millennium. In his fascinating poem, *The Second Coming*, the Irish poet W. B. Yeats expressed his dread concerning the prophecies of the second coming and their connection to the coming Antichrist. Writing of his despair he said, "Things fall apart; the centre cannot hold; mere anarchy is loosed upon the world ... surely some revelation is at hand; surely the Second coming is at hand." Yeats, who died as World War II began, connected the growing anarchy and mindless violence of this century to the ancient prophecies concerning the coming Antichrist. His lack of personal faith led him to view the approaching fulfillment of the Bible's prophecies with a sense of foreboding and doom. Contemplating the relentless approach of the false messiah he wrote, "And what rough beast, its hour come round at last, slouches towards Bethlehem to be born?"

For over two thousand years the religious writings of both the Jews and Christians have expressed a fascination and curiosity about this mysterious person known as the Antichrist. In the following chapters we will explore the tremendous Bible prophecies that reveal the remarkable rise and fall of Satan's Prince of Darkness.

4

Plans for a
New World Order

I dipt into the future, Far as human eye could see,
Saw the vision of the world,
And all the wonder that would be; ...
Till the war-drum throbbed no longer,
And the battle-flags were furled
In the Parliament of Man,
The Federation of the World.

ALFRED LORD TENNYSON

Poets, dreamers, mystics and kings have dreamed for centuries of uniting the nations into a worldwide empire. The horrors of two world wars with a hundred million casualties, the Holocaust and the threat of nuclear war convinced many that a one-world government is the only hope if humanity is to survive. This dream has inspired philosophers and politicians to develop strategies for a planetary government that would unite the world as it was in the days of ancient Rome. Two millennia ago a Roman citizen could travel in safety over a thousand miles of well-tended roads from Spain to Syria, crossing a huge empire with one language, one set of laws and a government that endured over the centuries. The military power of Rome's legions established a *Pax Romana*—"the Peace of Rome" over an enormous empire.

In the centuries following Christ, after a millennium of successful growth the Roman Empire's political, military and economic system began to disintegrate. Rome gradually lost her energy, her vision and her ability to control the vast empire of nations and races her armies had conquered. Following the final defeat of the Roman armies in A.D. 476, the invading barbarian tribes of Goths and Vandals looted the treasures representing centuries of Roman art and manufacture. When the final battle was over, the remnants of the Roman Empire began to disintegrate among competing tribal warlords. Chaos reigned for hundreds of years. The centuries-long period of war and anarchy which followed Rome's collapse ushered in the "Dark Ages." The literacy, economy, civil peace and lifestyle of Rome were lost as the empire fragmented into many disparate pieces. The light of Roman civilization went out and Europe descended into a long night of cultural darkness and despair. Through that dark period the only ones who maintained the culture, literature, and legacy of civilization were the Christians and their church libraries.

Out of this chaos, nation states emerged and gradually created the national political institutions that govern Europe today. A fierce sense of nationalism characterized the political process in the new nations created within the ancient boundaries of the Roman Empire. During the last fifteen hundred years the world has witnessed increasing independence in the emerging nation-states of Europe. Yet the dream of a revived Roman Empire continues to inspire great men of vision. Despite the valiant and often violent efforts of kings, emperors, popes and politicians, the European nation-states vigorously resisted any attempts to force them to come together into one overriding political empire. Two and a half thousand years ago the prophet Daniel predicted that no one would succeed in recreating the Roman Empire until the final generation when the Messiah would return. In A.D. 800 Charlemagne tried and failed to unite Europe under the Holy Roman Empire. Later Frederich Barbarossa, Napoleon Bonaparte, Benito Mussolini and Adolph Hitler each tried in vain to redraw the map of Europe to recreate the glorious days when the Roman Empire held sway for thousands of miles from the shores of Britain to the deserts of Syria.

Today, as we approach the year 2000, man has arrived at a great divide in human political history. In the last three years the world was astonished to witness the breakdown of political parties and superpower alliances that have defined international politics since World War II. The stunning reunification of the powerful German nation on October 2, 1990, transformed the political landscape of Europe. German reunification has tremendous implications for the emerging European superstate that will profoundly alter the balance of world power. The German writer Hermann Rauschning spoke of an ancient Germanic longing for world empire, "At bottom, every German has one foot in Atlantis, where he seeks a better Fatherland and a better patrimony." After forty-five years of self-imposed restraint the new generation of leaders of this German superpower have lost any sense of guilt for the World War II crimes of their fathers. As the Soviet Union rapidly disintegrated, a confident German-led European Community laid the foundations for the New World Order prophesied by the ancient prophets of the Bible.

AN ASSAULT ON NATIONAL SOVEREIGNTY

Today it is fashionable in the media to criticize the nation-state as the cause of many, if not most, of the world's problems. We are constantly persuaded by our media and politicians about the great advantages of joining supernational organizations and reducing our independence, patriotism and loyalty to our own country. The old nation-states are blamed for war, poverty, racism and lack of efficiency. One-world government is offered as the solution to many of the massive social, economic and environmental problems facing mankind. Globalism is promoted in schools, the media and speeches as the answer to the great challenges confronting our nations today.

The plan to build the European Community was organized around a well-planned assault on the sovereignty of the nation-states of Europe. For example, in France an appeal was made to the voters of the old provinces of the Roman Empire, such as Provence and Alsace Lorraine, etc., against the dictates of the central government of

Paris. Citizens were promised the efficiencies of a central Europewide market, local control of cultural and language matters, together with the diminishing of the power of the national capital. This appeal proved irresistible to many Europeans.

However, the growth of the New World Order is at the expense of the national governments that have preserved our freedoms and democracy over the years. We should remember that the nation-state is one of the oldest institutions in human history. While there have been thirteen years of war for every year of peace throughout history, the nation-state is not the problem. Because of the sinful nature of men, wars would have occurred regardless of the political organizations man created. It is worthwhile to note that the Bible does not predict the extinction of the nation-state in our future. In fact, the prophecies tell us that Christ will judge the nations on the basis of how they treated His followers and, as a result, they will be either blessed or cursed during the Millennium and beyond. The book of Revelation also tells us that in the New Earth "the nations of those who are saved shall walk in its light, and the kings of the earth shall bring their glory and honor into it" (21:24). Ultimately this assault on the nation-state will fail because the Scriptures prophecy that the saints shall rule the nations forever.

In the light of the significant historical role of nations in preserving individual rights, assisting cultural development, and providing democratic rights, it is imprudent to abandon the role of nations in human government. Without individual nations, if a future dictator ever gains power over such a world government, there will be no outside nation left to oppose him and provide the possibility of defeating tyranny. History reveals very few nations, if any, that successfully overcame dictatorship without the outside assistance of another nation. If all of nations were eliminated under the tyranny of a totalitarian world government, freedom could be extinguished forever.

However, the Bible tells us that, in the final generation of this age, the Antichrist will rule the entire world for more than seven years. Revelation 13:7,8 tells us the Man of Sin, empowered by Satan, will rule the planet for a time: "And authority was given him over every tribe, tongue, and nation. And all who dwell on the earth will worship him, whose names have not been written in the Book of Life of the Lamb slain from the foundation of the world."

In this century we have witnessed the tragic destruction of more than one hundred million victims of Communist and Nazi powerhouses. Now the greatest powerhouse in history is forming before our eyes. It appears under many names and guises but its purpose is always the same: the creation of an elitist world government that will dominate the nations and their citizens for the benefit of a few leaders and their followers.

The U.S. government has actively cooperated in plans for a one-world government. Former President George Bush announced to U.S. Congress on September 11, 1991, that he was working to create a "New World Order." President Bush used the term "New World Order" more than two hundred times in his speeches during his presidency. However, the president did not explain to the public what the New World Order really means. The truth is that the New World Order will encompass the creation of a global government under the United Nations with a joint American and Russian partnership. Tragically, the New World Order will ultimately lead to slavery for freedom-loving people throughout the world.

Former British Prime Minister Margaret Thatcher recently revealed the truth about the political merger in Western Europe. Thatcher said that "it would be the greatest abdication of national and political sovereignty in history." Unfortunately, people will not listen to the warning until it is too late—until hundreds of millions have yielded their freedoms to the socialist rulers of a new European superstate. Thatcher was forced out of office by her party because she resisted the surrender of British sovereignty to the European Community. Sir Geoffrey Howe, the deputy prime minister of the United Kingdom, and the new Prime Minister John Major planned the Iron Lady's overthrow. He admitted that the 1992 plans for the European superstate were originally conceived some thirty years ago.

The ultimate plans of the New World Order will develop in three major phases. The first phase involved the consolidation of military and political power. The active military involvement of all the major powers of Europe and the U.S.A. to defeat Iraq in Operation Desert Storm was the first military operation of the New World Order. While this military cooperation was the most public and acclaimed action furthering the New World Order agenda, the next two phases are equally important to the new emerging global order. The second phase involves the economic merger of the three major regions of the world under agreements like N.A.F.T.A. The economic phase will affect our lives far more than military exercises in far off countries like Iraq, Somalia or Bosnia. The third and final phase will bring about the political, economic and military merger of the three superpower areas into a one world government. Target date: A.D. 2000.

THE COUNCIL ON FOREIGN RELATIONS

The Council on Foreign Relations (C.F.R.) was established following World War I by the elite groups controlling the financial and political life in the U.S.A. in an attempt to make sure that the future foreign policy of America followed their private interests. It was founded by Colonel House, President Woodrow Wilson's advisor, to coordinate the political agenda of the major financial and business leaders of the Eastern Establishment. They began with a secret group of approximately 270 members from the political, business and academic communities. Today the C.F.R. includes more than 2,700 current members representing the elite who govern America from behind the scenes. Over the last seventy years they have commissioned studies, networked their people into the State Department, and built relationships with similar one-world government groups in Canada, Britain, Japan and Europe. In his testimony before the U.S. Congress in February, 1950, an international banker named James Warburg, another C.F.R. member, made this chilling prediction, "We shall have world government whether or not you like it—by conquest or consent."

The Council on Foreign Relations is committed to the elimination of national boundaries and the merging of all nation states into a one-world government. For the last forty years members of the C.F.R. and their European counterparts have shaped the foreign and defense policy of the United States of America, Britain, France, Canada, and Germany. The move towards world government is no accident. Every single step was meticulously planned by these secret groups. It's time to wake up and realize where they are taking us.

The list of major well-known media personnel who are members of the Council on Foreign Relations is staggering. Many of the major print and television media stars we listen to daily are members of this secret group. There is an interlocking membership of key players involving the Trilateral Commission, the Council on Foreign Relations, international banks and major corporations, the military, the State Department, and the White House. Very few make it into the higher power circles of government in Washington unless they first serve as members of the C.F.R. or the Trilateral Commission.

As a small example of the C.F.R. membership, David Rockefeller, the head of the powerful Chase Manhattan Bank, is the chairman of both the Council on Foreign Relations and the North American Trilateral Commission. Former Secretary of State Alexander Haig, former Secretary of State Henry Kissinger, former CIA head William Casey, former Secretary of Defense Caspar Weinberger, Senator Ted Kennedy and Robert McNamara, president of the World Bank were members. Past Presidents John F. Kennedy, Richard Nixon, Gerald Ford, Jimmy Carter, and George Bush were all members of the Council. The presidential elections are increasingly meaningless because Americans are only given a choice between Team A and Team B. The players wear different sweaters but the management and ownership are the same. Since the 1950s almost every president and most cabinet members belonged to the council. President Reagan was the only recent president who did not belong to the C.F.R. However, most of his cabinet members were members.

In the 1992 election the American public was asked to choose between three candidates: President George

Bush, Governor Bill Clinton, and Ross Perot. However, all three candidates were members of the Council on Foreign Relations. None have denied membership in the Council. President Bush and President Clinton also belong to the Trilateral Commission. Many cabinet members, senior military staff, and State Department officials in every administration are members of this secret group.

The international nature of business, investments, and the network of personal friendships has given these people a globalist perspective where they feel very little loyalty or patriotism to their own nations. Most think of themselves as elite "citizens of the world" with little regard for the average citizen or democracy. Many people are surprised to discover that these enormously wealthy financial leaders are often extreme socialists in their political philosophy. These powerful and wealthy elites usually prefer to deal with communist or socialist governments rather than democracies. Most socialist and communist governments are run by similar elites that use their position to amass enormous wealth and power. Therefore, it is easier for a multinational company to cut a dishonest monopoly deal with a corrupt communist or socialist dictator than a freely elected democracy. That is part of the explanation for the strange support for the Soviet Union and communist China for several decades by the C.F.R. dominated American State Department. It also explains the vigorous campaign of the U.S. State Department to destroy the pro-western government of South Africa and replace it with the communist led African National Conference of Nelson Mandela.

A Council on Foreign Relations study in November 1959, at the height of the Cold War, declared that their goal was the building of "a new international order [that] may be responsible to world aspirations for peace . . . for social and economic change." The study argued for a new "international order [that would include] states labelling themselves as Socialist." These globalist groups have tried to engineer a merger between the United States and the socialist and communist states for the last five decades. Obviously, they realize that the average patriotic American would never knowingly accept such a program. Therefore, these groups have chosen to work behind the scenes in major western countries to bring about a merger of our countries and systems without the knowledge or approval of the citizens.

Rear Admiral Chester Ward, who resigned from the C.F.R. after 16 years, warned America of the ultimate goal of this secretive organization. "The most powerful clique in these elitist groups have one objective in common—they want to bring about the surrender of the sovereignty and the national independence of the United States ... The Wall Street international bankers ... primarily want the world banking monopoly from whatever power ends up in control of global government."

The economic failure of Marxist-Leninism and its communist governments around the world is preparing the world for a new form of world government that will ultimately be established under the future Antichrist. The government of the Man of Sin will certainly be fascist. In the place of communism's economic failure, we are watching the rise of a new form of state socialism, also known as fascism in many countries including Russia. Many of us are conditioned by the experience of World War II to recognize fascism only if we see the Nazis Swastika, Gestapo secret police, or Mussolini's Black Shirts. However, we should remember that communism and fascism are quite similar. Both systems demand total governmental control and regulation of all activities of its citizens. The only major difference is found in their attitude toward private property.

Communism demands government control by regulations of all property and production. It also demands complete government ownership of property and production. This leads to inefficiency because no one has any motivation to produce for the state when they cannot own private property. Fascism, while it demands the same level of government regulation and control, does allow private ownership of property and production. Fascism understands that people will only work hard when they receive individual reward for their efforts. In fascism, the government will allow you to own your property but they will totally regulate what you can do with it. The growth of state socialism and fascism in Europe, Japan, North America, and Israel is absolutely unprecedented. The staggering increase in government regulation in the areas of taxation, safety, and environment is strangling the business community. For example, the U.S. Federal Register listed over seventy-five thousand new regulations issued by the U.S. government last year alone. One researcher concluded that over forty thousand regulations governed every stage of the process, from the farm to the restaurant, to produce a hamburger in America. The government allows us to own our homes, land or the shares of our companies but they totally regulate what we can do with them. This is state socialism or fascism.

THE TRILATERAL COMMISSION

Since World War II, secret groups of bankers, politicians, intellectuals and scientists have met regularly to plan the creation of a world government. These people do not trust democracy because they know the average patriotic American or Canadian would never willingly surrender his country and constitution to be ruled by faceless foreign leaders on some secret international committee. If we truly love our liberties and our country we need to resist this relentless move to surrender our sovereignty to the coming world government. As Patrick Buchanan stated, "We don't want to hand over our sovereignty for a cushioned seat at the committee table ruling the world."

After World War II the secret groups promoting globalism felt that a direct appeal to a one-world government would not be as effective as an indirect approach. In the early 1970s Zbigniew Brzezinski, President Carter's National Security Advisor, founded the Trilateral Commission under the financial control and direction of David Rockefeller, chairman of the Council on Foreign Relations. His books and confidential reports to these organizations have developed many of the basic strategies of the coming New World Order. In a recent television interview Brzezinski was asked about the real meaning of the phrase "the New World Order." Although he practically invented the modern concept, Brzezinski claimed he wasn't sure what the phrase meant.

As a result of Brzezinski's input they developed a

more subtle plan that appeared to create a competition between the three economic and political superstates. However, the hidden reality was that the United States, Germany, and Japan represented three branches of a single global enterprise. The plan required each of the three superpowers to take the first steps to dominate and finally merge the nations in their own area. Public opinion is being persuaded by the media to accept the loss of national sovereignty in return for the promised blessings of a stable international political and economic New World Order. Once this stage is successfully completed the final step will be the merging of the three superpowers into a one-world government. To illustrate their support for this concept, on January 30, 1976, 32 Senators and 92 Representatives signed The Declaration of Interdependence. This document was an attempt to create propaganda for the planned New World Order. This was their statement, "Two centuries ago our forefathers brought forth a new nation; now we must join with others to bring forth a new world order."

After failing to achieve military domination during World Wars I and II, Germany is now conquering the nations of Europe through economic and political means. In Asia, Japan is rapidly dominating the countries it tried to conquer in World War II and is now forming a new "Greater East Asia Co-prosperity Sphere." In the Western Hemisphere the United States has created the North American Free Trade Agreement to consolidate the economies of Mexico, Canada, and America. This "Trilateral" approach succeeded in creating the impression among many people that there is a true international competition underway between the U.S.A., Europe, and Japan. However, there is a fundamental agreement between the international power-brokers to restructure the globe into a world empire. The Trilateral Commission is accomplishing this restructuring through the merger of the three great economic superpowers: America, Europe, and Japan. It is no accident that the most powerful individuals within the major governments and multi-national business enterprises have joint memberships in the Trilateral Commission, the Council on Foreign Relations, the Bilderberg Group, and various other global think tanks.

The purpose of the Trilateral Commission and the Council on Foreign Relations is to infiltrate and dominate the decision making bodies of government. They use the academic community and the media to influence key people to adopt a new world order philosophy. In their 1951 annual report the Council on Foreign Relations explained its methods. "In speaking of public enlightenment, it is well to bear in mind that the Council has chosen as its function the enlightenment of the leaders of opinion. These, in turn, each in his own sphere, spread the knowledge gained here in ever-widening circles." The whole process depends on networking at the most sophisticated level.

THE BILDERBERG GROUP

A third secret group behind the rush toward world government is known as the Bilderberg Group, named after the hotel in Holland where they first met in 1954. This group's purpose is to coordinate the European portion of the New World Order plan to create the European Community. Much of the planning for the "Europe 1992" plan came from the Bilderbergers and their interlocking memberships involving the Council on Foreign Relations, the Trilateral Commission, and the British group known as Chatham House. Prince Bernhard of the Netherlands, Denis Healey of Britain, plus David Rockefeller and Dean Rusk from the United States met in that first meeting to co-ordinate the European contribution to the emerging world superstate. While the Trilateral Commission tends to focus on financial and political matters, the Bilderbergers are very concerned with military and strategic matters that impact on the coming world government. Because of the high government and business positions held by the men in these interlocking groups, they are in a unique position to promote like-minded junior members of their group to the highest governmental and industrial positions in their respective countries.

The World Bank and
International Monetary Fund

Another feature of this planned restructuring of the world involves the coercion by the globalist's World Bank and International Monetary Fund to force developing countries to follow the rules of the New World Order. These international institutions use the "carrot" of new loans and the "stick" of approval of debt-restructuring to force Third World countries into their assigned positions in the New World Order. In 1990 a study called A Report to the Trilateral Commission - Number 39 revealed their true intentions. "With due deference to local circumstances and sensibilities, the Trilateral countries should be frank in advocating the need for reform and modernization of Latin American economies. Such efforts are necessary both to achieve recovery and secure international support—particularly from the Trilateral private sector." In a startling revelation of the true agenda of the Trilateral bankers it concluded, "The purpose of this effort is to help Trilateral policy makers find a place for the societies of Latin America and the Caribbean in the future international order."

Only a few years ago Third World countries were threatening to default on huge national loans they owed to western international banks. However, the collapse of commodity prices destroyed the revenues of Third World economies. Since the collapse of the Soviet Union and the rise of the New World Order, the Trilateral bankers are in a position to dictate terms to the developing countries. With the overwhelming economic leverage possessed by international lending authorities, Third World countries are totally vulnerable to pressure to co-operate with the international bank's debt restructuring plan.

In April 1992, Russian President Boris Yeltsin tried to put the best face on his capitulation to the international bankers after accepting their restrictions in return for $45 billion in western loans. Yeltsin claimed, "We do not intend to work under the direct orders of the International Monetary Fund. We do not agree completely with this organization's viewpoint and we will stick to our point of view" (New York Times, April 29, 1992). While that was his public position for the ears of the Russian people, the reality is that Yeltsin is now dependent on international loans and aid. Despite his protests, Yeltsin must play the tune of the bankers by opening Russia up to Western investment. Russia must now repay more than $100 billion in outstanding loans to Western bankers from the 1980s.

Throughout Latin America "debt-for-equity" conversions are being entered into between governments and world bankers. Deeply discounted government bonds are traded for equity in newly privatized companies that were formerly government owned companies. "Debt-for-nature" swaps are another astonishingly creative high finance tool. Millions of acres of South American land and rain forests are traded in return for writing off the enormous foreign loans that were accumulated during the free-lending eighties. The huge international banking and industrial corporations of the West and Japan are steadily increasing their control over the land and resources of Third World countries in a new wave of colonialism.

The fifteen republics of the former Soviet Union are now lining up for membership in the World Bank and International Monetary Fund. At the end of World War II the United States single-handedly financed the Marshal Plan reconstruction of post-war Europe. However, during the decade of the eighties, America was transformed from the greatest creditor nation in the world to the largest debtor nation. Even America was forced by its weakened financial state to bring in the International Monetary Fund as a financial partner to begin rebuilding the Soviet Union's economy. The U.S.A. no longer has the financial clout to force other nations to automatically follow its lead. Today Germany, Japan and the oil-rich Arab nations often dictate the terms of discussion.

THE NORTH AMERICAN FREE TRADE AGREEMENT

As an example of the secret economic agenda of the New World Order, consider the new North American Free Trade Agreement (N.A.F.T.A.) that was signed in December 1993 by the U.S.A., Canada, and Mexico. In order to achieve global domination, it is essential that the three superpowers first achieve dominance over the nations of their respective regions. The New World Order will begin by engulfing its various regions, one by one, starting with the Western Hemisphere. The world is being restructured and divided into spheres of influence between three major economic players, the United States, Germany, and Japan.

The North American Free Trade Agreement has just been finalized. However, there are already advanced plans among governments and businessmen for an even larger trade agreement that will encompass the whole of the Western Hemisphere from the tip of South America to the North Pole. The target date: the year 2000. The consequences for the citizens and nations involved are awesome. In this new agreement the lowest wages and benefits paid in Honduras or Mexico will set the new standard for American workers. Huge multi-national companies will choose to produce their goods in these South or Central countries without high taxes or difficult environmental restrictions. Additionally, they will not have to pay for expensive health care systems, pensions or the higher wages expected by North American skilled workers. The N.A.F.T.A. plan will endanger the benefits built up over the last three decades by North American workers. Plants and jobs are moving south of the Rio Grand at an ever-accelerating rate. Chile is the first South American nation to sign initial agreements to participate in the new expanded Free Trade Zone. In the last two years, thirty-two secret trade agreements have been signed between the U.S.A., Canada, Mexico and a number of South American countries without public debate.

Where is the real support for the North American Free Trade Agreement when many believe the average worker will be harmed? The N.A.F.T.A. supporters, the lobbyists for the international bankers and multinationals, and their politicians are pushing us toward this New World Order. Former President Bush announced the plans for this Western Hemisphere agreement in June 1990 and called it the "Enterprise for the Americas Initiative." President Clinton's administration pushed the agreement through a reluctant Congress. The plan requires all countries to remove tariff, trade and financial investment barriers to international companies. Additionally, it requires these countries to submit the control of their economy to international bankers under strict debt-reduction schemes. Of course, foreign banks needed some method to recover the disastrous loans they made during the 1980s. N.A.F.T.A. is their ingenious solution. While recovering from the massive "bad" loans they made in the last decade, the banks are also ensuring the total domination of these countries' economies. Peru provides an example of how these schemes will work. Over $60 million in monthly interest payments are paid by Peru to the World Bank and International Monetary Fund. These interest payments exceed the new loans made by the western banks to Peru. In other words, Peru, like most Third World countries today, is now repaying more money to the West every year than the Western nations provide in aid and loans. Western aid and international loans have resulted in a new and onerous colonialism.

If nations refuse to agree to these arrangements of the New World Order they will be left out in the cold. If they agree they will lose control of their economy and, ultimately, their political destiny. International drug companies, worldwide banks, and multinational oil corporations will quickly dominate their local economies. The price which nations must pay to sit at the table with the World Bank and International Monetary Fund are to: (1) accept a free market economy; (2) pay off past international bank loans as demanded by the International Monetary Fund and World Bank; (3) eliminate nationalized industries; and (4) remove all barriers to international investment and trade. Opposition to these agreements is rising in America and Canada from concerned citizens who fear that our politicians are selling out our national interest in secret back room deals that benefit only the men behind the scenes. The group "Action Canada Network" wrote an analysis of the N.A.F.T.A. trade talks. They concluded: "Despite [Canadian Trade Minister] Wilson and [Prime Minister] Mulroney's attempt to hide it, they are negotiating a new economic constitution for North America, undemocratic and unaccountable to its citizens." The basic point to remember is that democracy and citizen input can only occur on a local or national level. Once our nations sign these complicated international agreements, the ability of the public to influence the economic or political situation is nil. By their very nature, international treaties and agreements preclude any democratic input. While few citizens realize it, international agreements legally supersede our national laws and constitutional rights. Decisions and actions taken by secret committees behind closed doors without public accountability will govern our lives. The power brokers want to eliminate the sovereign nation state because they will then have absolute control of our lives and resources. These trends are creating the preconditions for the final totalitarian world empire described by the ancient prophets.

In the next chapter we will examine the globalist agenda of those who plan to replace the nation state with a global government that will set the stage for the totalitarian government of the coming Antichrist.

5

The Globalist Agenda for World Government

ORGANIZATIONS OF THE NEW WORLD ORDER

The United Nations

The United Nations (UN) was formed during World War II by the allied nations in a hope that it could be used to prevent another disastrous world war. After more than sixty million died in WW II the victorious allies genuinely longed for a peaceful forum to work out their differences without resorting to war. However, in the last five decades more than thirty-seven million people were killed in 340 wars. Despite seven thousand disarmament conferences only five weapons systems were actually destroyed and eliminated. While we talk about peace, the world still arms for Armageddon. Despite the collapse of the Soviet Union, six hundred major Russian arms factories are running 24 hours a day. The Russians and their former republics continue to produce awesome amounts of conventional and nuclear weapons every year, claiming arms production is needed to provide employment. Throughout the world ethnic groups are arming and embarking on civil wars to achieve independence. Despite the talk of peace there is a greater danger of war today than at any other time since 1945.

The United Nations was founded on the basis of respect for the individual sovereignty of each member state. A fundamental principle of the UN was that the international body would never interfere in the internal affairs of a sovereign member state. This principle of non-interference enabled the UN to wisely avoid many internal crises including civil wars and public unrest during the last five decades. However, with the collapse of the Soviet Union and the growing support for a New World Order, this principle of non-interference has eroded to the point of extinction.

As an example, following the War in the Gulf, the UN massively intervened in Iraq's internal affairs to carve out an enclave to protect the Kurdish minority in northern Iraq from the armed attacks of Saddam Hussein. While the protection of the Kurds was very popular in the West, it is a fundamental shift in the way the United Nations conducts its affairs. Additionally, the UN has moved international nuclear and biological weapons inspection teams into Iraq. They are searching for weapons of mass destruction hidden by Hussein's forces. Once again, this action was applauded by the nations. Recently, the UN voted for an arms embargo, economic sanctions and, ultimately, the use of force against Libya if they refused to release two men suspected of bombing a Pan Am flight over Scotland. Note that these men, while probably guilty, have not been convicted in any court of law. They are simply terrorist suspects. Yet the UN has voted to interfere in Libya's internal affairs because Libya is an outlaw state with few friends.

However, even though these actions seemed warranted, the UN could easily use this legal precedent against our own nations. For example, imagine what would happen if civil unrest involving minorities arises in the future within Canada, the United States or Israel. How would we respond if the United Nations voted to send UN peacekeeping forces to carve out a "protected homeland" for our dissenting minorities? For the last two years, Yassir Arafat, the leader of the Palestinian Liberation Front, has called for the UN to pass resolutions demanding that Israel withdraw unilaterally from the West Bank, Gaza, and East Jerusalem, including the Temple Mount. Third World nations form a majority in the UN The new president of the UN general assembly is a Palestinian who was born in East Jerusalem. The secretary general of the UN, Boutros-Ghali, is an Egyptian. These Arab leaders want the UN to use the same sanctions and threats against Israel that it has used against Iraq and Libya. David Kay, the leader of the UN nuclear inspection team destroying Iraq's nuclear program, was reported as stating that he could hardly wait to finish the job in Iraq so that he and his team could launch a surprise nuclear inspection against Israel. Why would he make such a statement unless there were serious plans to use the power of the United Nations against Israel? A UN military attack against Israel to force it out of the West Bank and Jerusalem could easily trigger the War of Gog and Magog described in the Bible.

The International Peacekeeping Force

The New York Times published an article entitled "The New World Army" in March, 1992, calling for the creation of a permanent UN army. "The bill for 11 UN peacekeeping missions involving 77,000 blue helmeted UN troops could approach $3.7 billion this year. Never before have so many UN troops been committed to so many costly and diverse missions ... UN forces were asked to disarm guerrillas, conduct elections, and enforce human rights (Namibia, Cambodia, Yugoslavia, El Salvador). The Security Council recently expanded the concept of threats to peace to include economic, social and ecological instability." These actions are an astonishing expansion of the role of the United Nations. As demands grow for a permanent UN rapid deployment army, negotiations have commenced to include Russian, European, Canadian and American Special Forces in the core of the future new world order army. The New York Times, a veritable public relations agency of the New World Order, called for the major nations to contribute their forces. "One promising possibility is to make fuller use of the UN Charter. Article 43 already calls on members to make available 'armed forces assistance and facilities' necessary to maintain international peace." Amazingly, the New York Times article suggested that American tax dollars be diverted from the U.S. defense budget directly to the UN military budget.

One of the most dangerous things about the UN Charter and various other international treaties is that they literally supersede the constitutions of our democratic countries. As an example, the U.S. Constitution states that treaties signed by the Senate supersede the Constitution. Therefore, if there is a conflict between a UN treaty and the laws of the United States, the Supreme Court will demand that the government obey the dictates of the United Nations treaty.

A UNITED NATIONS SPY AGENCY

In early 1992 several top UN officials called for the United Nations to set up its own intelligence and surveillance agency. The purpose would be to provide the UN Security Council with independent intelligence acquisition and analysis to enable it to accurately monitor complicated situations arising around the world. The former head of the CIA, William Colby, talked enthusiastically about the need for an "enhanced data-gathering capability" for UN politicians and planners. UN Secretary-General Boutros-Ghali stated, "What is important is that the UN must have its own intelligence. This would help us maintain ... independence, and a more important presence in the different countries and regions where there will be a possibility of military confrontation." The U.S.A., Britain, Japan and many other nations constantly provide the UN with comprehensive intelligence reports, so there is very little objective need to enlarge the power of the UN by creating its own spy agency. The real purpose is to establish the first international intelligence agency of the New World Order whose spies will owe no loyalty to any particular nation. The intelligence agents will spy on various nations and will report directly to the world government.

Another goal being promoted is to establish a United Nations arms control monitoring system that will identify arms dealers, the types and number of weapons, together with the sources of international weapons transfers. The breakup of the Soviet Union has opened a Pandora's box of conventional and nuclear weapon sales to unstable regimes and terrorists. The number of high-tech fighter planes, biological, and chemical weapons sold to Third World countries is staggering. However, there is no secret about where these arms sales originate. The UN already knows that the vast majority of sophisticated arms sales to the Middle East and Third World countries are made by major powers including the United States, Russia, Canada, Britain, Germany, France, and China. These demands to expand the UN's powers are just one more strategic step in the plan to use the world body to bring about the world government prophesied by the Bible.

THE COUNSEL ON SECURITY AND COOPERATION

In Eastern Europe, we have witnessed the official dissolution of the Warsaw Pact that once coordinated the military strategy of Russia and her Eastern European colonies. The Council on Security and Cooperation in Europe has been strongly supported by the Soviet Union and the communist governments. They see it as a vehicle to bring about a consolidated security arrangement encompassing all of Europe's nations and the emerging nations of the Commonwealth of Independent States (CIS). Russia has suggested that strengthening the powers of the fifty-one nation Counsel on Security and Cooperation could provide a vehicle to guarantee the security of all states in the area. Initially the Russians and East Europeans demanded that NATO disband after they had formerly withdrawn from the Warsaw Pact. However, the Russian Red Army remains in Poland, the Baltic States, and the eastern half of Germany.

In a later chapter we will see that, although the West is disarming, very little has changed on the Russian military side. Now they suggest that Russia and Eastern European countries join NATO. Amazingly there is a growing level of support in the European Community for this merger. This will prove to be a disaster for NATO because a defensive alliance needs to focus on a potential enemy if it is to have any purpose or cohesion. President Yeltsin wants to convince the Europeans to merge NATO's armed forces with Russia's under the umbrella of the Council on Security and Cooperation in Europe. In any such arrangement, Russia's five million-man army would obviously dominate the West's smaller forces. The result would be the effective neutralization of Europe and the total isolation of America. This has been one of Russia's major strategic goals for fifty years.

If this plan succeeds, Russia will have neutralized the West without firing a shot. As the ancient Chinese military scholar Lao-tzu wrote in his Art of War, "All warfare is based on deception." He also advised that the best way to win a war was by strategic deception that avoided fighting. The Russian leaders have studied Lao-tzu well. After Europe is neutralized and cut off from America there will be very little chance of stopping Russia and her allies from a lightning strike into the Middle East. In one surgical strike the Russian generals would achieve their centuries-long dream of capturing the Persian Gulf, the oil fields, and the strategic land bridge of Israel connecting three continents.

THE CLUB OF ROME

The Club of Rome was formed in 1968 as a European "think tank" to study various complicated issues involved in preparing the nations to accept the coming New World Order. An Italian industrialist, Aurelio Peccei, closely connected with the Bilderberg Group, brought together leaders from ten nations to study the problems. From the beginning, the Club of Rome has used its studies and reports to promote the belief that the only way out of our intractable problems is to abandon our national sovereignty to a world government. Some of their studies include "The Limits to Growth," the "RIO Report" and "Mankind at the Turning Point." Each study presents massive new world problems and offers world government as the only possible solution. Many members of the Bilderbergers, the Trilateral Commission, and the Council on Foreign Relations are also members of the Club of

Rome. There is a strong New Age flavor to the terminology and philosophy expressed through Club of Rome reports.

The Ten Kingdoms

It is interesting to observe that many organizations connected with the coming world government have divided the world into "Ten Kingdoms," as Daniel revealed in Nebuchadnezzar's vision of world empires. The Club of Rome, the Trilateral Commission, and the Council on Foreign Relations each use a "ten kingdom" administrative model in their plans for the coming world government. In the book of Revelation the prophet John revealed that the Antichrist, the Beast, and his ten-nation confederacy will rule the world for seven years during the coming Tribulation period until the Messiah returns to establish the Kingdom of God on earth. "And the ten horns which you saw are ten kings who have received no kingdom as yet, but they receive authority for one hour as kings with the beast" (Revelation 17:12).

The Colonization of Africa

The major colonial powers of Britain, France, Germany, Portugal, and Spain withdrew from their African colonies at the end of World War II in the hope that these newly independent nations would learn to govern themselves. Tragically, most of these countries have descended into a veritable hell of famine, corruption, torture, tribal warfare, epidemics, and one-party dictatorships. According to interviews and polls the first "one-man-one-vote" election in South Africa will give power to Mandela and the ANC. Past African experience and the enthusiastic commitment to communism expressed by the ANC and Nelson Mandela suggests that this first election may be the last. There are no democratic governments in Africa north of the borders of South Africa. Many African countries have ceased to operate normally as governments or nations. Outside their capitals, huge countries like Zaire, the size of Western Europe, have collapsed to the point where the only government that exists is that of local warlords and army officers ruling corruptly from the barrel of machine guns. Countries like Ethiopia, Sudan, and Somalia were devastated by corruption, civil war, human rights abuses and famine. Many of their leaders have amassed hundreds of millions in stolen loot from diverted western aid and payments for raw materials. When the dictators finally flee their country to live in Switzerland with their ill-gotten gain, the new governments usually find the treasury empty.

The United Nations Food and Agriculture Organization predicts a virtual catastrophe in the 1990s as civil conflicts, famine, and AIDS take their terrible toll on Africa's 480 million population. Many experts have finally come to the realization that billions in additional aid will not provide the answer. The billions of dollars that have been given in aid have not produced stability or self-sufficiency that we intended. The African continent has fallen into an abyss with little hope of escape through their own efforts. This seemingly hopeless situation has led some to suggest that the West should simply abandon Africa to its misery. However, this solution is both immoral and unacceptable. The television cameras of CNN and other networks provide instant access to the horrifying pictures of Africa's misery. The electronic media allows wars, famine and epidemics in Africa to be witnessed by millions in the West as if it is happening next door. Calls to reconsider our traditional approaches are rising from both conservatives and liberals. The unprecedented collapse in Somalia, Sudan, and Ethiopia has led to calls by foundations, banks and international institutions to reinstitute a colonial mandate or trusteeship over the African continent until it can develop the human and institutional resources to properly govern itself. This is playing right into the hands of those who wish to establish a world government.

The *New York Times* carried articles suggesting that "United Nations troops be sent to the Horn of Africa (Somalia) to restore order and supervise the distribution of food supplies." Unfortunately, the intervention of UN troops in Somalia has degenerated into a quagmire. Far from applauding UN intervention, many Somalis see the UN troops as the enemy. This is only the first of many planned interventions to try to bring about some degree of order in nations that cannot govern themselves. An article in the *European* newspaper suggested, "To some extent, Africa has already been recolonized by the International Monetary Fund and the World Bank, which has forced its free-market medicine on a host of Third World countries without much more than a murmur of protest. These agents of 'new imperialism' also insist on good governance and human rights" (May 10, 1992). The groups that are committed to the New World Order agenda see this appalling situation in Africa as an opportunity to illustrate how their elitist approach can transform society and create order out of chaos.

THE NAZI'S SATANIC MOTIVATION

Satan tried to dominate the world in the 1930s and 1940s through the Adolph Hitler and German Nazi Party. Ample historical evidence proves that Adolph Hitler, Heinrich Himmler, and Joseph Goebbels were surrounded by occult and satanic influences. Hitler was involved in mediumistic trances for many years and referred to demons that directed his activities. The dreaded SS secret police organization was a secret religious body that initiated members with satanic blood oaths to Lucifer. Following their conviction as war criminals during the Nuremberg War Trials a number of top Nazis requested occult religious rituals prior to their execution. At Nuremberg the leaders of the West, including Churchill, decided to suppress the evidence of the true occult motivation of the Nazi leaders attempt to conquer the world. Winston Churchill and other western leaders felt that the public could not handle the truth. Instead, the trials simply concentrated on the evil crimes of the Nazis without exploring the satanic motivation for their monstrous genocide.

The Nazis planned to create a world empire through fire and blood. In a speech to his followers Hitler declared, "National Socialism will use its own revolution for the establishing of 'a new world order.' " Hitler was consumed with an evil need to dominate humanity. Though very few people realize it, Hitler had sold his soul to the devil in an appalling occult ceremony. While in his early twenties he surrounded himself with witchcraft, drugs, and satanic sacrifice. After gaining power Hitler participated in grotesque occult rituals in his mountain top retreat where he dedicated himself and Germany to his satanic new world order. In the closing days of the war, when he realized he had failed, Hitler demanded that his officers destroy all factories, railways, farms, and food reserves throughout Germany. As the Russians launched their final attack he ordered the flooding of the Berlin underground in an attempt to drown tens of thousands of German civilians hiding from the bombs. This was essentially an occult act of evil, black witchcraft to invoke the wrath of the gods by a "deluge" and sacrifice of the German people. Satan motivated Hitler's hatred of the Chosen People that manifested in the Nazi attempt to annihilate the Jewish people through the Holocaust. The devil knows Bible prophecy reveals his defeat at the hands of the coming Messiah in the generation that witnessed the rebirth of Israel. By destroying the Jews, Satan hoped to defeat God's plan to redeem Israel and the nations. Because the devil is not omniscience like God, he could not anticipate that the horrors of World War II would motivate the Jews and the nations to create Israel in 1948, partially in revulsion to the horrors of the Holocaust.

ISRAEL'S ROLE IN THE NEW WORLD ORDER

Israel plays a key role in the secret plans for world government because of its geostrategic location on the vital land bridge between Europe, Asia and Africa. Whoever controls the land of Israel can dominate the Persian oil fields and the Suez Canal that is vital for European and African trade. That is why Russia and America both demanded the right to co-sponsor the Middle East Peace talks. It also explains the tremendous financial support and enormous arms shipments by both superpowers to this volitile area over the last four decades. Of the top twenty arms importing nations in the world, seven are in the Middle East. Though Israel is one of the smallest nations in the world and its land is mostly desert, even the distant nations of China, India, and Japan are moving to take their place at the peace table to determine the final settlement. The European Community recently demanded that they join the middle East Peace talks as a co-sponsor.

Israel, with only eight thousand square miles and a population of five million citizens, contains less than one-tenth of one percent of earth's population. Despite its insignificant size, a multitude of debates, conferences and resolutions focus on this small country every year. The leaders of the nations recognize that if Armageddon comes it will undoubtably start here. Jerusalem, the spiritual home of three great religions, has captured the attention of the world's citizens. The prophet Zechariah foretold twenty-five centuries ago that the nations of the world will come against Israel and Jerusalem in the last days. "Behold, I will make Jerusalem a cup of drunkenness to all the surrounding peoples, when they lay siege against Judah and Jerusalem. And it shall happen in that day that I will make Jerusalem a very heavy stone for all peoples; all who would heave it away will surely be cut in pieces, though all nations of the earth are gathered against it" (Zechariah 12:2,3).

In the chapter "Israel in the Valley of Decision" we will explore the incredible prophecies about that nation's role in the events that will shortly unfold as the planet rushes to its final appointment with destiny.

THE NEW AGE AGENDA

It is not my intention to complete an in-depth review of the New Age movement. Others have done excellent research in uncovering the coordinated New Age assault on the Judeo-Christian values that have made our nations great. However, it is important to point out how these New Age practitioners have made common cause with the planners of the New World Order. The pagan philosophy behind the New Age movement has been working behind the scenes throughout this century to destroy democracy and create a world government. There was an explosion of occult groups and eastern religions in Europe in the early 1900s. Hundreds of satanic cults appealed to the aimless European men and women whose lives were dislocated by the horrors of World War I and the Great Depression that followed. One of these obscure occult sects, the Thule Group, rose to prominence in the 1920s in Germany and Britain. The Thule Group and the Golden Dawn society inspired many of Hitler's followers. It was dedicated to furthering the plans for a one-world government that would destroy all traces of Judeo-Christian morality. Occult groups including Free Masonry and the Illuminati attempted to undermine the existing political and religious order during the last two centuries. The evidence of an unholy alliance between the supporters of the New World Order and the New Age occult groups is overwhelming. Many of those leading the current rush toward world government are committed to a pagan and occult vision totally opposed to the Judeo-Christian morals and democratic values of the average western citizen.

THE ATTACK ON CHRISTIAN VALUES

The New World Order political groups and the New Agers are both aiming at the year 2000 as their target date for imposing a one-world government that will eliminate every Judeo-Christian moral value we cherish. A concentrated attack has been launched against our children's values as indicated by the rampant paganism occurring in children's television, games and comics. A majority of children's television programs on Saturday morning contain graphic violence together with constant New Age themes of occult, supernatural powers. The prevalence of the "Third Eye" of Eastern mysticism in cartoons is overwhelming. Take a Saturday morning and force yourself to watch this garbage for several hours with a notebook to record every instance of violence, immorality, profanity and occult activities. This exercise will be both shocking and enlightening to realize the sustained occult propaganda that is directed at our children in these television programs. This is not accidental. There is a sophisticated New Age agenda behind this programming.

Teachers from kindergarten and up are attending seminars on professional development days to learn how to teach your child to enter a trance state and explore occult visualization. Astral travel, experiments in clairvoyance, and dream interpretation are commonly offered to elementary children without their parents knowledge or approval. School boards and teachers fight with all their ability to prevent any Christian or biblical influence within the school under the spurious argument of "separation of Church and State." However, these same teachers and boards are actively promoting New Age and Hindu religious beliefs disguised as meditation.

As an example of the war of values being waged today, Proposition 10 is actively being pushed by educators in every state. It demands that teachers educate our children to believe that homosexuality is a valid choice because "ten percent of humans have already chosen this lifestyle." However, a number of studies in several nations reveal that less than 2 percent of the population are homosexual.

New Age philosophy and techniques are successfully infiltrating the business world today. Salesmen and managers are often forced to attend Transcendental Meditation (TM) courses and new age visualization exercises even though it violates their personal religious beliefs. Failure to attend these sessions often leads to dismissal. Transcendental meditation is directly founded on pagan Hindu religious beliefs and practices. Each participant is taught his own special "mantra" that must be endlessly chanted in a meditative trance state. However, there are only a few such "mantras" that are given to students. Each of these mantras is the name of a Hindu god or demon. Although they are often ignorant of the fact, as TM students chant their mantras they are worshiping demons. Yet TM is deceptively presented to business and education groups as a non-religious, harmless relaxation therapy.

TED TURNER AND CNN

Ted Turner, the owner of CNN, the world's largest and most influential news organization, made a speech to the Hollywood Radio and Television Society in Beverly Hills. The *Washington Times* reported his comments to the media. He offered his alternative Ten Commandments to the world to replace the Ten Commandments of the Bible. These Ten Commandments require the promise: "1. To love the Earth. 2. To love mankind. 3. To treat everyone with dignity. 4. To have no more than two children. 5. To save what's left of our natural world in its untouched state. 6. To use as little non-renewable resources as possible. 7. To use as few toxic chemicals as possible. 8. To contribute to those less fortunate than ourself. 9. To reject the use of force, especially military force; to support the total elimination of all nuclear, chemical and biological weapons; and finally, 10. To support the United Nations and its efforts to collectively improve the conditions of the planet."

Ted Turner created a popular Saturday morning action-adventure cartoon series called "Captain Planet" designed to promote his Ten Commandments to children viewers. Ted Turner's CNN is the single most powerful television media in the world today. It is totally committed to a so-called "even-handed" approach between America, Russia, Somalia, or Iraq. In other words, it will take no sides in any conflict involving America. The CNN coverage of the war in the Gulf was ample proof of CNN's philosophy. CNN and a large part of the media are philosophically committed to a socialistic, New Age orientated, one-world government where unelected foreign leaders will control the lives of North American citizens.

There are many high level personalities and leaders promoting the New Age-New World Order agenda. Prince Philip of England has praised New Age paganism for creating an "environmental consciousness." His son Prince Charles denounced God's command that man was to have dominion over the earth. Instead, Prince Charles claimed that man should renounce the biblical concept of "dominion" and embrace the concept of "stewardship."

The starvation in Third World countries with poor crop yields is often due to their antiquated, inefficient farming methods. However, while peasants threshed fields with horses in the background, Prince Charles praised "traditional methods" of production because they were "natural." The fact that their inefficiency also leads to millions of deaths by starvation is apparently not a concern.

Teilhard de Chardin was one of the philosophers who laid the foundation for the New Age movement and world government. His statement sums up their plan to unite these groups into an overwhelming force for change. "Nothing in the Universe can resist the cumulative ardour of a sufficiently large number of enlightened minds working together in organized groups."

THE ENVIRONMENTAL-POPULATION STRATEGY

The Club of Rome and other supporters of the New World Order realize that the environmental issue is a perfect cover to allow them to take over global powers. In their reports they openly discuss the need to "exaggerate" the environmental crisis and world population problems. Once people are filled with panic these groups can demand the surrender of our nation's sovereignty to a world government as their proposed solution. This strategy explains the current media hype and hysteria about environmental problems. While many serious environmental problems exist, the New World Order propaganda plays on people's exaggerated fears to force them to accept draconian laws designed to limit their freedom. As an example of their dishonest strategy, consider this quote from *The First Global Revolution* sponsored by the Club of Rome. "The common enemy of humanity is man ... In searching for a new enemy to unite us, we come upon the idea that pollution, the threat of global warming, water shortages, famine and the like would fill the bill. In their totality and in their interactions, these phenomenons do constitute a common threat which demands the solidarity of all peoples ... The real enemy is humanity itself ...

The Club of Rome has, from its beginning, realized the need for such an approach" (page 115).

This statement is astonishing in its cynical presentation of plans to exaggerate problems to create the perceived need for a totalitarian world government led by the Club of Rome and the Trilateral Commission. Take careful note of their statement, "The common enemy of humanity is man." This is the satanically inspired, communist man-hating doctrine that seeks to destroy individual liberty and happiness in the pursuit of a "higher idea" of the greater good. The bloody history of this century's four major experiments to create a "new humanity" were disastrous beyond anything ever experienced in history. The Russian Soviets butchered over sixty million citizens in their attempt to create the "new Soviet man." The Nazi Party drenched Europe in the blood of over fifty million in Hitler's plan to create "a master race." Red China is still killing thousands every month in their concentration camps to add to their thirty-five million past victims. The Marxists in Cambodia slaughtered more than one-half of their population, some four million men, women and children.

After a sobering examination of these ideologies and their socialist experiments throughout this century, we would be well advised to take such people's statements seriously. These New World Order leaders mean precisely what they say. These evil people literally hate humanity. They see individuals as impediments to be killed if they get in the way of their grandiose plans for a New World Order. Their constant preoccupation with plans for population control should alert you to their ultimate intentions. The New Age movement openly talks of the need to eliminate billions of excess people to achieve "harmony" with Mother Earth. A number of New Age and New World Order publications have suggested that the earth can only sustain a population of between one and two billion. Reading between the lines, you can see that some of these people actually plan to reduce the population of the globe to a "more manageable" two billion. They truly believe the world has over three billion excess people. What will happen to the rest of mankind? Strangely these New Age - New World Order strategists passionately want to "save the whales" yet enthusiastically support the right of a mother to kill her unborn child right up to the moment of birth.

These trends are leading us inexorably toward the world government foretold by the ancient prophets so long ago. In the next chapter we will examine the growing threat to the freedoms we cherish coming from those who are planning this world government that is setting the stage for the coming of the Antichrist.

6

The Assault on
Your Freedoms

The approaching New World Order will need to maintain surveillance on all its citizens. The book of Revelation tells us the Antichrist will institute a universal system of population control involving the mysterious Mark of the Beast and the number 666. Recent advances in the technology of surveillance will make this ominous prophecy possible for the first time in history. Massive corporate and government computer databases, fingerprint and DNA records, electronic funds transfer and the monitoring of all phone calls already exist. Much of your privacy and personal freedom has already been lost.

NATIONAL HEALTH AND IDENTITY CARDS

There is a great danger to our liberties as citizens from the introduction of a national identification system. Yet, exploding health costs have triggered a crisis that will force a national health identification system on all Americans. President Clinton has shown a sample biometric identification card on television to prepare citizens for the introduction of this system. These biometric systems will contain your electronic fingerprint or voice print within a tiny computer chip on the card. When you place your card in the reader it will compare your fingerprint or voice against its electronic memory to verity your I.D. When you hand your "smart" computer identification card to your pharmacy or hospital they will have access to your complete medical records. While Americans have resisted such identification cards in the past, the government wants its agencies to be able to track all citizens. This system will make it possible to impose a police state throughout North America overnight.

All citizens in Spain are issued a National Identity Card. A new law will make it illegal for a Spanish citizen to refuse to produce his identity card to officials. Under the proposed law, Spanish police can search cars and houses without a warrant and arrest people for not carrying their National Identity Card. This is not Nazi Germany or Russia, this is democratic Spain, a member of the European Community. If this law is successfully passed, the passage of similar laws throughout the European Community and North America may follow. The pressure to introduce national identity cards is already building in America with the rising crime rate, illegal immigration, the tragedy of abducted children, and the increase in counterfeit credit cards. A letter published in the Union Leader November 11, 1991, illustrated the obvious argument for such identity cards. "Why not ID cards? To identify 300,000 runaway teenagers annually; to identify 9 million illegal aliens; 700,000 phony welfare recipients; 150,000 fugitive criminals." The value of such a universal system to the police is obvious. However, a national identity card will one day pave the way for the totalitarian system of the Antichrist.

FINGERPRINT AND DNA GENETIC IDENTIFICATION

The FBI maintains fingerprint records and computer files on more than fifty million American adults. There is a strong call for all school children to be fingerprinted due to the tragedy of missing and abducted children. Proposals now call for DNA genetic identification. Each cell in your body contains DNA that is absolutely unique to your body. It is the most accurate identification system to date. An oral swab or hair sample from each person could be frozen on identification cards and stored in a vacuum-sealed package. Such a system would eliminate the "unknown soldier" if any blood or body tissue remains. Current proposals call for the automatic DNA testing of all soldiers and prisoners. The FBI would have positive identification of criminals if a hair or blood sample is found at a crime scene. A universal DNA system would provide a future dictator with the technology to find anyone who resisted their plans.

THE MONITORING OF PHONE CALLS

Most people still innocently believe that their phone calls are private. Unfortunately, virtually anyone can obtain a small inexpensive device that will secretly record your phone calls without your knowledge. Government agencies worldwide possess sophisticated surveillance equipment that can record your phone conversations without directly tapping your phone. All long distance phone calls are routed through central stations and satellites back to earth. The National Security Agency (NSA) and its sister agencies in other western countries now monitor every single phone call, fax, and electronic mail transmission in the world. Even secret coded transmissions of foreign governments and corporations are routinely listened to by American intelligence. As an example, the air-to-base radio messages of Iraqi pilots were recorded and used to distract the pilot during air combat in the Gulf War.

A BBC special television report on intelligence and the British government's use of the "Dictionary" program revealed the massive monitoring of all phone calls. Recently accusations were made that a citizen using a radio scanner had intercepted an indiscreet phone call Prince Charles made to a lady. This was nonsense because they would have sold the recording to the tabloids the next day for a million dollars. The call in question was made in 1989, but the British tabloids did not receive the transcript until 1992. The British House of Common's investigation of MI5, British Intelligence, revealed that MI5, British intelligence, were monitoring the phone calls of the Royal Family. Someone in the intelligence community who disliked the Royal Family took the three-year-old surveillance tape and anonymously gave it to the tabloids.

Obviously, it is impossible to listen to millions of simultaneous phone calls, fax, and electronic mail messages. Nor is it necessary. A huge array of sophisticated machines record millions of microwave telephonic voice and digital computer signals passing through the air. These signals are downloaded to a group of Cray IV super computers that completes an instantaneous word analysis. The "Dictionary" computer program listens for specific words from a list of three hundred selected key words, numbers or addresses. All calls that do not include these key words are immediately erased without being listened to by a human. However, if any of these words appear the computers will download that phone call for later human analysis. For example, if someone used any of these words: assassinate, drugs, President Clinton, White House, coke, missile, nuclear, biological, or any of several hundred such key words, the computer would select that call for human listening. Obviously, the vast majority of calls containing those key words are totally harmless—someone is discussing a novel or movie plot. However, the computer might pick up on an assassination plot or a terrorist plan to bomb a defense plant. From that point on, any calls to or from that particular telephone number will be monitored by a human intelligence analyst for evaluation.

VOICE PRINT TECHNOLOGY

Major advances in speech recognition techniques make it possible to control your computer through voice commands. My computer, a Macintosh 840 AV, the fastest personal computer in the world, responds to my voice commands and can repeat aloud anything I write on the computer screen. This advanced speech recognition technology enables intelligence services and corporations to monitor the phone calls of any targeted individual. Advanced Voice Print technology monitors the resonance, density and decibel level of an individual's voice identifying their particular stress, pattern and rhythm. Since each voice is as unique as a fingerprint, high speed computers can identify your voice within seconds from millions of simultaneous phone calls routed through central exchanges or satellites. Telephone companies and police investigators now use voice prints to apprehend and convict perverts making obscene or threatening phone calls. However this technology can also be used by the government or corporations to monitor every phone call made by a targeted individual. This person's voice can be detected instantly, even when calling from a public phone booth or a borrowed phone anywhere in the world. The call can then be secretly monitored, re-directed or terminated.

There were over fifteen hundred terrorist bombings annually in the U.S. five years ago. Each year thereafter the number of incidents dropped dramatically so that in 1992 there were less than ten terrorist bombings. Obviously, the American intelligence community is doing a superb job of intercepting these terrorists before they can accomplish their evil schemes. The FBI recently appealed to phone companies to alter their new optical cable systems that will carry thousands of phone calls on a tiny fiber the size of a human hair. The FBI was concerned that new advanced technology might interfere with their existing ability to easily monitor anyone's phone call. Currently, negotiations are underway to insure that the FBI and other intelligence agencies will still be able to listen in on your phone calls at will. While honest citizens applaud government efforts to catch criminals and terrorists, these technologies pose an ominous threat to our freedoms if a dictator ever seizes power in our nation.

BIG BROTHER IS WATCHING YOU

Computer records around the country contain a staggering amount of personal information on every private citizen. Despite the fact that some of this information is out of date or erroneous, very little data is ever removed. In

1990 the U.S. General Accounting Office discovered that 910 major computer databases contained billions of files on private citizens. A surprising amount of this government data is traded with other government offices, sold to commercial companies, or stolen. The Federal Bureau of Investigation, Defense Intelligence Agency, Central Intelligence Agency, and the powerful National Security Agency possess sophisticated technology capable of secretly accessing any of this data without a trace.

Most companies store personnel records on computer files. The majority of these computer systems are equipped with telephone modems for communicating with computers outside the office. These modems allow a determined computer specialist to steal private information from your file. While these systems are supposedly safeguarded by elaborate passwords, most people use passwords they can easily remember. These passwords are often a variation of their own or their family's birth dates, telephone numbers or Social Security numbers. Anyone with the password can access these inadequately protected interconnected computers with a telephone modem. A high speed computer program can quickly search various possible combinations, or a computer hacker may simply guess the password and access the most sophisticated computer network. The majority of security breeches are never reported because the companies are embarrassed they were penetrated. In addition, new technologies allow intelligence agencies to literally "read" data from magnetic variations on your computer screen while agents are parked in a van across the street from your office. It would astonish you to know how easy it is for a computer professional to access computer files holding the most intimate details of your private, medical, and financial life.

CREDIT REPORTING AGENCIES

Retail credit agencies contain computer records on 170 million U.S. citizens. While your income tax records exist in supposedly secure government computers, a copy of your tax file is often required by your bank when you apply for a loan or mortgage. Your bank balance, bill-paying history, and even unsubstantiated derogatory comments by nosy neighbors are in the computer files of credit reporting agencies. A 1991 Consumers Union study found that 48 percent of the files of credit reporting agencies contain errors. More worrisome is the fact that 19 percent contain errors that might result in your being denied credit.

In July, 1993, *MacWorld* magazine investigated the privacy of your computer records. As a test, two computer writers tried to acquire as much data as possible on eighteen prominent people in business, entertainment, and political fields. They worked from their home computers with a telephone modem accessing legal public databases. These neophyte investigators input only the names and addresses of their subjects. Seventy-five minutes later they found the following information: Birth date, home address and phone, neighbor's address and phone, Social Security number, driver records, marriage record, tax liens, campaign contributions, real estate owned, civil court filings, voter registration, vehicles owned, commercial loans and corporate ties. The average cost? $112.

Obviously a private investigator or government agency, with greater expertise and resources, could discover a lot more. The New York Department of Consumer Affairs discovered that 35 percent of credit reporting agencies were willing to sell your private financial credit reporting file to private investigators in violation of state security and privacy laws. A Lou Harris poll indicates over 80 percent of citizens feel their privacy is threatened. They are correct. I have seen the information that can be acquired in only twenty-four hours by a dedicated computer investigator. If you think privacy still exists in our world, think again.

The buying and selling of information is now a huge business. Several major companies, as supermarkets of information, acquire vast amounts of data from government and private sources for resale to their customers. An unfortunate by-product of our system of credit cards, debit cards, and electronic funds transfers is the total elimination of financial privacy for consumers. Your bank, the police, and credit investigators can track virtually every single purchase you make. The truth is that financial privacy no longer exists for anyone in the Western world. Any knowledgeable person with access to a computer, a telephone modem, and the right access codes can tap into the widely interconnected financial computer systems to bring up your personal files—your medical records, financial records, etc.

THE INTERPOL CONNECTION

The International Police Organization provides a massive police computerized information network connecting 158 national police forces throughout the world to track down international criminals and terrorists. Police computer records of American and Canadian citizens are available to the police forces of other countries through terminals accessing the Interpol Computer System.

However, during World War II, Interpol records were captured by the Nazis. The records were transferred to Germany and were used to round up resistance members and thousands of European Jews. The head of Interpol during the war was Reinhard Heydrich, the leader of the Nazi Storm Troopers. The infamous Wannsee Conference that developed the "Final Solution of the Jewish Problem" was convened at Heydrich's office on January 20, 1942. Following Germany's defeat Interpol helped protect ex-Nazis who fled to South America. After the war Interpol's records were recaptured by the allies. However, despite repeated protests by Israel, Interpol adamantly refused to destroy these records on thousands of innocent Jewish citizens. Interpol has refused to cooperate with Israel in capturing terrorists such as the killers of the Israeli Olympic athletes. Although few western citizens are aware of it, the communist nations of Eastern Europe became members of Interpol long before the so-called "revolutions" in the early 1990s. Since 1990, when Russia joined Interpol, KGB agents can legally access Canadian and U.S. police records on you and your neighbors. In 1991 the Maastricht Treaty created Europol, a European Police Organization, to link the police computers and communications of the twelve nations of the European Community. These organizations, while necessary to fight international crime, are moving us step-by-step towards the totalitarian dictatorship described in the book of Revelation.

LASER AND OPTICAL SCANNING

The laser scanning technology that is used in grocery stores gives you some idea of the ease with which such a control system as the Mark of the Beast could be implemented. Scanning devices, including long distance optical readers, are now used in many buildings, highways, and high security areas. In San Francisco an optical scanner reads the license plates of all cars crossing the Golden Gate Bridge. While you innocently drive across the bridge, enjoying the beautiful view, an instantaneous check of motor vehicle records, parking citations, and outstanding warrants is run against your car's license number. If you have neglected to pay your speeding and parking tickets, a California Highway Patrol officer with a radio-computer link awaits you in a chase car at the end of the bridge to introduce you to some of the dubious benefits of modern technology. Welcome to the world of Big Brother!

When you drive up to many border posts and stop at the red line, an optical scanner reads your license plate. It instantly runs your number through the motor vehicle registry and police files of Canada or the U.S. In the five seconds before you cross the red line the computer also accesses the Immigration and Customs-State Department computers. When the pleasant customs officer asks you where you live, he already knows the answer! His computer shows that you were born in Chicago, you live in Los Angeles, the car you are driving is registered in your name and gives your address. It also shows that you took two trips to Canada in the last five years. Custom and immigration computers record every time you enter and leave the country. If your answers to questions about your place of birth and address do not agree with the computer record, then the suddenly unfriendly customs official will ask you into the customs station for a further investigation.

Miniature computer sensors can now be placed in any object from a product to a car that will allow that object or person to be monitored unobtrusively from a distance. The Detroit and Winnipeg police departments can now track the exact location of every police vehicle on a computer map of their city from a satellite in geostationary orbit over North America. In the future, a detective will simply place a tiny computer sensor in a suspect's car or briefcase and track a kidnapper electronically from either satellite or helicopter. The new surveillance technologies are awesome. For example, during the Waco, Texas tragedy, the FBI inserted special pinhole cameras and microphones through the exterior walls of the compound which then transmitted every sight and sound by radio. In addition the Strategic Air Services from England sent a specially equipped plane over the compound that could photograph every person in the building by sensing their presence through the ceilings and floors through thermal imaging. The government agencies knew what the Branch Davidians were doing at all times. Special surveillance cameras can now photograph in total darkness. Microwave detectors can detect a conversation inside a room three miles away by measuring microscopic vibrations of the windows responding to your voice.

ENVIRONMENTAL LAWS LESSEN OUR FREEDOM

The continued environmental degradation is leading to calls for harsh environmental protection laws. The greed of some corporations and the indifference of many political leaders has brought the world to the point where many species are on the point of extinction. However, one of the great dangers facing freedom today is the widespread introduction of draconian environmental laws. As an example, violations of the Clean Air Act can produce sentences of over four hundred years in prison and fines of up to $25,000 per day. This is bizarre when you consider that individuals committing violent robbery or rape often serve less than five years in prison. These environmental laws also offer $10,000 to informers for telling the government about a suspected violation. This scheme resembles the informer systems that communist and fascist police states use to control their citizens. The government of Ontario, Canada, is proposing a law whereby a farmer can be charged with a criminal offense for cutting down a tree on his farm without a government permit. A farmer can be prevented from allowing his cattle to drink from a stream on his own property because the cattle might "pollute" the water for cottage dwellers downstream.

The disaster of socialism in Eastern Europe and the Soviet Union has led many socialists to disguise their political agenda by dressing it up in environmental language. These drastic laws criminalize actions that used to be mere civil violations. The underlying political agendas of some in the environmental movement is to eliminate private property rights.

Global warming is the great new crisis that the New World Order proponents are using to force nations to submit to international controls. Despite thousands of scientific studies they still cannot determine whether or not the globe is truly warming. It is possible that the variations we have witnessed in the last fifteen years are simply part of a natural cycle. Some scientists believe that a warming trend of one or two degrees would cause increased ocean evaporation that will naturally produce additional cloud cover that will cool the earth back to its original equilibrium. In other words, God created the planet with a self-regulating climatic control system. However, over the next ten years, the Clean Air Act will cost industry over $20 billion in a vain attempt to reduce global carbon dioxide levels. I use the word "vain" because only 2 percent of the 760 billion tons of carbon dioxide produced every year comes from industry. The rest of the CO_2 (98 percent) is produced naturally and cannot be controlled or altered. A total shutdown of industry worldwide would only reduce carbon dioxide emissions by 2 percent. The World Court in Europe passed a resolution in 1988 that has the force of law internationally. The resolution demanded the creation of a "super national agency within the framework of the United Nations that could impose sanctions against any country negatively impacting the environment." When our diplomats sign such agreements they place or own constitutions and laws under the control and oversight of the World Court. In reality they are signing away our freedom and sovereignty without ever asking the people if this is what they wish. The demand for environmental laws is a apple pie and motherhood issue that attracts the support of almost all parties. However the ultimate effect is to transfer our rights and freedoms into the hands of socialist groups that fundamentally oppose private property and free enterprise.

THE WAR AGAINST DRUGS CAN ERODE OUR FREEDOM

The devastating drug epidemic continues to ravage the cities and families of our nation. In addition to the destruction of lives directly attributed to drugs, this scourge has produced the greatest crime wave in history. The need for cash to fund their drug habits encourages addicts to sell drugs or engage in violent crime to get the money to pay for their drugs. The direct and indirect cost of this drug plague amounts to untold billions in stolen property, medical bills, drug enforcement and prisons. However, the greatest cost of drugs may be the loss of our liberty and freedom to the growing demands for totalitarian police methods to fight the drug epidemic. In the pursuit of drug dealers our legislators have passed laws that seriously erode the basic liberties that our democracy is founded upon. The U.S. Supreme Court ruled in 1990 that police can arbitrarily stop cars without cause at roadblocks to randomly search for possible drugs or drunk drivers. This police action is very similar to the laws in totalitarian countries. The premise of such arbitrary searches is that citizens are guilty until proven innocent. Wide-ranging search warrants and intrusive wire tapping are increasingly common as the drug war escalates.

The United States Bill of Rights promises that the citizen will be protected against arbitrary intrusion from government agents. The experience of arbitrary searches by the British soldiers in pre-revolutionary America angered the founding fathers of America. This created an overwhelming desire to prevent any such arbitrary police powers in their new country. The Fourth Amendment of the U.S. Constitution states: "The right of the people to be secure in their persons, houses, papers, and effects, against unreasonable searches and seizures shall not be violated." If we are not very careful the greatest victim of the drug wars could be freedom itself. While honest citizens applaud police efforts to catch drug dealers we are in danger of losing the civil liberties we cherish. The road to world government is paved with good intentions of efficiency and cost savings. However, these systems are setting the stage for the totalitarian rule of the Antichrist.

7

The Financial Road to World Government

One of the most obvious indications that we are moving toward a new world order can be seen in the massive changes to our financial systems. Credit cards, electronic funds transfer, debit cards, bar coding, personal ATM and plans for a single, worldwide currency are preparing the way for the totalitarian control and surveillance of society.

THE MOVE TO A CASHLESS SOCIETY-CREDIT AND DEBIT CARDS

Years ago, banks and financial institutions began a campaign to introduce credit cards to every household. This "buy now - pay later" system has resulted in a huge personal debt load for the average citizen. From the late 1960s until 1985 I worked with a number of banks, insurance companies, and other financial institutions. My access to internal reports and studies of financial corporations allowed me to evaluate their long-range plans for credit cards and electronic funds transfers. These studies and discussions with bank executives revealed that banks did not introduce credit cards for credit transactions only.

Rather, they intended that the universal use of credit cards would prepare us to ultimately abandon the use of checks and paper money entirely in favor of electronic funds transactions. Transporting millions of paper checks from bank to bank through clearing centers is time consuming, costly and inefficient. Instantaneous electronic transfers will speed up financial transactions.

Banks are now introducing debit cards across the country. Debit cards will allow a consumer to buy goods without carrying cash. He will offer his debit card to a clerk and the sales price will be instantly debited from his personal account. The system produces a monthly record of his purchases while eliminating checks and cash. If he is overdrawn the system obtains funds from his credit card account. The bank will collect service charges on every transaction and record every purchase of their customers. Financial institutions knew it would take decades to condition people to abandon cash and trust electronic banking. The massive introduction of credit cards and ATM banking is part of that conditioning.

ELECTRONIC FUND TRANSFER

Because of mail thefts, robberies of welfare recipients, and mail strikes in Canada, the general public easily accepted the idea of having their checks automatically deposited in their banks. Commercial departments of many banks encourage their corporate customers to pay their employees by automatic funds transfer each month. Municipal, state and national governments already use the electronic funds transfer system. Government personnel and other recipients of government checks now have their funds deposited directly to their accounts.

Several years ago a security conference met in Washington to discuss rapidly evolving surveillance technologies that enable governments and investigators to observe any citizen twenty-four hours per day if required. As an exercise, the security teams were asked to recommend the most efficient and inexpensive method to monitor a whole population. They could choose among various options including a huge secret police force, informers, phone taps, television surveillance in all streets and rooms, etc. The security teams concluded, surprisingly, that the most efficient method to totally observe the movements of a complete population was the universal introduction of an Electronic Funds Transfer (EFT) system. They determined that such a system would instantly record every purchase of a newspaper, taxi, or subway ride, and all other economic transactions. The system would unobtrusively track every citizen of interest to the security forces. You cannot move or live in our society without spending money. If the EFT system reveals that two individuals made a purchase in the same street or building you could track their relationship and movement. The planned EFT system and bar-coding of the currency will eliminate financial privacy by creating an electronic record of our daily transactions.

Governments throughout the world are currently involved in experiments to eliminate cash in financial transactions. Several military bases in Canada and the United States (Paris Island, S.C.) are involved in the experiment. Soldiers must turn over all cash when they enter participating bases. Once he enters the base, every transaction from the purchase of clothes at the Post Exchange to the buying of a newspaper is made by an electronic funds transfer card. This special "smart card" is a combination credit-debit card with a miniature computer chip that automatically debits his purchases. Without the card, a soldier on the base "cannot buy or sell." Military bases were chosen for the experiment because they are a "closed" society that allows banks and the government to adjust the system and closely observe the results without interference. Governments and financial institutions plan to use the knowledge gained in these experiments to introduce this "cashless society" throughout western Europe and North America.

THE UNDERGROUND CASH ECONOMY

The greatest problem facing the government is their desperate need to generate additional tax revenues. Huge welfare costs and massive interest payments on the national debt have created staggering deficits. However, the resistance of voters to higher taxes has put the government in a difficult position. Studies reveal a huge amount of the economic and financial transactions are not being recorded or taxed at all. Increasingly, people are using cash in an attempt to escape high taxes. In Canada a recent study noted by the *Western Report* on November 25, 1991, suggested that the untaxed underground economy is approximately $110 billion. The figures for the U.S. economy will be ten times that, or approximately $1 trillion every year. If a significant part of this underground economy was taxed, the budget deficit would disappear and our government could begin to pay down the national debt. Some economists estimate that one-third of the economy escapes taxation.

Five-hundred top police specialists met in Ottawa, Canada, in April 1992 for a conference on fighting a new wave of sophisticated international counterfeiters. Modern criminals are equipped with photographic-quality color copiers, 1000 DPI laser printers and electronic color scanners. This high-tech equipment, in the hands of clever criminals, is capable of turning out counterfeit money, passports, phony checks, and false documents that are so perfect they can fool the experts. Only a few years ago it took a genuine master printer or engraver to produce high quality documents or counterfeit money. Today, the latest technology allows criminals to produce inexpensive, genuine looking documents. This high-tech crime wave is forcing governments and banks to examine the possibility of rapidly converting to a true cashless society with electronic bar coding and embedded computer identification systems to eliminate fraud. As an intermediate step on the way to a cashless society the government plans to introduce a new currency.

The U.S. government has modified its larger currency by inserting a magnetic thread into its $50 and $100 bills that contains the denomination of the bill in microscopic letters. Despite official denials, the magnetic threads in the bills can be detected by airport scanners if a smuggler carries more than $5000 in large bills together. It is also reported that agents with a special scanning device in a van parked outside a building can detect these magnetically marked bills in amounts exceeding $10,000.

Bar Coding the U.S. Currency

One of the most startling of the U.S. government's plans to fight tax evaders is the introduction of a new bar-coded currency. Just as the Universal Product Code on packages can be read instantly by a laser bar code scanner, all new currency will be issued with a bar code. In Europe several countries have introduced bar coded currency. The United States Senate authorized the issuing of new bar-coded currency to "efficiently track U.S. currency—bill by bill—without any undue administrative burden."

When the plan is implemented, the government can easily track the new bar-coded currency. When you go to the bank to withdraw a thousand dollars in cash, a laser scanner would instantly read the bar codes of the bills given to you by the teller or the automatic teller machine. Later that month you may pay three hundred of these dollars to a friend who deposits them in his bank in another state or uses them to buy a suit. The scanner in his bank or store will record the bar codes of the currency he uses. Then the national tax computers of the U.S. Treasury will compare the two transactions concluding that the man received those particular bills directly or indirectly from you. High speed super computers will monitor such transactions and determine whether the amount of cash spent by someone agrees with the income he reports on his income tax form. If there is a discrepancy an audit will follow. The advantages of this system to a cash-starved government are irresistible. Another advantage is that this system will detect drug dealers who operate with large amounts of cash. Introducing such a system worldwide would almost eliminate money laundering.

If you examine the U.S. currency in your wallet you will discover that the smaller denomination bills are the oldest bills you have ever seen. In fact, up to a third of such bills are so faded they can no longer be read correctly by the optical scanners in vending machines. A representative of a vending machine company revealed that the problem is so bad that the vending industry is requesting that the government introduce a new one dollar coin for use in their machines. The reason the money is so old is that the Federal Reserve Banks are no longer collecting old currency bills each day and burning them as they have for decades. Instead they continue to re-use the old faded bills until the government moves to introduce the new bar-coded currency, already approved by the Senate. One reason for the delay in implementation was fear of a political backlash against this attack on financial privacy. Obviously such a bar-code system will forever eliminate the financial privacy of any citizen. A complete computer record of every cash transaction will be in the hands of the government.

A WORLDWIDE CURRENCY

Prior to converting to a cashless society governments plan as an intermediate step to issue new currencies worldwide to replace all national currencies. The European Community, the U.S. Federal Reserve Banks, the International Monetary Fund, and the World Bank are working together to introduce this new currency system. On January 1, 1993, the European Community introduced the new European Currency Unit (ECU). This new European currency will co-exist with other national currencies until 1997—at the latest. At that time all European Community national currencies will be eliminated. The sole currency of the European Community, the world's greatest economic superpower, will be the ECU, the premier currency of the world. The likelihood of Canada and the United States remaining outside of this monetary union by 1997 is between slim and none. The economic argument for a one-world currency will be overwhelming in the late 1990s as one nation after another is forced by economic necessity to abandon their pride in their national currency to join the New World Order. Currency union is another part of the globalist agenda to transfer the citizens' loyalty from his country to the world government. Recent polls in Europe show that young people see themselves as Europeans rather than as Frenchmen or Germans. Interestingly, while the globalists in North America use the softer expression "New World Order," Europeans openly refer to the "World Government."

Europa and the Bull - the Symbol of Europe

It is fascinating to examine the new European Currency Unit. In the past, most countries placed an engraving of a political leader or national symbol on their currency. However, the European Community planners chose a new symbol for their new E.C.U—a woman riding a beast with two horns. This is startling in light of John's prophecy in Revelation about the False Prophet and the revived Roman Empire. "Then I saw another beast coming up out of the earth, and he had two horns like a lamb and spoke like a dragon" (Revelation 13:11). John also foretold an unholy alliance between the false ecumenical church and the revived Roman Empire in the last days. The false church was represented by the "Mother of Harlots" riding on a beast which symbolized the Roman Empire. "So he carried me away in the Spirit into the wilderness. And I saw a woman sitting on a scarlet beast" (Revelation 17:3).

The conscious motivation for the European politicians to choose this particular symbol arises from the ancient Greek myth about Europa and Zeus, the leader of the pagan gods. This ancient myth describes the origin of Europe. According to mythology Zeus wanted to seduce Europa, a beautiful maiden who would have nothing to do with him. He transformed himself into a beautiful bull that later became the pet of Europa. One day, when she was riding the bull he took her across the sea to Crete, revealed himself as Zeus and seduced her. However, it is amazing to see this prophetic symbol of the "Mother of Harlots" and the revived Roman Empire appear on the new currency of the European Community. This same symbol was also engraved on the new stamp commemorating the election of the European Parliament. Both the E.C.U. and the stamp are illustrated in the photo section of this book. The Brooks Instrument Company of the

Netherlands was featured in a recent European magazine noting that it had received the coveted Quality Award issued by the European Standards Committee. After being audited in seven areas of financial health and environmental concern this company could now display the Quality symbol on its letterhead, packaging and product. The Quality Symbol is a woman riding the beast with two horns. If a company wants to be a supplier to a government of the European Community one of the first questions will be, "Do you have the Quality Mark?"

THEY ALREADY HAVE YOUR NUMBER

We have received reports about a massive new computer system in Europe that connects 950 of the world's largest banks and transfers over $5 trillion every day electronically. Our European source claims the system has already assigned an eighteen digit number to every human in the western world in preparation for the coming cashless society. The first set of numbers relate to your sex, your birth date, your social insurance number. The following numbers will indicate your street address. During the last decade special satellites have mathematically mapped every street in the western world. Your number contains your identification and the street you live on.

COMPUTER CHIPS BENEATH THE SKIN

One of the obvious limitations of EFT and credit-debit cards is the problem of theft or loss of the card. Individuals often forget their Personal Identification Number (P.I.N.) and are unable to use the automated teller machines at the banks. Furthermore, when a wallet is stolen, the thief often finds the victim's P.I.N. number hidden in his wallet. By the time the victim reports the theft, the robber has taken thousands of dollars from the bank machines.

A *USA Today* article on April 20, 1992, calculated that "more than $1 billion was lost last year because of misplaced, stolen or counterfeited credit cards." One of the largest banks in the world, Citibank, recently introduced "photo identification" on their VISA and MasterCards as a method of minimizing their losses due to lost and stolen cards. The photo ID credit cards will initially be offered as an option to their thirty million American credit card customers. Other credit card issuers are expected to follow Citibank's lead.

Another way to protect consumers would be to implant a bar code device beneath your skin that would contain your complete medical records as well as financial records. Furthermore, such devices would provide absolutely secure identification for children and mentally handicapped individuals. This device could hold over forty-five billion bits of information that can be accessed by an electronic scanner inducing a current in the passive coil computer chip. Initially these passive coil devices, encased in an one-eighth-inch long plastic capsule, were inserted beneath the skin of the neck of dogs using a needle injector device. The computer chip contained information on the owner and medical information on the animal. The device, unlike dog tags, can not be lost or removed from the animal. According to the *Toronto Star*, May 5, 1992, all animals adopted from the Toronto Humane Society will automatically be implanted with a computer micro chip inserted under their skin to enable owners to trace their new pet. A photo of this device appears in the photo section.

Some have suggested that an even smaller modified device could be placed beneath the skin on the hand of a human. Whenever he wanted to prove his identification or to authorize a purchase, the person would simply extend his hand and the laser scanner would read the data invisibly through his skin. It would authenticate his identification and the store computer would debit his bank account by direct computer access. At the same moment it would modify the data in the computer chip in his hand to reflect the fact that his purchase had debited his bank account by the appropriate amount.

These trends are leading us closer and closer to the totalitarian world government foretold by the ancient prophets. A fundamental principal of democracy is that the price of freedom is eternal vigilance. Many of the worst threats to our freedom appear disguised as progressive steps to create a better world. Unless we wake up to the ultimate agenda of these globalist groups, we will lose the freedom and liberties that make life worthwhile.

8

The Rise of the
European Super State

"The fourth beast shall be a fourth kingdom on earth, which shall be different from all other kingdoms, and shall devour the whole earth, trample it and break it in pieces. The ten horns are ten kings who shall arise from this kingdom" (Daniel 7:23,24).

REVIVING THE ROMAN EMPIRE

Twenty-five centuries ago the prophet Daniel foretold that four world empires would arise in turn to rule the world until the Messiah would appear to establish His eternal Kingdom of righteousness. Daniel prophesied that the fourth great empire (Rome) would revive in the last days to rule the world once more. Thousands of years ago the prophet saw a revived Roman Empire rising in Europe from the ruins of the ancient empire of Rome. In the centuries following the fall of Rome a fierce sense of nationalism arose among the emerging nation-states in Europe. During the last millennium many tried to recreate the Roman Empire that once ruled from Britain to the deserts of Syria. Despite the violent efforts of kings, emperors, popes, and politicians to force them to unite, the European nation-states vigorously resisted— until now. Finally, in our lifetime, the Roman Empire is being revived. Following the devastation of World Wars I and II the ravaged nations of Europe began the first tentative steps toward establishing the foundation of a super state.

THE EUROPEAN COMMON MARKET

In 1957 the Treaty of Rome created a new Common Market in Europe. It evolved from the initial European Coal and Steel Community following World War II. Nationalism and petty bureaucracies made the Common Market initially ineffective. The astonishing vigor of the new European Community makes people forget that only ten years ago most people thought that Europe would never again rise to become a world power. The *Economist* magazine ran a fascinating article in 1982 on the twenty-fifth anniversary of the Common Market. The prospect at that time was so depressing that the magazine's cover showed a tombstone engraved with "European Economic Community." The fear was that without radical change, Europe was doomed to lose its international stature and power to America, Russia, and Japan. The weak independent states of Europe could not guarantee the security of Europe on their own. Some also feared that reliance on the nation state would ultimately lead Europe back into the nightmare of nationalistic wars that had devastated the continent for the last few centuries. Many felt individual European nations would never be strong enough to compete globally. Their only hope was to unite the incredible manpower, intelligence and resources of the nations of Europe into a closely integrated supranational state. The twelve-country community included: Italy, Netherlands, Germany, Ireland, France, Portugal, United Kingdom, Luxembourg, Belgium, Denmark, Spain, Greece.

Jacques Delors's Vision of a New Europe

In 1984 Jacques Delors, a brilliant French finance minister, was looking for a new challenge. When he failed in his goal to become the prime minister of France, Delors was offered the presidency of the lackluster European Economic Community (EEC) as an alternative. Despite the bleak prospects Delors believed the EEC had the potential to transform Europe and regain the ascendancy over the Americans and Japanese. He explained to the various member states that they faced a historic opportunity. "Europe's choice is between survival and decline." The only solution was to break down the antiquated laws, customs, taxes and bureaucratic nightmares that held back business. Delors had a vision of a Europe that would operate economically, defensively and politically as one gigantic super state while still allowing the cultural and language diversity necessary to satisfy the citizen's fundamental needs.

The president of the European Community Commission rules Europe from the thirteenth floor of the Berlaymont, the enormous headquarters office in Brussels, Belgium, that serves as the political center of the emerging European super state. Jacques Delors plans for the European Community to become the greatest power on earth as we approach the new millennium. The goal is to regain the dominance Europe held for most of the last two thousand years from the rise of the Roman Empire till World War II. In interviews he often speaks of the combination of Roman law and Greek spirit as the basis of the "European idea." While his vision of European union is relentlessly futuristic, the plan will produce a modern revival of the ancient Roman Empire that spanned the continent as a powerful super state for almost a thousand years. The 1992 plan for Europe represents an attempt to recreate the past at the same time it reaches out to an unknown future. Magazines in Europe often refer to the EC as "an embryo European government" and "Jacques Delors's European Super state."

It is fascinating to examine the ancient prophecies of the Bible concerning the rebuilding of the Roman Empire in the last days in light of the practical plans underway today to create this European super state. "Behold a fourth beast, dreadful and terrible, exceedingly strong. It had huge iron teeth . . . and it had ten horns. I was considering the horns, and there was another horn, a little one, coming up among them, before whom three of the first horns were plucked out by the roots" (Daniel 7:7–8).

In a pivotal meeting held in 1984, Jacques Delors made four fundamental proposals that would transform the face of Europe forever. The first reform revamped the EEC's institutions to provide a powerful political and organizational base for the community. He proposed major changes to empower the European Commission in Brussels with executive powers under his presidency. The second reform created a common European Defense and Security Policy to eliminate military dependency on America. Delors' third policy reform proposed a true European Monetary Union and a new European currency. This revolutionary idea was resisted by the nationalists, especially Britain, until 1989 when major steps were taken to facilitate the creation of a European financial currency called the European Currency Unit (ECU). The fourth reform was the most fundamental—the creation of an enormous "home market" included more than 320 million consumers. Delors created a truly "unified single internal market" that would operate as if the twelve nations were a single country. At the stroke of the pen a unified Europe became the world's largest market.

THE SINGLE EUROPEAN ACT—THE 1992 PLAN

Although it garnered little world attention at the time, the Single European Act profoundly altered the original Treaty of Rome. It created the legal basis of "the 1992 Plan"—the unification of Europe. A White Paper detailed 275 specific directives to produce the unified market. How long would it take to complete the final integration of markets and political institutions? Jacques Delors said "1992." The "1992 Plan" was born. While some suggested an astrologer or some elaborate computer calculation set the 1992 date, the truth is simply that Delors figured it would take several four-year terms as president of the EEC to accomplish the job. Once the plan was publicized it developed a momentum and life of its own. Today, newspapers and magazines run numerous articles on the progress towards implementation of European unity. The business leadership of Europe is solidly behind the plan to unite Europe. For the first time the pressures for political, economic, social, military and monetary union combined to produce an overwhelming move toward creating a new super state. As the EEC developed into a political and military union the name was changed to the European Community (EC). One of the most startling indications of the new state of affairs in Europe is that on January 1, 1993, all internal border controls were eliminated for European Community citizens. A European Community citizen can now travel from Greece to Italy to France and Britain without ever being asked about his identity or facing questions from customs agents.

The growing environmental concerns in Europe are accelerating the demand for Europe-wide solutions as the close proximity of their countries allows pollution from one country to effect three or four neighboring countries. The EC is now able to respond across national borders and impose solutions that were previously impossible. The fantastic growth of tourist travel in Europe also facilitates the new sense of belonging to a "common home." Few Europeans visited other countries prior to World War II. Today, over 50 percent of Germans and Frenchmen have visited their neighbor country. The Treaty of Rome calls for the "free movement of people" and it is occurring today for the first time in history. This tourism creates a sense of being a "European" rather than being a Frenchman or German. Millions now carry a new European Community Passport rather than their former national passport.

THE TREATY OF MAASTRICHT—THE MOVE TO FULL EUROPEAN UNION

On December 10, 1991, members of the EC signed the Treaty of Maastricht vastly expanding the powers of the

European Parliament and the EC itself. It created a historic political and monetary union that is changing the face of Europe and, ultimately, the world. The new treaty moved Europe beyond the economic and political sphere into the area of complete monetary and military union. Margaret Thatcher warned about the dangers in an article in the European newspaper on May 24, 1992, "The Maastricht Treaty passes colossal powers from parliamentary governments to a central bureaucracy. A dispassionate observer could perhaps be forgiven for wondering whether it is we in the West who are trying to convert the East to democracy or they who are converting us to bureaucracy." Thatcher also revealed the community "is committed to the creation of a single currency no later than 1999. A single currency means a single interest rate, a single monetary policy, a single economic policy, and eventually a single minister. But control over economic policy and the supply of money to the executive is at the heart of parliamentary democracy."

The twelve members have ratified the treaty bringing European union into full effect. The EC parliament of 518 members meets in Strasbourg, France, and is directly elected by popular vote across Europe. Under the new rules the European Parliament has a greater voice in the EC laws on the single market, education, training, environment, consumer rights and health programs. Additionally, the parliament will be consulted on who will head the all-powerful Executive Commission, and will approve the new team of commissioners. The unusual situation of the parliament meeting in Strasbourg while the Executive Commission meets in Belgium will be resolved shortly by moving the parliament to Brussels, Belgium. One of the largest buildings in the world, the new European Community Parliament will cover some four million square feet and cost over one billion dollars. More than twelve thousand employees work for the Executive Commission controlling every facet of life in Europe. The European Court of Justice rules on the interpretations of the decisions and laws of the Commission. German Chancellor Helmut Kohl recently claimed, "We have reached a major milestone on the way to one of the great dreams of our century— political union on a federal basis." Margaret Thatcher, in a speech about the increasing powers of the European Community, warned about the dangers to democracy and freedom if we abandon the sovereign nation state. She called the Maastricht Treaty "the worst abdication and voluntary transfer of political sovereignty and power in western history." In a lengthy article in the *European* newspaper on May 24, 1992, Thatcher wrote, "Will it [the treaty] ensure and enhance democratic government? The answer must be no, for it involves enormous transfers of powers from national governments to a centralized bureaucracy. It speaks of a common foreign and security policy. It extends Community authority in a host of fields and provides for majority voting in many of them."

As Europe unites, many nations fear that they will be shut out of the New World Order and all of its supposed economic advantages. Russia, the Ukraine and many of the former Soviet republics are now negotiating the best deal possible with the EC. First Gorbachev, and now Boris Yeltsin, are talking about a "Common European Home from the Atlantic to the Urals." In the chapter on Russia we will explore the grim possibilities that the Russians, with their still overwhelming military forces, are still planning a sophisticated Trojan Horse strategy to subvert and conquer Europe. Other nations are rapidly forging new international treaties, forming their own regional groupings, including the League of Arab States, the Islamic League, the South Pacific Forum and the North American Free Trade Agreement. The only real competitors to the newly expanded European Community will be the new Western Hemisphere bloc and the Japanese-led Pacific Rim nations. The ultimate merger of these three great alliances will produce the one-world government predicted by the ancient prophets of the Bible.

THE EUROPEAN FREE TRADE ASSOCIATION (EFTA)

On January 1, 1993, the European Community expanded their economic and political union once more to become the world's greatest supranational state. The European Free Trade Association (EFTA) included seven nations that previously formed their own common trading area outside the EC. The seven states included: Norway, Iceland, Sweden, Austria, Finland, Switzerland, Liechtenstein. These EFTA nations have now agreed to join forces to create an enlarged European Community uniting nineteen European nations. The expanded European Community contains half a billion people linking nations from Scandinavia to the Mediterranean.

This new economic colossus now accounts for over 46 percent of world trade, making the EC the largest trading block in the world. Another six nations including Turkey, Hungary, and Poland, with an additional 120 million people, are asking to join this "common European Home." At the present rate of integration and growth, the expanded European Community will have a gross international product greater than $9 trillion by the year 2000. The European Community will increase its gross international product by 5 percent (or over $250 billion) as a result of increased market efficiencies produced by full integration in 1992. The integration of Europe will produce an increased economic growth between now and the year 2000 that will exceed the gross national product of the U.S.A. today. This astonishing economic growth is equivalent to adding another America to the economic world in less than seven years.

A number of Christian church groups in Norway and other countries have expressed concerns about the European Community. They fear that the 1992 Plan will herald the long-prophesied kingdom of the Antichrist described in the book of Revelation. Arthur Berg, a former editor of a Norwegian Christian newspaper warns, "There is a chance that the European Community is making the throne on which the Beast could sit, covering not only Europe, but the whole world." While these Christians are derided by the media and politicians, they warn the people of the dangers in the direction Europe is taking.

The New European Super State

The 1992 Plan for full integration of Europe came into force on December 31, 1992. For the first time in over two thousand years we are witnessing a true "United States of Europe." The unique characteristics of this emerging European Super state supersede any previous alliance or confederation in history. The Europeans now have:

1 European Citizenship and Passport
1 High Court
1 Central Bank and Currency
1 Foreign Policy and European Army
1 Political, Economic, and Military Control

The combination of these factors has produced the world's first truly integrated confederation of nations. Just as the Bible prophesied thousands of years ago, during the generation that the nation of Israel is reborn, the Roman Empire will arise again in the form of a ten-nation confederacy. This confederated super state is destined to rule the world under the dictatorial control of the coming Prince of Darkness, the Antichrist.

Europe's great advantage is its enormous pool of well educated and motivated workers determined to make Europe the world economic leader. German banks and industry are leading the way to dominate the huge new markets of Eastern Europe and the former states of the Soviet Union. They need everything from consumer goods to new industrial plants and transportation. Eastern Europe and the new Commonwealth of Independent States are economic basket cases. However, they possess large numbers of superbly educated engineers and workers, together with the world's largest deposits of natural resources. German reunification created an enormous economic, political and potential, military power in the heart of Europe. The reunification of Germany has provided the model for the massive economic integration of Eastern and Western Europe. Western Europe is now positioned to exploit these unprecedented opportunities. If Europe can successfully integrate its diverse economies and penetrate Eastern Europe and the former Soviet states with its financial and marketing strategies, the EC will be the dominant global power in the years ahead.

The European Parliament Stamp

The European Community's Parliament in Strasbourg created a unique postage stamp to commemorate the December 31, 1992 date that sealed the unity of the European super state. This curious stamp contains the most amazing symbol in light of the ancient prophecies of the book of Revelation. The stamp's engraving shows a woman riding on the back of a two horned beast that is rising above the sea. The prophet John described the coming kingdom of the Antichrist in his vision of a "beast with two horns." In another passage he described "a beast arising out of the sea." In Revelation 17, John described another vision showing the unholy alliance between the false world church of the last days and the rising kingdom of Antichrist. This prophecy revealed the false church as the Mother of Harlots, or as the King James Version describes her, Great Whore of Babylon, riding upon a "scarlet beast" representing the ten nation confederacy of the revived Roman Empire. "Then I stood on the sand of the sea. And I saw a beast rising up out of the sea" (Revelation 13:1). "Then I saw another beast coming up out of the earth, and he had two horns like a lamb and spoke like a dragon" (Revelation 13:11). "And I saw a woman sitting on a scarlet beast which was full of names of blasphemy, having seven heads and ten horns" (Revelation 17:3). An illustration of this European Parliament stamp is included in the photo section.

The North Atlantic Treaty Organization

NATO's sixteen-nation organization successfully defended Western Europe and North America for almost five decades against the vast arms buildup of the Soviet Union and the communist nations of Eastern Europe. Now that the Warsaw Pact has officially disbanded and the Commonwealth of Independent States (CIS) has replaced the Soviet Union, many in Europe are rethinking the future role of NATO. Some suggest that the organization should be eliminated. Others recommend that NATO be transformed into a political and foreign relations coordinating body. However, the civil war in former Yugoslavia has threatened Europe with the first real war since the end of World War II. Although the original NATO treaty prohibited the action of its armed forces outside the basic Western European theater of operation, NATO's armed forces are now being used under the auspices of the United Nations to assist in peacekeeping in Bosnia. Some suggest that NATO troops be used to control the civil war between Armenia and Azerbaijan in the former Soviet Union. This startling proposal was actually approved by some members of the Russian government. It would transform NATO's role from defending Europe and North America to becoming the armed forces reserve for the United Nations and the European Community. This action would please the Russians because their long-term goal has always been to remove NATO as a bulwark against a Russian invasion of Europe. The nations of Eastern Europe, escaping from decades of Soviet domination, requested NATO membership to protect themselves against a resurgent Russian imperialism. Naturally Russia has protested against this move. Tragically, both American and Western Europe have rejected immediate NATO membership for these states out of fear that they might offend Russian sensibilities.

In an article on the European Community, commentator Larry Abraham warned about the implications of the 1992 Plan: "All of Europe—not just Russia or the Eastern block—is in the process of perestroika, or 'restructuring.' The first step is already finalized with the 1992 common currency for the EEC. This will be followed by the gradual surrender of national sovereignty to the European Parliament" (March 1990, *Insider Report*). He also pointed out that the Russians and the Eastern European nations "will ultimately join this 'Urals to the Atlantic' federation. These steps are being initiated with meetings and agreements with the Conference on Security and Cooperation in Europe. Watch for this organization to take on increased importance."

THE ROLE OF AFRICA AND
MEDITERRANEAN NATIONS

During many years of teaching about the Bible's prophecies of the revived Roman Empire, I pointed out that the present European Community encompasses only the nations of the western portion of the ancient Roman Empire. Daniel 2 described the prophetic symbol of the Roman Empire as a metallic image of a man with two iron legs, representing the Eastern and Western Roman Empires. In its final form the symbolic image contained two feet with ten clay and iron toes. This image, with five toes on each foot suggests that final revived form of the Roman Empire will include nations from both the former Western and Eastern Roman Empire. Turkey, Syria, Lebanon, Israel, Egypt, Libya, Tunisia, Morocco and Algeria belonged to the Eastern Byzantine Empire for a thousand years from the fourth century until 1453. Therefore I pointed out the possibility that the kingdom of the Antichrist will ultimately expand to encompass some of these nations as well as Western Europe.

Israel and Egypt are now associate members of the European Community. It is fascinating to observe the new EC negotiations developing strategic and economic ties with the north African nations of Mauritania, Morocco, Tunisia and Algeria. These Mediterranean countries are to receive special assistance from the EC. An executive commission is examining the advantages of joining the Mediterranean countries of north Africa into a new common market associated with the European Community. The massive legal and illegal immigration of millions of north Africans into Europe in search of jobs and a better life is producing tremendous social problems. Over 6.5 percent of the population of France are legal immigrants, but officials estimate that there are at least 2.5 million illegal immigrants. The EC Commission has reported that the population growth in North Africa will vastly exceed any possible economic growth in the area. The population of Algeria, Morocco and Tunisia alone will explode from a current 60 million to more than 112 million in the next thirty years. This means their economic standard of living will continue to fall, producing a huge wave of immigrants desperately seeking a better life in Europe.

Many young Europeans are unwilling to do the basic infrastructure jobs of society. Where will Europe find the nannies and maids, the restaurant and garbage workers needed to keep the cities functioning? The answer is obvious: the willing and able immigrants from north Africa. But there is a price. The governments of north Africa are demanding a seat at the table of the European Community. Negotiations have commenced regarding associate membership in the EC ultimately leading to full membership. As Europe considers the problems of Africa, the community has committed an emergency aid package of $265 million to deal with the growing famine conditions affecting the Sub-Sahara region. Some sixty million in Africa now face the worst famine in this century.

King Juan Carlos of Spain and King Hassan of Morocco successfully negotiated the construction of an eighteen-mile-long bridge linking Africa and Europe for the first time in history. This tremendous historic engineering project is slated to be completed by the year 2000. It will link Morocco and Spain at an estimated cost of $10 billion and will open vast amounts of trade between the two continents. The suspension bridge will be supported by enormous steel piers spaced a mile apart to allow the safe passage of some fifty thousand ships each year that enter or exit the Mediterranean at the Straits of Gibraltar. The World Bank and the EC will oversee the international funding of this incredible project. It will revitalize the transportation networks of north and central Africa and provide an inexpensive trade route between the two continents. Step by step, the rebuilding of the Roman Empire continues.

THE KINGDOM OF THE MESSIAH

European leaders are unaware of the ancient biblical prophecies which warn that the reunion of Europe will prepare the way for the rise of the Antichrist. Step by step, exactly as the Bible predicted, the Roman Empire is reviving before our eyes. The good news is that, after the terrible seven-year tribulation period is completed, the whole world will finally unite, not under the control of evil men, but under the righteous government of the coming Messiah. The Kingdom of the Messiah will produce the joy, peace, prosperity and justice man has dreamed about for so long.

Daniel was unique among the prophets of Israel in that God allowed him to foresee the time of the coming Messiah with great precision. He received a revelation of the ten nations reforming the Roman Empire. Then God showed Daniel that Christ would establish His kingdom in the lifetime of the leaders who would reestablish the Roman Empire. "And in the days of these kings the God of heaven will set up a kingdom which shall never be destroyed; and the kingdom shall not be left to other people; it shall break in pieces and consume all these kingdoms, and it shall stand forever. . . . God has made known to the king what will come to pass after this. The dream is certain, and its interpretation is sure" (Daniel 2:44,45).

According to the Jewish commentators the phrase "in the days of these kings" indicates that the prophecy will be fulfilled in the lifetime of the men who are re-creating the Roman Empire. The reunification of Europe gives us hope that our generation will witness the fulfillment of the prophecies leading to the triumphant return of Christ to establish His eternal Kingdom. The coming Messiah will "set up a kingdom which shall never be destroyed."

9

Israel—The Key to World Government

"Multitudes, multitudes in the valley of decision! For the day of the Lord is near in the valley of decision" (Joel 3:14). Israel is the key nation to watch if we want to understand God's unfolding plan to redeem the earth. The prophet Joel prophesied of the coming great day of the Lord when God will bring the nations to meet Israel in "the valley of decision." This appointed battle will occur in the great Valley of Jezreel in northern Israel that lies before the ancient city of Megiddo. God will gather the nations of the world together at the Battle of Armageddon to determine who will rule the world. In the chapter on Armageddon we will explore the Bible's prophecies about this incredible battle.

THE RISE OF ANTI-SEMITISM

"Then they will deliver you up to tribulation and kill you, and you will be hated by all nations for My name's sake. And then many will be offended, will betray one another, and will hate one another" (Matthew 24:9–10). In these tragic and prophetic words, Jesus warned His disciples that rising anti-Semitism would be one of the final signs of His second coming. This implacable hatred of the Jewish people is the mark of a civilization unredeemed by the love of God. Satan inspired a growing hatred of the Jews in Germany that finally culminated in the Holocaust with the deaths of over six million Jews. During the 1930's the Nazi propaganda machine of Dr. Goebbels produced racist cartoons and diabolical film portrayals of the Jewish people to convince Germans that Jews were sub human. It is frightening to witness the same evil portrayals created today in Russia and Arab countries to encourage hatred of the Jews. The depth of the hatred for Jews displayed in articles in Arab newspapers is chilling.

Satan hates the Jews because God picked Israel to be His Chosen People. They acted as God's messengers to mankind giving the world the Ten Commandments, the written Word of God, and the birth of the Messiah. God changed Jacob's name to Israel because it means "Prince with God." Satan knows that God plans to redeem the planet from his evil rule including the redemption of His chosen people Israel. The devil can read prophecy in the Bible as well as you. He knows that the rebirth of Israel in 1948 began a chain of prophetic events that will inevitably end in this generation with his destruction at the hand of Jesus the Messiah. This knowledge motivates Satan's unrelenting hatred of Israel.

Christ's prophecy of a terrible persecution of Jews in the final generation is already beginning to be fulfilled in desecrations of Jewish synagogues and cemeteries around the world. Even in Japan, with only a thousand Jews living in the country, racist anti-Semitic books, including the forgery entitled *The Protocols of the Elders of Zion* are best sellers. The "Protocols" an anti-Semitic propaganda book, was forged by the anti-Semitic Russian secret police prior to World War I. It purports to be a plan by a group of Jewish conspirators to take over the world. Amazingly, despite its proven source as a forgery, this evil book continues to be a best seller throughout the Arab world and many other countries. Tragically, several patriotic American groups still quote from this forgery as if it were true.

Dozens of nations, within and outside the Arab

world, and thousands of companies participated whole-heartedly in the illegal Arab boycott of Israel since 1948. Though illegal, many nations and companies still comply with the boycott, refusing to do any business with Israel, in order to gain access to the Arab countries' petro-dollars.

REPLACEMENT THEOLOGY—A REJECTION OF GOD'S COVENANT WITH ISRAEL

Another tragic sign of the last days is the revival of a re-placement theology that refuses to grant Israel its rightful place in the Bible and in God's prophetic plan for the fu-ture. Some Christians still reject the clear teaching of the Old and New Testaments about the role of Israel in God's plan for the redemption of the planet. The Bible declares that Israel's covenant with God is unbroken. Is-rael is still the key to the unfolding prophetic events lead-ing to the second coming of Christ. Since these prophetic Scriptures are unshakable, the only way to escape their clear message is to arbitrarily change the meaning of the Bible's words. This is the same method used in the medi-aeval period to ignore and eliminate Israel. Today, the movement appears under a number of names including Replacement Theology, Restoration Theology, Kingdom Now, or Dominion Theology. Their basic premise is that God's covenant with Israel has been broken and the Christian Church has "replaced" Israel forever in God's plan. There is a major division growing between churches and denominations over Israel's role in God's plan today. While many of the supporters of this theol-ogy are not themselves personally anti-Semitic, this doc-trine can prepare the ground for an anti-Semitism within the Church.

Vehement hatred for Israel manifests itself in blatant anti-Semitism and widespread unbalanced media report-ing on the Middle East. When Israel expelled 415 Hamas terrorist members, the world's media universally con-demned this action and sympathetically interviewed the terrorists. At the same time Egypt executed many Muslim terrorists while Algeria summarily sent over a thousand extremists to camps in the desert. Not a single Western media voice condemned these actions by Arab states in their war against Islamic terrorism. If Middle Eastern oil is cut off in a future Arab-Israeli crisis we could witness a massive reaction and hatred against Israel. Rather than blame Israel, the real culprit will be the economic and political choices of our governments that left our countries dependent on cheap Middle Eastern oil. We should have supported a higher gasoline price policy that would create a strong independent domestic oil business. This policy would provide America with a guaranteed energy self-sufficiency based on using the huge oil resources God provided in this North American continent.

The media have repeatedly criticized Israel for its efforts to stop Arab terrorism in the territories. The reporters claim that Israel's soldiers are using excessive force in arresting Palestinians. However, these Arab terrorists started arming themselves with guns recently, leading to a number of armed battles in West Bank villages. Knowledgeable Arab sources claim that less than 25 percent of the Arab "collaborators" tortured and killed by the PLO are connected with Israel's security services. Many innocent individuals are tortured and murdered because a personal enemy informed on them to the intifada leadership. In the first four months of 1992 the army arrested fourteen hundred Palestinian terrorists and leaders of the intifada. Many of these men were armed and were charged with torturing and killing other Arabs believed to collaborate with Israel. Only thirteen of the fourteen hundred arrested suspects were killed during their capture, less than one per cent, despite the fact that many of them were armed. These figures indicate that the Israeli army is exercising incredible care in a difficult situation. Compare this result with the disastrous casualties sustained at Waco, Texas.

American State Department officials have belittled Israel's value to America as a strategic ally since the end of the Cold War. This criticism is part of a well-planned strategy to distance America from active support of Israel. As an example, former National Security Advisor Zbigniew Brzezinski, a leading member of the Trilateral Commission and the Council on Foreign Relations, derided Israel's vast contributions to America in the area of intelligence cooperation. Brzezinski stated, "I can state categorically that the value of the intelligence that the U.S.A. transfers to Israel . . . exceeds what the U.S.A. obtains from Israel." This false statement reflects the distaste for Israel projected by many New World Order leaders. The leading authority on the value of the intelligence which Israel transferred to America is General George Keegan, the former U.S. Air Force Chief of Intelligence. He declared: "We have benefited from Israeli Intelligence in the equivalent of billions of dollars . . . I could not have acquired this [intelligence] with five CIA's and a $50 billion budget . . . I can say without reservation that for every dollar [the U.S.A.] has given to Israel, we have gotten a thousand dollars of benefit in return."

One last example of White House manipulation of the media against Israel concerns the astonishing "leaks" from the administration that Israel had illegally transferred Patriot Missile technology to China. This charge of treason was released to the press and not denied by the White House. Yet they knew it was false. The Chinese tripled their intelligence penetration of American defense industries in the last three years and may have acquired Patriot technology through their spy network. China is the prime supplier of missile technology to Israel's Arab enemies. Why would Israel sell Patriot technology to China who would use it to modify their Silkworm and other missiles they sell to Syria and Iraq to later attack Jerusalem? The charge was both evil and nonsense. The White House allowed the "leak" to damage Israel's reputation in the minds of American citizens for several months. Then, after the damage was done, the White House admitted that there was no evidence whatsoever to support the charge. However, out of the millions of citizens who listened to the original charge of treason against Israel, less than 10 percent will ever hear that the accusation was false and that Israel was blameless. The damage was done.

THE FINAL WAVE OF PERSECUTION
UNDER ANTICHRIST

The book of Revelation tells us that during the Great Tribulation the Antichrist, empowered by Satan, will attempt to destroy Israel and the Jewish people. "And she bore a male Child who was to rule all nations with a rod of iron. And her Child was caught up to God and to His throne. Then the woman fled into the wilderness, where she has a place prepared by God, that they should feed her there one thousand two hundred and sixty days." (Revelation 12:5,6). The woman in John's vision is Israel who "bore a man child," namely Jesus of Nazareth, who will someday "rule all nations with a rod of iron." Israel's "male Child" Jesus was "caught up to God" almost two thousand years ago. Many times in the Old Testament God used the symbol of a woman to indicate His relationship to Israel. The woman in Revelation 12 cannot represent the Church because Jesus preceded and formed the Church; not the other way around. The Church did not give birth to Jesus, the "male Child." Historically and prophetically, the "woman" Israel gave birth to Jesus the Messiah.

Jesus warned His disciples that Satan would attempt to destroy the Jews during this tribulation period by persecuting all who will not accept the Antichrist as Messiah. The passage in Matthew 24:15 describes the awful tribulation when the Antichrist will defile the rebuilt Temple in Jerusalem. "Jesus said, 'Therefore when you see the "abomination of desolation," spoken of by Daniel the prophet, standing in the holy place' (whoever reads, let him understand), 'then let those who are in Judea flee to the mountains. Let him who is on the house top not come down to take anything out of his house. And let him who is in the field not go back to get his clothes. But woe to those who are pregnant and to those with nursing babies in those days! And pray that your flight may not be in winter or on the Sabbath' " (Matthew 24:15–20).

Christ warned that the persecution will commence the moment the Antichrist defiles the Holy of Holies. Many righteous Jews will recognize the Man of Sin at that time as a false Messiah and will reject him. Apparently the persecution will begin so quickly that Jesus warns the Jews to literally flee without stopping to "take anything out of his house." The warning implies that Antichrist's persecution will have a demonic supernatural element to it requiring extraordinary escape measures. Revelation 12:6 tells us that "the woman," Israel, will flee into "the wilderness" to escape the punishment that the Antichrist will inflict on those who reject his claims to be God. The Lord will prepare "a place" for her in the wilderness as a special protection from Satan's attack. While many suggested Petra in Jordan as the place of protection in the wilderness, it is probable that the refuge will involve more than the ancient desert city of Petra. The size of Petra would prevent its use as the sole refuge for more than a small fraction of the Jews of Israel. It is likely that the majority of Jews will flee to many nations, including Egypt. The prophet Isaiah spoke about five cities in Egypt that will speak Hebrew in the last days. "In that day five cities in the land of Egypt will speak the language of Canaan" (Isaiah 19:18). This situation may come about as a result of Jewish refugees fleeing to Egypt to escape the Antichrist's persecution in Israel. Christ taught, Matthew 25, about the judgment of the "nations" on the basis of their treatment of His Jewish and Gentile followers during the terrible persecution. This suggests that individuals in many nations, including America and Canada, may be involved in an effort to provide sanctuary for the Jews during the Great Tribulation. Even after the rapture of the Church to heaven there will be many people whose Judeo-Christian background and love of liberty will motivate them to provide protection to the Jews and Gentiles fleeing the totalitarian forces of the Antichrist.

John's prophecy in Revelation assures Israel of God's miraculous protection as Satan attempts to destroy them. The prophet describes a future supernatural battle in the heavens when Satan will be violently cast down to the earth. "And war broke out in heaven: Michael and his angels fought against the dragon; and the dragon and his angels fought, but they did not prevail, nor was a place found for them in heaven any longer. So the great dragon was cast out, that serpent of old, called the Devil and Satan, who deceives the whole world; he was cast to the earth, and his angels were cast out with him" (Revelation 12:7). The passage indicates that Satan will be cast to the earth at the mid-point of the seven-year tribulation period leading to the Battle of Armageddon. The Bible speaks of great spiritual battles in the heavenlies of which we are only dimly aware. The Scriptures indicate that as many as one-third of the angels joined Satan's initial rebellion against God in the dateless past. A small hint of this spiritual warfare appears in Genesis 6 concerning Satan's attempt to subvert mankind through the fallen angels. The book of Revelation prophesies about demonic attacks during the tribulation period led by a demon spirit named Apollyon.

The prophet John warned of the horror that will follow when Satan attacks Israel. "Woe to the inhabitants of the earth and the sea! For the devil has come down to you, having great wrath, because he knows that he has a short time. Now when the dragon saw that he had been cast to the earth, he persecuted the woman who gave birth to the male Child" (Revelation 12:12,13). The attack on Israel will be ferocious because Satan, aware of the prophecies, will know he has only 1260 days until his final defeat at the hands of Jesus Christ. Revelation 12:14–16 describes Satan's supernatural attempts to destroy the Jews and Israel's divine protection. "But the woman was given two wings of a great eagle, that she might fly into the wilderness to her place, where she is nourished for a time and times and half a time, from the presence of the serpent. So the serpent spewed water out of his mouth like a flood after the woman, that he might cause her to be carried away by the flood. But the earth helped the woman, and the earth opened its mouth and swallowed up the flood which the dragon had spewed out of his mouth."

Possibly the Antichrist will use a weapon, such as an underwater thermonuclear device, to create a huge tidal wave in an attempt to overthrow the fleeing Jews. The fact that Scripture specifically states that the "earth opened its mouth, and swallowed up the flood" may indicate that the devastation of such a tidal wave will be averted by a supernatural earthquake that will open a chasm to absorb the water. Possibly the word "water" refers symbolically to some other method of destruction that Satan will use at that time. However the prophecy is fulfilled, the Bible tells us that God will protect Israel during the 1260 days of persecution.

As Revelation 12:17 declares, after this deliverance of Israel, Satan will turn to attack those Gentiles who have accepted the Messiah, the "rest of her offspring." John prophesied: "And the dragon was enraged with the woman, and he went to make war with the rest of her offspring, who keep the commandments of God and have the testimony of Jesus Christ." Despite the terrible persecution, multitudes of the Jews and Gentiles will become believers in Jesus as Messiah during the Great Tribulation. These believers will respond to the message of the Two Witnesses, the 144,000 Jewish witnesses and the three angelic messengers mentioned in the book of Revelation. The prophet John describes this huge harvest of tribulation saints as follows, "After these things I looked, and behold, a great multitude which no one could number, of all nations, tribes, peoples, and tongues, standing before the throne and before the Lamb, clothed with white robes, with palm branches in their hands, and crying out with a loud voice, saying, 'Salvation belongs to our God who sits on the throne, and to the Lamb!' " (Revelation 7:10).

God will never leave the earth without a witness. Even though the rapture of the Church will translate the Christians to heaven before this point, the clear testimony of the prophet is that millions will respond to the message to repent "make straight the way of the Lord" during the tribulation period. The identity of these millions of new tribulation believers in this "great multitude" is certain: "Then one of the elders answered, saying to me, 'Who are these arrayed in white robes, and where did they come from?' And I said to him, 'Sir, you know.' So he said to me, 'These are the ones who come out of the great tribulation, and washed their robes and made them white in the blood of the Lamb' " (Revelation 7:13,14). During the

Tribulation, the Antichrist and the False Prophet will attempt to destroy those who reject him, often with beheading (Revelation 20:4). Millions will pay the ultimate price of martyrdom for their faith in Christ during the persecution in the Great Tribulation.

The Antichrist will first gain power over three of the ten nations of the emerging revived Roman Empire. Then, following a future crisis, according to the prophet Daniel, he will obtain total control over the remaining seven nations composing the ten nations of the final Gentile world empire. The strategic role of Israel will be critical in the plans of the Antichrist to cement his control over the nations of the world. Daniel tells us that the Antichrist will confirm a treaty with Israel for seven years. "Then he shall confirm a covenant with many for one week; but in the middle of the week he shall bring an end to sacrifice and offering. And on the wing of abominations shall be one who makes desolate, even until the consummation, which is determined, is poured out on the desolate" (Daniel 9:27). Initially he will be accepted by many of the Jews and Gentiles as a Messiah-figure. However, the "prince who is to come" will reveal his true satanic nature three-and-a-half years after the treaty signing when he will stop the daily sacrifice in the rebuilt Temple in Jerusalem. Satan hates the Temple of God and the sacrifice that reminds men that Jesus, the Lamb of God, shed His blood for us as the one true, effective sacrifice for sin.

The Antichrist will be slain in the mid-point of the seven year treaty. "And the dragon gave him his power, his throne, and great authority. I saw one of his heads as if it had been mortally wounded, and his deadly wound was healed. And all the world marveled and followed the beast" (Revelation 13:2,3). Immediately after telling of the Antichrist's death and resuscitation, Revelation 13:5 tells us that "he was given authority to continue for forty-two months," a period of three and one-half years that will end at Armageddon. Some writers have questioned whether or not this death wound to "one of his horns" truly relates to an actual death of the Antichrist. Others wonder if this refers symbolically to the "death" and revival of a nation. However, John's further words clarify that he must be referring to an actual man, the Antichrist. Revelation 13:12 declares that the False Prophet "causes the earth and those who dwell in it to worship the first beast, whose deadly wound was healed." It is obvious that people do not worship a nation, empire or ideology. John confirmed that the one who dies is a man, the Antichrist, by telling us, "And he deceives those who dwell on the earth by those signs which he was granted to do in the sight of the beast, telling those who dwell on the earth to make an image to the beast who was wounded by the sword and lived" (Revelation 13:14). The False Prophet's satanic power causes this supernatural statue, "the image of the beast," to "speak" in imitation of a man.

Since the Antichrist will stop the daily sacrifice in the Temple, it is possible that the one who kills him with a death wound will be an Israeli Jew enraged at his blasphemy against God when "he sits as God in the temple of God, showing himself that he is God" (2 Thessalonians 2:4). As Revelation declares, the Antichrist will satanically rise from the dead and live. Some writers doubt that the Antichrist will actually die and be resurrected. However, the Scriptures clearly describe a real death with a sword wound and a resurrection. Somehow God will allow this act to occur to fulfill the prophecies. Remember that the evil magicians in Egypt manifested satanic supernatural powers in duplicating some of the plagues.

If his death and resuscitation occurs thirty days after he stops the daily sacrifice, this may account for the puzzling fact that Daniel refers once to 1260 days and then to a period of 1290 days. The Hebrew phrase "a time, times and half a time" indicates 1260 days because a "time" equals a year of 360 days, "times" equals two years and "half a time" equals half a year of 180 days. Daniel therefore describes a "time, times and half a time," as a period of precisely 1260 days for the duration of Antichrist's power over the tribulation saints of God. This period of 1260 days is the last three and one-half years of the seven-year treaty period (Daniel's Seventieth Week of years). Yet he tells us in another passage that there are precisely 1290 days from the stopping of the daily sacrifice until the end. Daniel 12:7 records that "it shall be for a time, times, and half a time; and when the power of the holy people has been completely shattered, all these things shall be finished." In Daniel 12:11 he states, "And from the time that the daily sacrifice is taken away, and the abomination of desolation is set up, there shall be one thousand two hundred and ninety days." Both periods terminate at the Battle of Armageddon with the victory of the Messiah over Antichrist. In other words Antichrist will stop the daily sacrifice 1290 days before Armageddon. Thirty days later, he will be killed by someone. Then he will be resurrected satanically. The Antichrist will persecute the tribulation saints for the remaining 1260 days until his defeat by Jesus Christ.

If a Jewish believer kills the Antichrist and Israel resists the Man of Sin's defilement of the rebuilt Temple, this may trigger the terrible persecution of the Jews during the Great Tribulation. As Jeremiah the prophet declares, "Alas! For that day is great, so that none is like it; and it is the time of Jacob's trouble, but he shall be saved out of it" (Jeremiah 30:7).

ISRAEL—A TEST CASE FOR THE NEW WORLD ORDER

Why is Israel so critical in plans for world government? As President Clinton and his advisors make their plans for the New World Order they desperately need to solve the crisis in the Middle East. It is one of the most difficult and intractable of the issues upsetting the delicate balance of power in the emerging world government. The War in the Gulf was the first real test of this New World Order. The United Nations punished Iraq for defying the expressed will of the Security Council. As the UN passed a series of resolutions punishing Iraq's aggression, the U.S.A. and its allies decided to use all the power necessary to punish Iraq as a renegade power. The measures used against Iraq after the conclusion of hostilities overturned decades of self-imposed rules by the United Nations against interfering in the internal affairs of a sovereign nation. In the forty-five years since World War II the UN has followed a fundamental principle of refusing to involve itself in internal conflicts or problems within member countries.

However, the rules changed dramatically following the War in the Gulf. To establish the power of the New World Order is was essential to transform the United Nations into a vehicle to manipulate member nations according to the wishes of the great powers. In the past, raw power was exercised by a great power through gun-boat diplomacy, subversion, or military action. Today, mass media attention and world political sensibilities require the marshalling of coercive military and political power under the auspices of the respected United Nations. In the aftermath of the War in the Gulf the United Nations sent inspection teams deep into Iraq against Hussein's wishes to search for nuclear, biological, and chemical weapons of mass destruction. While this was a desirable goal when dealing with a dictator like Saddam Hussein, a very dangerous legal precedent was established. The UN now has the authority and legal power to force its will on a member state and violate its sovereignty in a search for weapons. David Kay, the American leader of the UN nuclear inspection team, told reporters that he could hardly wait to complete his work in Iraq because he really wanted to inspect Israel's nuclear program. Israel? Why would he talk about Israel? He obviously knew that senior people in the UN proposed using the expanded power of the world body to try and "denuclearize" Israel. This would make it vulnerable to the overwhelming conventional and chemical weapons of its Arab enemies.

In a related area the United Nations also carved out "Kurdish zones" or enclaves in northern Iraq to protect the Kurdish refugees against the terrors and retaliation of Hussein's army. While this was a laudable goal, another dangerous legal precedent was established. Now the UN General Assembly could use the Iraqi precedent to argue in the future that the UN would be acting according to international law in carving out zones or enclaves to "protect" the Palestinians against Israel in the West Bank or Gaza. PLO Chairman Yassir Arafat has repeatedly called for the United Nations to pass resolutions against Israel. He wants the UN to use its peace-keeping troops in the West Bank and Gaza to "protect Palestinians" against Israeli troops.

THE EUROPEAN COMMUNITY AND ISRAEL

The European Community is strongly pushing for involvement in the Middle East peace negotiations. As reported by the *Jerusalem Post* on May 10, 1992, the Italian Foreign Minister Gianni De Michelis offered "incorporating Israel into the European Community economic zone in return for an agreement to involve the European Community in the Middle East political process." As the article pointed out, "The Europeans want Israel to help them gain parity with the U.S.A. and Russia in the region's political process." This is only the beginning of a process that will ultimately culminate in the revived Roman Empire making a seven-year defense treaty with Israel as described by the prophet Daniel.

ISLAM AND THE UNITED NATIONS

In assessing the barrage of hateful speeches in the United Nations against Israel, it is worthwhile to consider the nature of many of the third world nations composing the majority of the UN General Assembly. Of the 181 member states of the United Nations, Islam is the major religion in thirty-five of them (22 percent). Judaism is the major religion in only one nation, Israel. The Palestinians claim that the only place where they could possibly establish a Palestinian state must be in the tiny area of the West Bank or Gaza. However, vast areas of undeveloped land are available in the Middle East among their oil-rich Arab brethren that would easily provide the land and resources needed for a Palestinian state of their own. To gain a realistic perspective on the question of "land for peace," consider the following facts.

THE RELATIVE SIZE OF THE ISLAMIC NATIONS, THE U.S.A. AND ISRAEL

	Square Miles	Population
Islamic Nations	8,879,548	804,500,000
United States	3,540,939	252,000,000
Israel	8,000	5,000,000

When the Palestinians demand that Israel surrender "land for peace," consider that Israel is so small that you could fit thirty-two nations the size of Israel into the state of Texas. Even Saudi Arabia is more than 107 times larger than Israel. The total land area of the thirty-five Islamic nations is more than 1107 times larger than Israel. When the media suggest that the only place where the Palestinians could possibly settle is in Israel, they are ignoring the fact that Islamic and Arab countries possess vast empty areas. The Arabs also own enormous oil reserves that could easily provide the basis for rebuilding productive lives for these people. Those Arabs in Israel and the territories that are willing to live in peace with the Jews would be welcome to stay. However, for those that insist on Arab sovereignty, there are ample territories in the Islamic states where they could establish their autonomy while living side by side with their Arab and Islamic brothers. In this century of devastating wars, over fifty million refugees from many nations were successfully resettled in other countries. No one ever suggested that the millions of displaced Germans, Poles, Vietnamese and other refugees return home. These refugees created a new life for themselves as citizens in their new countries. It is only in the case of the Palestinians that the UN and Arab governments cynically demanded they be held in refugee camps for over four decades against the impossible chance that history can be reversed so they could return to the places they abandoned so long ago.

In the 1948 War of Independence Egypt and Jordan militarily occupied the West Bank and Gaza. Until 1967 the Arabs of the West Bank and Gaza insisted that they were Arabs belonging to Greater Syria. However, after they lost control of the territories during the Six Day War, they invented the fiction that the Arabs in the territories are a distinct race called Palestinians, existing "from time immemorial" in the Holy Land. The truth is that the name Palestinian was applied almost exclusively to the Jewish people of the Holy Land until 1967. As an example of the Jewish use of the word *Palestinian*, the Jewish *Jerusalem Post* was called the Palestine Post during the first five decades of this century. As an example, from 1948 to 1967 Jordan occupied the West Bank. There is not one article or speech given before the 1967 Six Day War in which any Arab called for the creation of an independent Palestine or claimed that the Arabs in the territories were a distinct race. The speeches of the West Bank Arabs before 1967 called for the creation of a Pan-Arab nationalism encompassing all Arabs in the Middle East as brothers. The concept of an ancient Palestinian race, separate from the Arabs of Jordan, Iraq or Saudi Arabia, is a recently created fiction that has proved to be an extremely useful propaganda tool in their attempts to dislodge the Jews from the Holy Land.

The world receives a very distorted view of events in the Middle East. Israel is constantly condemned by the UN, the U.S.A., and Canada for expelling convicted Arab terrorists. Yet during the same period, Kuwait expelled over 350,000 innocent Palestinians from its country after the War in the Gulf for the sole crime of being Palestinian. The world's response—nothing. The Arab nations response was equally silent. No one cared. When I questioned individual Arabs in the Middle East about the terrible Kuwaiti injustice to their Palestinian brothers, their response was a shrug and the comment, "These things happen." The Arab governments have no great love for the Palestinians. They cynically support them as a tool in their war with Israel but they often repress the Palestinians living in their country.

ISRAEL AND THE UNITED NATIONS

The Arab-African-Communist bloc of nations at the United Nations General Assembly continuously attacked the Jewish state with formal censures from the moment Israel was created. Since 1972 this Arab-led alliance has passed an incredible total of 430 anti-Israel resolutions, an average of two resolutions per month. During the same period the UN Assembly never once censured any of the terrible regimes and their dictators such as Pol Pot, Idi Amin, Hafiz Assad, Nicolae Ceausescu or Saddam Hussein. Every one of these leaders was responsible for the deaths of thousands of citizens. Why are there no censures?

Not only has the General Assembly passed anti-Israel resolutions, the UN Security Council voted to condemn Israel with three "expressions of concern," seven "warnings" and forty-nine "condemnations." With the single exception of the Iraqi War in the Gulf, the Security Council never criticized any Arab nation for decades of torture, civil rights abuses, and murders of thousands of their citizens, not even President Assad of Syria's murder of twenty thousand men, women, and children in the town of Hom.

RESOLUTION 3379—"ZIONISM IS RACISM"

In 1975 the United Nations saw its blackest day. Led by the Arab bloc, communist and third world nations joined to cynically vote for the infamous "Zionist is racism," Resolution 3379. However, Zionism is the legitimate aspiration of the Jewish people for a national homeland. After two thousand years of murderous exile, surely the Jews deserve the right to return to their Promised Land. The Jews have suffered from racism more than any other people in history. Zionism is the movement to return the Jews to protection in their ancient homeland Israel. To equate this with racism is a mockery of justice. Finally, on December 16, 1991, after years of behind the scenes American diplomacy, 111 countries voted to repeal the hateful Resolution 3379. However, the Arab nations, while supposedly negotiating peace with Israel, refused to vote for repeal. The vote did not even identify the resolution by name in deference to the hatred of the Jews expressed by many Third World nations. Their continued hypocritical condemnation of Israel is an incredible indictment of the morals of the United Nations. This hatred of Israel is one more sign of the fulfillment of Bible prophecy.

Yet, on the very day that this small moral victory occurred, 152 nations of the UN voted to call all member states to withdraw their embassies from Jerusalem. Only Israel voted against the resolution. America and Canada were silent. It is a fundamental point in international law that any nation can choose its capital, but the nations of the world refuse to acknowledge Israel's right to choose even western Jerusalem as their capital. The prophet Zechariah warned that in the last days the nations would gather against the city of Jerusalem. "And it shall happen in that day that I will make Jerusalem a very heavy stone for all peoples; all who would heave it away will surely be cut in pieces, though all nations of the earth are gathered against it" (Zechariah 12:3).

ISRAEL'S COVENANT WITH DEATH

For the last forty-five years the Jewish State was forced to arm for Armageddon as it faced a huge alliance of Arab nations that steadfastly refused to accept Israel's right to exist as a nation. The Jewish state is the only nation in the world that is faced with the extinction of its government, its institutions and the lives of its entire population if its enemies ever conquer its territory. This unprecedented situation forced Israel to become an armed camp surrounded by implacable enemies. Through many miracles, plus the motivation of Israel's soldiers and its technological edge, Israel has been able to survive and prosper. Yet its fundamental purpose is to bring home the Jewish exiles from around the world. The enormous defense expenditures have drained over 40 percent of the nation's budget for several decades. "They have also healed the hurt of My people slightly, saying, 'Peace, peace!' When there is no peace" (Jeremiah 6:14). God declared in several prophecies, including this one in Jeremiah 6:14, that men would cry out for peace in the days leading to the greatest battle in history. Today the word "peace" is on the lips of many world leaders. However, secretly, many of these same countries are quietly arming for war. Of the top twenty arms importing countries in the world, seven of them are in the Middle East. The staggering amounts invested in armaments and the massive cost of their standing armies could have been used to transform the Middle East into a veritable paradise. The tragedy is that the Arabs and the Jews are brothers. They are both the children of Abraham. These ancient nations are locked in a tragic death struggle that will end only through the direct intervention of God. There can be no true and lasting peace until the Lord supernaturally changes the hearts of Jews and Arabs and replaces their hate with love for their brothers.

The Jewish citizens would love to find a formula for peace that would produce justice for all peoples, Jews and Palestinians, along with secure and recognized borders. However, as long as the Arabs and their governments entertain the illusion that Israel will someday be destroyed, they will never enter into a true peace conference with the Jews. Unfortunately, the Arabs are currently only seeking an armed truce that will allow them to improve their strategic position to ultimately drive the Jews into the sea.

THE PLO-ISRAELI PEACE AGREEMENT—A COVENANT WITH DEATH

In the last few months the leaders of Israel and its deadly enemy, the PLO, signed a peace treaty that promised an end of the deadly warfare that has characterized the Middle East for four decades. Yasir Arafat and Yitzhak Rabin took the first tentative steps towards a possible peace treaty in the Middle East. Does this mean true peace is at hand? Or, will a false peace lead inevitably to the war prophesied by the ancient prophets of Israel?

The Arab governments and the PLO now offer Israel "peace for land." But what kind of "peace" are they offering? There are two concepts of "peace" in the Arab language. One represents true peace such as we enjoy between Canada and the U.S.A. where we genuinely wish our neighbours well. The other concept of peace is more like "an armed truce." During the crusades the leader of the defeated Muslim armies, Saladin, offered the English general, Richard the Lion-Heart, a peace treaty. However, two years later, after rebuilding his armies, Saladin broke his agreement and defeated the English armies. In Yasir Arafat's speeches to Arab audiences, he explained that he will offer Israel "the peace of Saladin." This proves that he is offering Israel "an armed truce" rather than true peace. The PLO have not relinquished their commitment to conquer all of the land of Israel. All Palestinian groups uses emblems, flags and letterhead that contains maps showing that all of Israel and the territories must be conquered from the Jews.

The PLO have often declared that their long-term strategy is to eliminate Israel in a plan called "liberation in phases." Since 1974 Yassir Arafat decreed that during the first phase of his "Phases Plan" the PLO will establish a beachhead in Gaza and the West Bank. In the second phase their armies will take over Jerusalem. In the final phase, they will build up their strength in Gaza and the West Bank to finally conquer all of Israel. On Sept. 1, 1993 Arafat confirmed to an Arab audience that his peace accord was part of his "Phases" plan. During interviews many Arabs declare they will never be content until they recover the entire land of Israel from the Jews. Arafat stated in 1980: "Peace for us means the destruction of Israel." The Koran teaches that, if a land was ever occupied in the past by Muslims, then it must be recovered by Jihad, or holy war. Although Yasir Arafat has pledged to eliminate references to the destruction of Israel from the Charter of the Palestine Liberation Organization, it is significant that he has refused to call for a conference to do so. Furthermore, most of his Arab allies refuse to relinquish their goals to destroy the Jewish state.

Thousands of years ago the prophet Ezekiel (Chapter 38 & 39) predicted that a huge confederacy of Arab nations under Russian leadership will join together to attack Israel after the Jewish exiles have returned to their homeland. Despite massive changes in Russia the hardliners in the KGB, the army and military-industrial complex are trying to maintain their power. The prophet declared that a future military leader of this alliance will say "I will go up against a land of unwalled villages; I will go to a peaceful people, who dwell safely, all of them dwelling without walls, and having neither bars nor gates." For the last forty-five years Israel did not "dwell safely." Israel has remained an armed camp for decades surrounded by two hundred million Arabs. It is forced to spend more on defense than any other country. However, this recent peace accord may create a false sense of security and safety over the next few years that will allow Israel to relax its defenses and "dwell safely." This peace agreement may set the stage for the fulfillment of the great War of Gog and Magog prophesied by the prophet Ezekiel.

THE STRATEGIC IMPORTANCE OF TERRITORY

Israel requires military control of the Golan Heights, Gaza and the West Bank in order to provide the strategic depth to defend itself against the overwhelming military force of its Arab enemies. Every military study in the last twenty five years has concluded that Israel cannot be defended by conventional forces and weapons if it loses military control over these vital territories. The U.S. Joint Chiefs of Staff 1992 study confirmed Israel could not give up the Golan, Gaza or the West Bank and survive an Arab invasion. Without the West Bank Israel will be less than nine miles wide at its center near Tel Aviv where almost eighty percent of its population lives. In a future conflict enemy armies could cut Israel in two parts by attacking from the PLO controlled high ground of Judea and Samaria (West Bank). The Jewish state could be overrun in a matter of days. In a future war Israel will be forced to resort to nuclear weapons when it finds its small diminished territory about to be overcome by enemy armies. The Israeli army calls this "the Samson Option" because it would destroy the Middle East, just as Samson brought down the temple on his enemies. Despite this grim reality the present Israeli government has agreed to relinquish these strategic areas. For the first time since its creation in 1948 Israel's conventional army and air force will not be able to successfully defend its vital territory and population from an armed invasion.

THE FINAL COVENANT WITH DEATH—A TREATY WITH ANTICHRIST

The United Nations and the Arab states continue to call for the elimination of Israel's nuclear weapons. The introduction of Iranian nuclear weapons and the growing possibility of Libya, Syria and Iraq joining the nuclear club has altered the strategic balance. It is difficult to see how a balance of nuclear terror could continue for very long between Israel and the Islamic states dedicated to its destruction. Plans to ban nuclear weapons from the Middle East may tempt a future Israeli government to agree to relinquish its nuclear option. Israel realizes that an unstable Arab regime might be tempted to use their atomic warheads even though it would result in mutual assured destruction. In Islamic religious philosophy they would gain paradise if they died a devastating war to cleanse the "infidels" from Jerusalem. In a few years these events will set the stage for a superpower to guarantee Israel's security and borders.

When Europe finally unites under ten kings led by the Antichrist, they will offer a seven-year treaty to Israel guaranteeing her security. For the first time since 1948 the Jewish state will finally be able to lay down her arms. Israel dreams of directing her resources to the "return of the exiles" and plans to build a just and prosperous society. The cost of housing and employing the returning immigrants from Russia will require all of the talents and money available in Israel. These factors will motivate Israel to make an "agreement with death" with the "prince that shall come."

The prophet Isaiah spoke of this peace treaty and Israel's false confidence in the Antichrist. "You have said, 'We have made a covenant with death, and with Sheol we are in agreement. When the overflowing scourge passes through, it will not come to us, for we have made lies our refuge, and under falsehood we have hidden ourselves'" (Isaiah 28:15). The leaders of Israel will cynically make this seven-year treaty with the dictator of Europe believing that he will protect them from the devastating wars during that terrible time. However, this treaty will fail. In

Isaiah 28:18 the prophet reveals God's judgment on Israel's treaty with the Antichrist: "Your covenant with death will be annulled, and your agreement with Sheol will not stand; when the overflowing scourge passes through, then you will be trampled down by it." After three-and-a-half years the Antichrist will betray Israel and break his treaty. He will enter the rebuilt Temple in Jerusalem claiming to be god. When he demands that Israel worship him, most of the Jews will rebel against him. The book of Revelation describes Israel fleeing into the wilderness for 1260 days (three and a half years) after this betrayal. In the following chapters we will explore the incredible events that will occur during this seven-year period leading up to the Battle of Armageddon. True peace will elude the nations until the Messiah, the Prince of Peace comes to rule the earth. While we rejoice at the prospects of a peace agreement in the Middle East we need to recognize that the ancient prophets warned that a false peace would set the stage for the momentous events that conclude with the Battle of Armageddon.

10

America and the Coming Economic Crash

America has played a tremendous role in fulfilling the Great Commission in the last two hundred years. The United States founded missions throughout the world, bringing hundreds of millions of nationals to a belief in Christ as their personal Savior. The generosity of North American Christians provided the funds for an enormous outpouring of the gospel in print, radio, and television that has transformed the world's awareness of Christ.

America has led the way in the development of the philosophy and institutions of the New World Order. The huge banking and investments groups created educational foundations to provide the leadership for the coming one-world government. The Council on Foreign Relations and the Trilateral Commission, that we examined in another chapter, were founded in America. Both institutions are key players in the move towards an abandonment of national sovereignty that will ultimately produce the kingdom of the Antichrist. Much of the technology for the electronic surveillance and planning for the one world currency is produced in the U.S.A.

THE DISARMING OF AMERICA

As President Clinton implements his vision of the New World Order his administration believes that Russia can be brought into the fold of the new world government. The United States has embarked on a unilateral disarmament program that is eliminating the great military strength which the Reagan administration built up to protect the West against foreign enemies. Weapons funding is down 50 percent and is projected to drop even more. They recently shut down Mountain Home Air Force Base in Idaho one of two radar command centers that track Russian bombers flying toward America. The second one in Bangor, Maine, remains open only part of the time. The $1 billion Over-the-Horizon Backscatter Radar System, designed to peer two thousand miles off the U.S. coast covering a six-million-square-mile area to detect incoming Russian missiles and warplanes, is being shelved by the White House.

While disarming America's military the administration is engaged in a massive arms sale to other countries. Last year the U.S.A. became the number one arms supplier to the Third World. In 1990, U.S.A. foreign arms sales rose to a staggering $18.5 billion dollars compared to Russian sales of only $12.1 billion. The U.S.A. now accounts for 44.8 percent of all foreign arms sales. American leaders often preach peace to the world and piously suggest that Europe stop fueling the Middle East arms race. Meanwhile, America sold $14.5 billion in weapons to Saudi Arabia alone in 1991, more than Russia sold to all other Third World countries combined. The White House justifies these massive arms sales to volatile regions by claiming it will help the defense industry adjust to the American disarmament program.

PREPARING FOR THE COMING ECONOMIC CRASH

The simple truth is that you cannot borrow or spend your way to prosperity. America has been living beyond its means for decades. The bill collector is finally coming to close us down. As the graph shows the national debt is rising astronomically as government borrows billions more every month. Experience tells us we reap what we sow. It's called "the Coming Economic Crash" and it will destroy our economy through a stock market crash, a banking credit collapse and finally, hyper inflation.

THE COMING STOCK MARKET CRASH

The first economic crisis facing us is a massive stock market crash that will dwarf the crash of 1929. However, the Bible indicates an economic collapse will prepare the way for the rise of Antichrist. James warned that "Your gold and silver are corroded, and their corrosion will be a witness against you and will eat your flesh like fire. You have heaped up treasure in the last days" (James 5:3). As I examined the prophecies of the economic changes that the Antichrist will introduce together with economic intelligence reports, I believe we are on the verge of a stock market collapse such as we have never witnessed before. The Dow Jones average stock is now trading at forty-three times current earnings, almost three times higher than the market hit before the 1929 crash! However, the average Dow Jones stock is paying less than 3 percent in dividends. Many investors are thrilled with receiving 17 percent or more on their stocks and mutual funds in recent years. However, the danger signs are everywhere.

We are in the greatest speculative stock market bubble in history while the underlying economy is in shambles. The average savings rate is pathetic and the national deficit is staggering. When the market collapses it will take the American economy into a great depression of the late 1990s. Stocks could easily lose 50 percent to 60 percent of their value wiping out mutual funds, pension funds, and the life savings of unsuspecting investors. In an exact parallel to 1929, the stock market is in an incredible speculative boom with brokers receiving massive infusions of over one billion dollars in new cash daily. The stock market has risen to such unrealistic speculative levels due to a tidal wave of new funds that poured into brokers as investors abandoned the low interest rates of the money market funds and CD's. Over $400 billion of new money was transferred into the stock market from CDs and money market funds in the last twelve months. Fifty-nine million Americans are pouring their life savings into this speculative market, many of them through 4300 mutual funds. A recent poll indicated that up to 70% of the investors in bank mutual stock funds mistakenly thought their money was guaranteed by the Federal Deposit Insurance. They are unprotected. The underlying profits to support such high stock prices are simply not there. Prudent investors should remember that "What goes up, comes down!"

The government tells us the economy is recovering and that all is well. The truth is precisely the opposite. Millions of jobs are being eliminated permanently as plants close forever or transfer to Mexico. Corporate indebtedness has risen to the point where many businesses won't be able to repay these loans. Business earnings have dropped to the lowest levels since 1929. Meanwhile the government has lost control of its spending as mandated welfare transfers, social program, and interest costs skyrocket. The average consumer is in the worst shape ever due to fears of losing his job, low investment returns, huge Clinton tax hikes, and the rising cost of living. Bankruptcies soared in 1993 as almost one million companies went out of business. These bankrupt firms represent the loss of dreams, products, and jobs for millions. According to surveys, thirty states suffer from economic recession or depression. Meanwhile President Bill Clinton has introduced the largest tax grab in history together with Hilary's $90 billion health plan. These initiatives will bankrupt many small businesses while discouraging others from hiring new employees.

THE APPROACHING CREDIT COLLAPSE

The second of three great economic crisis is the approaching collapse of credit. The savings and loan crisis will cost the American taxpayer one trillion by the time everything is wrapped up. But the worst is still to come. A banking crisis is now shaping up that will dwarf the S & L crisis and bring down some of the largest banks in the country. The U.S. Office of Management and Budget has warned the government that the largest banks in the country are in danger of failing according to the top financial rating services. After decades of irresponsible loans to the Third World and real estate ventures, the banks are awakening to the reality of their crisis. The West finally realizes that loans to the socialist and communist economies were dropping money into an economic bottomless pit. To date, Western nations have lent over $1.2 trillion dollars to Russia, Eastern Europe, and the Third World. The odds that these loans will ever be repaid are between slim and none. Remember, it is your savings deposits that the banks are lending to Brazil and Russia. How will your money ever be repaid?

The 1993 deficit exceeded $400 billion forcing the government to borrow some $630 billion to pay for this year's deficit and debt rollovers from last year. As the *McAlvany Intelligence Report* indicates, "That is more than twice the total savings of the U.S. economy last year." This borrowing will use up over 80 percent of the country's savings and investment funds. This situation produced a dramatic drop in private credit availability. Many banks and trust companies have few funds to loan out. Instead of rolling over loans normally, many banks are demanding repayment in full when a five-year mortgage comes up for renewal. With many banks in bad shape we will likely see massive bank failures following the S & L disaster. Now is the time to check out your banks financial health. Right behind the banks stand our insurance companies. For decades insurance companies were the strongest financial institutions in America. However the 1980s decade of greed afflicted the insurance industry as well. Instead of relying on premium income and conservative investments, the insurance industry moved into risky real estate loans and junk bonds to enable them to offer higher rates of return. Growing numbers of insurance companies fail every month. Investors with large pensions and annuities should check out their company's health.

EXPLODING GOVERNMENT DEBT

"Democracy cannot exist as a permanent form of government. It can only exist until the voters discover that they can vote for themselves largess from the public treasury. From that moment on, the majority always votes for the candidate promising the most benefits from the public treasury, with the result that a democracy always collapses over loose fiscal policy, and is always followed by a dictatorship" (Alexander Tyler, 1776).

After decades of free spending by Congress, the chickens are finally coming home to roost. The inevitable result of the accumulating deficits is an approaching financial crisis beyond anything ever faced in our history. The American government at all levels—federal, state, and municipal has consistently spent money at a level far beyond its limited resources. Today over 13.4 million Americans are on welfare with one in seven people in Los Angeles receiving government benefits. The total welfare bill for last year exceeded $185 billion. This was financed through a combination of international and domestic borrowing plus robbing the Social Security System and other government pension plans and trust funds. However, the various dodges invented by clever government accountants and politicians have just about run out.

THE INFLATION CRISIS

The third great crisis is the danger of hyper inflation destroying our economy. For the last few decades until now, the U.S. Treasury borrowed from Japan, Germany, or the Arabs, but these countries are now reluctant to buy U.S. Treasury bills. When these international financial sources dry up, the only option left to the U.S. government will be to monetize the debt by inflating the currency. They will be forced to "print money" in a variety of ways. As a small example of things to come, recently the Japanese and Arabs refused to purchase several billions in T-Bills that are offered for sale by the Treasury every week. After an emergency call the U.S. Federal Reserve Bank stepped in to purchase $26 billion of U.S. Treasury Bills. They paid the Treasury with a slip of paper, an I.O.U.—saying "I owe you $26 billion." This is the equivalent of a bankrupt family attempting to solve its financial problems by the husband and wife writing each other I.O.U.'s and listing these pieces of paper as valid assets. This is simply printing money out of thin air. As the government continues this practice it will produce uncontrolled inflation by 1997 or sooner. The official Clinton deficit this year will be over $400 billion. However, the truth is much worse. The administration tried to minimize the figures because the true deficit is closer to $550 billion. The government will have to borrow half a trillion dollars to cover the deficit and debt rollovers from 1993.

Officially, the national debt of the United States amounts to $4,054,000,000,000 (according to the line budget). This staggering figure is beyond the ability of normal human beings to grasp. However, the official debt of four trillion and fifty four billion dollars is only the tip of the debt iceberg. The true national debt is closer to $7 trillion dollars when you add in the "off-budget" costs such as liabilities for the Social Security Trust Fund, military and government pensions, etc. How big a number is this? How much money is this? If you burned two hundred thousand dollars every single hour—or five million dollars every day for over four thousand years from the time of Abraham until today, you would still not have burnt up as much money as the true U.S. national debt of $7,000,000,000,000. The $7 trillion national debt amounts to twenty-six thousand dollars for every man, woman, and child. The interest charges on the national debt are equally staggering: at 9 percent they amount to $630 billion per year! This equals $1.7 billion every day or $71 million every single hour. If this wasn't bad enough, the government is accumulating $1.5 billion of additional new debt every day for welfare, education, etc.

The taxes paid by the average American are rising every year while their true after-tax disposable income is declining. The average taxpayer will work from January until May 10th before he has paid the taxes demanded by all levels of government. Our taxes will continue to skyrocket. Irresponsible politicians refuse to cut back on the entitlement programs that transfer dollars from working taxpayers to benefit non-working recipients. They are afraid such cutbacks would cost them votes. Even conservative politicians, once in power, find it is impossible to vote to cut spending programs.

The experts agree that the total tax revenues of the U.S.A. government will not be sufficient to pay even the growing interest charges on the national debt by the year 1997. After paying the interest on our national debt, there won't be a single dollar left from our huge taxes by 1997 to pay for a soldier, a road, welfare, or the court system! Every dollar raised in taxes will be needed to pay the interest charges on past debt. The government cannot simply repudiate the national debt because 83 percent of it is owed to American banks, pensions, insurance companies, and individuals. By that point America won't be able to borrow money abroad. The Japanese and the Arab oil sheiks will not lend to America when there is no prospect of getting their money back. Long before then, America will be forced to monetize its debt. In other words, the U.S. will inflate its money to pay off the debt with devalued currency. The result will be staggering inflation beyond anything seen in American history. The situation is identical in my own country, Canada.

The government will be forced to monetize the debt. America will have to inflate its currency by printing money in a vain attempt to postpone economic collapse. If you think it can't happen here, consider the history of Germany in 1923, Argentina in the 1970s, or Yugoslavia today. Recently banknotes of 10 billion dinars (worth $6) were distributed. The average inflation rate is 20% a day in a country with an average salary of $10 U.S. per month. There are no clever moves left to avoid this coming inflation. Every other option has been tried and failed. Unlike past inflationary spirals in America that were quite gradual, this inflation will accelerate very quickly. In this situation inflation and interest rates can soar rapidly from 10 percent to reach 30 percent, 50 percent, 100 percent and 1,000 percent. This will trigger the collapse of our sophisticated economic system with reverberations throughout the world's financial centers. The approaching world economic crisis may present an opportunity for a brilliant economic and political genius to arise with proposals of a totally revolutionary economic and political system. A New World Order will emerge from the financial chaos based on radically changed laws, electronic transfers eliminating physical cash, and a new international currency. Daniel the prophet wrote about the Antichrist, that "through his policy also he shall cause craft (economy) to prosper in his hand" (Daniel 8:25).

FINANCIAL STRATEGIES FOR THOSE LIVING IN THE LAST DAYS

Before the Lord led Kaye and I into full time ministry I spent eighteen years as a professional in the area of financial planning, insurance, taxation, and wills. As we consider the coming economic crisis in the light of Bible prophecy we need to also examine biblical principles of financial stewardship. While these are basic and sound financial principles everyone must analyze their own situation and consult a qualified professional regarding any individual financial or investment decisions you wish to make. One of the first steps toward financial independence is to get out of debt. Pay down your highest interest loans such as credit cards and car loans as quickly as you can. Avoid credit like the plague. If you can't afford to buy an item for cash you can't afford it. Start saving 10 percent of your income immediately. Pay yourself first by depositing 10 percent of your income into a savings account and pay your bills with whatever is left. That is the only way to begin to see light at the end of the tunnel. Another fundamental biblical principle is to begin to tithe 10 percent to your local church where you are being spiritually fed. The Scriptures tell us, "Honor the Lord with your possessions, and with the firstfruits of all your increase; so your barns will be filled with plenty, and your vats will overflow with new wine" (Proverbs 3:9). These two principles, saving and tithing, are fundamental to any plan for financial independence.

Americans who naively depend on banks, insurance companies and pensions to faithfully pay their annuity and pension checks may face financial disaster in the years ahead. As a practical step we should make certain that we do not keep large amounts of cash in any one institution. Place your savings in a number of financially sound banks. You can send to Weiss Reports, Bests Reports or other financial reporting services for a report on the health of your financial institutions. As Christians we are commanded to be wise stewards of the resources God has placed in our hands. While owning your own home is a sound investment, the next few years will not be kind to investment real estate such as apartments or commercial buildings. Prepaying your home mortgage often produces the largest investment return available.

To avoid the dangers of a stock market crash prudent investors should consider transferring their funds out of stocks and mutual funds into secure investments that will preserve your capital. Consult with a professional advisor for recommendations but the decision must be your own. Although they pay low interest, government Treasury Bills, U.S. Savings Bonds, Bond Funds and Commercial Deposits with strong banks will protect your life savings during the next few years. Obviously, when hyper inflation arrives in a few years government securities will not be a sound investment then. Once the stock market crash occurs investors will be able to buy stocks and real estate for a fraction of their price today. In an economic crisis the person with liquidity is well positioned to protect himself and respond to contingencies.

WHERE IS AMERICA IN BIBLE PROPHECY?

Just where does America fit in Bible prophecy? The short answer is that the U.S.A. is not a major player in the prophecies of the last days. America does not play a pivotal role in the final end time prophecies because the Bible's purpose is to focus on the events primarily in Europe and the Middle East that will culminate in the return of Jesus Christ. Some have tried to fit America into the ten-nation confederacy formed in Europe out of the ruins of the Roman Empire. However, America was never part of the Roman Empire. The Bible is quite clear that the ten-nations will be formed out of the remnants of the old

Roman Empire. In many ways we can be thankful that neither America nor Canada are part of the ten-nation confederacy because the wrath of God will be poured out on the kingdom of the Antichrist. Certainly our countries will fall under the sway of the Antichrist for a portion of the tribulation period, as Revelation tells us that "power was given him over all kindreds and tongues and nations" (Revelation 13:7). However, the Antichrist will not be able to totally dominate North America as much as he can in the revived Roman Empire. Jesus Christ may refer to our nations when He declared that He would judge the sheep nations and goat nations on the basis of how citizens treat the Jewish and Gentile tribulation saints fleeing the persecution of the Antichrist (Matthew 25). At the end of the tribulation period the Man of Sin will gather the armies of the West together against the Kings of the East for the final Battle of Armageddon. The armies of the United States, Canada and the other Western nations will be present in the Valley of Decision for their appointment to meet Christ on the Great Day of the Lord.

The prophet Ezekiel may refer briefly to America and Canada when he describes the response of the western nations to the Russian-Arab invasion of Israel in the coming war of Gog and Magog. In Ezekiel 38:13 he refers to the "merchants of Tarshish, with all the young lions thereof." Many scholars believe that Tarshish may refer to England and that the "young lions" may refer to the nations that used to belong to the British Empire such as America and Canada. The prophet describes these nations responding to Russia's attack by asking, "Have you come to take plunder. Have you gathered your army to take booty?" In other words, the western nations lodge a diplomatic protest rather than defending Israel.

Is America the Babylon of Prophecy?

Some teachers suggest that the Bible's prophecies about Babylon's sins and pride refer to the coming judgment of God on America's sin. In addition they believe the prophecies about Babylon's destruction refer to God's final judgment of America. I believe they are mistaken. While we can learn the principle of God's hatred of sin from these passages about the evil of Babylon, America is not Babylon. America and Canada are two of the only nations in history to be founded by men of God on biblical principals. Isaiah 13 and Revelation 18 clearly refer to the actual rebuilt city of Babylon in Iraq. It is destined to become one of the capitals of the Antichrist's future empire. The prophets warn that Babylon will be utterly destroyed by God and that the fire and smoke will ascend from her ruins forever. As indicated in my *MESSIAH* book, the city of Babylon is being rebuilt by Saddam Hussein beside the ancient ruins at a cost of over $850 million to date. The city lies on top of an ancient lake of asphalt and oil that will burn forever when God destroys her as "Sodom and Gomorrah" on the "day of the Lord" (Isaiah 13:1,6,19). A picture of the rebuilding of Babylon appears in the photo section of this book.

JAPAN IN PROPHECY—THE LAND OF THE RISING SUN

Twenty years ago Japan was an aspiring Asian industrial country with only one-half of the gross national product of the United States. Yet, in only two decades the Japanese have exceeded the American economic miracle until today they have an economy over one-fifth larger than the U.S.A. More amazingly, the Japanese economy is growing more quickly than America. The Japanese have spent 270 percent more in overseas investment than the U.S.A. The cumulative effect of this massive compounding investment in real estate, major industries, joint ventures, and financial institutions has created an economic colossus. Each day, thousands of Japanese executives board planes to fly around the world to supervise over $400 billion in foreign investments for Japan Incorporated. Their annual investment in research and development exceeds the investments of the United States and Canada by over 50 percent. The Japanese spend three times more on equipment and factory investment per employee than the States and almost twice that of Europe. Consider the startling trade balances as a measure of Japanese power. In a few short years, America reversed its role as the world's largest creditor nation to becoming the world's largest debtor nation. On the other hand, Japan now is the largest net creditor nation with the largest trade surplus in the world—over $121 billion per year.

Despite Japan's advantages, they face severe problems. Its hugely inflated real estate market recently collapsed dragging down banks, trust companies, and real estate developers. Over 70 percent of mortgage payments on real estate loans in Japan are in default. The Japanese will still face the tremendous problem of relying on exports for sustained growth. Other nations are unlikely to allow Japan to continue to overwhelm their local industries forever. Japan faces severe problems as the financial leader of the world. Just as they led the economic boom in the 1980s Japan led the crash of the 1990s. The Japanese stock market recently dropped 60 percent of its value, losing an astonishing three trillion dollars. Before the crash, Japanese stocks traded at a speculative sixty-six times earnings, instead of the usual ten to twenty times earnings. However, Japan's underlying strengths will prevail and she will rapidly recover her dominant economic position in Asia.

Although Japan eliminated its military following their loss in World War II, the U.S., Europe and the UN are calling for Japan to re-arm and contribute troops to UN peacekeeping operations. The West will regret asking Japan to become a military power again. Her incredible industrial capacity, high technology industries and strict discipline will produce an awesome military force. The Bible warned that the "kings from the east" (Revelation 16:12) will destroy one-third of the population as they march relentlessly across Asia towards their prophetic destiny in the place called Armageddon.

Asia's Young Dragon Nations

Japan is not alone in this rise to economic dominance. There are eleven "dragon nations," including Taiwan, South Korea, Hong Kong, Singapore, Malaysia, and others. These are countries that want to copy the economic miracle of post-war Japan. North Korea is a growing military power and a major arms exporter. The CIA states they have produced several nuclear weapons. These Pacific rim countries are producing many emerging high tech industries and creating tremendous markets. They will produce the industrial base for the "kings from the east" mentioned by the prophet John in the book of Revelation. The Bible indicates that a group of Asian nations, known as the kings of the east, will confederate together in the last days to oppose the dictatorial worldwide rule of the Antichrist and Western nations.

THE KINGS FROM THE EAST

"Then the sixth angel poured out his bowl on the great river Euphrates, and its water was dried up, so that the way of the kings from the east might be prepared" (Revelation 16:12). According to prophecy, the "kings from the east" will be the greatest opponent of the Antichrist when God gathers the armies of the whole world to the Battle of Armageddon. In a later chapter of *Prince of Darkness* the details of the final conflict of the nations will be examined. After seven years of domination by the Antichrist the nations of Asia will be desperate to throw off the chains of oppression from this Western dictator and his False Prophet. First, the Antichrist will send his armies to the Middle East to destroy the armies of the king of the north and king of the south who attacked him in Israel. Seeing their chance, the kings of the east, the Asian nations led by China and Japan, will gather their awesome military forces to cross Asia and launch the greatest military invasion in history.

Intelligence reports estimate the enormous military manpower of China and Japan, including standing armies and reserves, could number almost 200 million by the year 2000. When Kaye and I traveled to China in 1986 we were amazed at the absence of girls. A recent television documentary called "The Missing Women of China" confirmed the evidence we documented in my book *Armageddon—Appointment With Destiny*. Under the

One-Child Policy, since 1978, population control authorities forced Chinese couples to have only one child. However, many parents prefer a boy to continue their family name and support them when they are older. Now an amniocentesis test will enable them to determine the sex of their unborn infant. If the unborn child is female the couple will usually choose to abort the baby and try again for a boy. Many Chinese daughters are killed after birth. As a result, China has a terrible population imbalance between male and female births. In Beijing I talked to Chinese officials who agreed that this unique sexual imbalance in births has produced nine boys for every girl since 1978. This will produce an excess population of 125 million young Chinese men of military age in the late 1990s without any young women for them to marry. Northern India and North Korea have the same phenomenon. The Toronto Star reported on February 4, 1993 that there is an amniocentesis and ultrasound clinic in every village in India to determine if the unborn child is female so the mother could abort. Over 99 percent of all abortions were of female babies. Tragically, this hatred of girls extends even to young female children. A medical study found that 50 percent of the families in over 100 villages admitted killing their second and subsequent daughters usually by strangling! The huge surplus of young males in Asia may very well provide the bulk of the manpower for the 200 million man army of the kings of the east.

"Now the number of the army of the horsemen was two hundred million, and I heard the number of them" (Revelation 9:16). Japan and China have a thirty-year friendship treaty and are currently engaged in massive trade and technology transfers. Combining the manpower and natural resources of China with Japanese managerial expertise, industrial capacity, and huge financial resources will produce the strongest military force in history. John foretold that this awesome army will march across Asia to attack the Antichrist's forces in Israel. Recent reports confirm that China and Pakistan are continuing to build a large military highway heading across Asia directly toward the Middle East. Over the last decade, Chinese construction troops built this rugged highway through the most inaccessible and dangerous mountains in southern China, Tibet, and Pakistan. Sources in Pakistan revealed that foreigners are forbidden to visit or photograph where the highway is being constructed. There is no known commercial purpose for the highway.

In addition, Revelation foretold the incredible detail that the great Euphrates River will be "dried up" to allow this huge army of the kings of the east to cross in their march towards Armageddon. "Then the sixth angel poured out his bowl on the great river Euphrates, and its water was dried up, so that the way of the kings from the east might be prepared . . . For they are spirits of demons, performing signs, which go out to the kings of the earth and of the whole world, to gather them to the battle of that great day of God Almighty" (Revelation 16:12,14). Two years ago the massive Ataturk Dam was completed in Turkey. At the press of a button the raging Euphrates River can be dried up stopping the flow of the river through Syria and Iraq. We can now understand how this awesome prophecy will be literally fulfilled in our generation.

11

The Great Russian Deception

The real powers behind the scenes in Russia, the KGB and Communist Party, have embarked upon the greatest deception plan in history. Daily we are told in the media that communism is dead in Russia and Eastern Europe. The politicians assure us the Cold War is over. Supposedly, the West has won without a final struggle. We are asked to believe that, after seventy-four years of brutal totalitarianism, the Soviet communists woke up one day and realized the error of their ways. They announced that they have abandoned Marxism and want to join the western democracies in a historic partnership. Their announced goal is to create a "common European home from the Urals to the Atlantic." You have heard the expression "It's too good to be true." Well, this Russian fairy tale is too good to be true.

THE BEAR IS ONLY SLEEPING

If Russia had truly abandoned communism, millions of well-armed communist soldiers, intelligence agents and loyal party members would have ripped the Soviet Union apart in a civil war. Their armed resistance to this "betrayal" of Marxism would have made the Russian Civil War of 1918 to 1922 pale in comparison. Why is there so little resistance to this radical reversal of political philosophy? Over twenty million citizens of the Soviet Union were well-indoctrinated communist party members, soldiers and KGB agents. It is beyond belief that all of these people would universally and genuinely see the light of democracy and free enterprise simultaneously. However, these dedicated Marxists know that glasnost, perestroika and democracy are simply disinformation designed to deceive the West. This explains why the party, the army, and the KGB have gone along with the perestroika changes in so docile a manner. The false coup against Gorbachev in August 1991 and the October 1993 struggle between the Parliament and Yeltsin convinced the West that Russia has truly reformed and abandoned Communism.

ALL WARFARE IS BASED ON DECEPTION

In ancient times the Greeks used a gift of a Trojan Horse to penetrate the strong defenses of the city of Troy. From its beginning the communist movement, led by Russia, was founded on deception and disinformation. Deceptive propaganda provides false information to their own Russian citizens and to the West to prevent them from understanding the true situation. Their purpose is to deceive the observer by presenting the situation as something quite different from reality.

Sun Tzu was a brilliant military strategist of ancient China. His classic study on military strategy and the need for deception, *The Art of War*, laid out the key principles to follow to defeat your enemy through deception. He believed that deceiving your enemy about your intentions and strengths was essential to victory. Sun Tzu claimed twenty-five hundred years ago that "all warfare is based on deception." Senior Red Army military and political officers take extensive examinations on the principles of Sun Tzu. One of his most fundamental techniques is summed up as follows: "When you are weak, pretend strength. When you are strong, pretend you are weak." If you examine Russian history in light of these principles you are less likely to be deceived. Tragically, most of the western media and public are totally unaware that the best propaganda chiefs since Hitler's Dr. Goebbels have been manipulating western opinion for the last seven decades. The Russian strategists plan to keep the West deceived about their true evil motives until they can use their massive armed forces to overwhelm our weakened western defenses.

A fundamental principle of totalitarian regimes is to establish and control their own opposition. Rather than allow secret groups of political opponents to grow independently, the Soviets would establish false-front anticommunist resistance groups led by deep cover KGB officers. While pretending to oppose communism these leaders would attract any potential opponents into their group where they could be controlled, watched and, finally, eliminated. Whenever any genuine anti-communist groups formed the KGB would infiltrate and destroy the true non-communist leaders. Thus, for decades, the KGB literally controlled dissident and anti-communist reform groups in their plan to utilize them to deceive the West. An article in the *Washington Post* on February 11, 1992 stated: "It is now known that the KGB infiltrated the independence movements and democracy parties that sprang up around the Soviet Union as a result of liberalizing policies of former Soviet leader Mikhail Gorbachev. Since many of these parties have now come to power, it means that KGB agents and informers are represented in the highest levels of government." Intelligence sources confirm that the secret police created and still lead the reform groups that have achieved power in Russian and Eastern Europe. "At a parliamentary meeting last week, Russian security chiefs acknowledged that the pro-Yeltsin Democratic Russia faction includes numerous KGB agents." The number of politicians in Eastern Europe who have worked for the communist intelligence organizations is legion. Efforts are now being made to suppress the release of these secret police files lest it "embarrass" the new "democratic" leaders of these nations.

For over seven decades the Russian Orthodox Church was totally controlled by the KGB. All priests and bishops were approved by the party and forced to report on their parishioners. In this light it should surprise no one that the Russian Orthodox Church has influenced the government to introduce restrictive legislation severely limiting the activities of western religious groups. For years I have encouraged Christians to get the Bibles into Russia and Eastern Europe while the door remains open. Interestingly, key leaders in the underground church have warned that the Lord revealed years ago that the door of freedom would only remain open for a few years before it would close again.

THE AUGUST 1991 COUP—RUSSIAN THEATER AT ITS BEST!

What about the August 19, 1991, coup against Gorbachev? The KGB deserve an Academy Award for the staging and plot development of this so-called "coup." Private polls in Russia reveal that some 62 percent of the citizens believe that the coup was staged for the political benefit of Gorbachev. To place this "coup" in its proper context we must remember that the KGB and Soviet communist special forces studied and mastered the art of coups for over seventy years. This is how the Bolsheviks originally came to power in 1917. The October Revolution was actually a brilliant coup by only 184 Bolshevik plotters. It succeeded in overthrowing the first democratically elected government in Russian history! Yet the August 1991 coup was the most inept military-political operation in the history of coups. It simply defies belief that this was a genuine coup against Gorbachev.

Consider these points about the failed coup. Why did the coup leader call himself the "acting president" if he truly intended overthrowing President Gorbachev? In every other coup in this century the rebels immediately attack the telephone system, water supplies, electricity, media access, airports and transportation. Not one of these targets was attacked. The telephones, radio and television stations, airports, and media broadcasting continued normally throughout the coup. The water, electricity, and phone lines to Yeltsin and the Russian Parliament also stayed open. Why did the plotters not attempt to kill Yeltsin, Gorbachev, and the other reformers since the Soviet Union had 250,000 superbly trained special forces Spetznaz troops available? The eight plotters were personally appointed by Gorbachev after being carefully vetted by the KGB. Even the president of Georgia and former Foreign Minister Eduard Shevardnadze claimed that the coup was staged. Citizens in the Crimea claimed that the "three rings of troops surrounding Gorbachev's house" did not exist except in the dreams of propaganda writers. Why would the coup leaders leave Moscow in the middle of the coup to confer with Gorbachev in the Crimea? The *Toronto Star* reported in 1993 that each of the plotters claimed that Gorbachev planned the coup with them for three weeks before the crisis. On June 24, 1992, the *European* newspaper reported that "Vasily Starodubtsev, who was held for his part in the abortive coup attempt in Moscow, had been released pending trial." Is this the normal tender way Russia deals with state traitors? The last question is the most devastating. Why have the trials of the plotters been delayed, evidence "lost" by the KGB, and a veil of secrecy been drawn over the proceedings? Two and a half years later not one of the coup plotters has gone to trial! Recently the Russian state judge fired all of prosecutors working on the case.

The real reason Gorbachev and the KGB planned the "coup" was to deceive the West about their true intentions. They knew some skeptics in western intelligence and military circles doubted the sincerity of their recent conversion to democracy. Some in the West warned of the dangers as Russia continued to massively arm its military while we disarmed believing the Cold War was over. The Soviets also knew that the New World Order planners in the Council on Foreign Relations and the Bilderbergers desperately wanted to believe that Russia was truly abandoning hard line communism. As Sun Tzu suggested: "Offer your enemy a bait to lure him; pretend disorder. Then strike him." The coup was planned to convince the West that Russia had truly reformed and communism was finished forever. When the reformers "won," as they naturally did, they would still need Gorbachev to deal with the West and the hard liners would go underground and out of sight. They hoped the failed coup would encourage the West to drop our reservations to the Soviet continued buildup of military power. Their goal was to encourage us to provide the high technology and western aid desperately needed by Russia. The western nations are providing billions in aid and investments. The "failure" of the coup supposedly proved that the "hard line communists had lost" and were now out of power. The West could safely disarm and ignore the largest military build-up in history because the new democratic leaders of the C.I.S. would never dream of using their superior weapons against the West.

THE BREAKUP OF THE SOVIET UNION

In my book *MESSIAH*, written a year before the August 1991 coup and published in May of 1991, I suggested that we would witness a future coup against Gorbachev, a breakup of the Soviet Union into fifteen republics and a possible "genuine repudiation of communism." My interpretations of the Bible's prophecies concerning Russia's future are found on pages 58 to 67 of *MESSIAH*. "In the event that Gorbachev is overthrown, most commentators expect his replacement will be a military or KGB candidate. . . . The military, upset by the soaring crime rate, growing shortages of food, and escalating ethnic unrest, will be tempted to ally themselves with hard-line KGB and old Communist Party elite to overthrown Gorbachev's reformers. . . . As the fifteen republics of the USSR continue to disintegrate into rebellious entities, there is a growing danger that, at some point, military and KGB forces will intervene and reestablish dictatorial and military control. . . . Even if the other fourteen republics should successfully break away, the largest republic— Russia—would still retain the bulk of the population, land and military-industrial assets of the union. . . . The prophet Ezekiel does not declare that 'Communist' Russia will come down against the mountains of Israel; rather he says that 'Magog,' which is Russia, will lead an alliance of nations against the Jewish state. Even if Russia should genuinely repudiate communism it would not change the fact that God has declared that Russia's appointment with destiny will not be postponed."

My anticipation of several key events in the breakup of the Soviet Union does not suggest that I am a prophet. I am not a prophet or the son of a prophet. As a matter of fact, ours is a "non-prophet" organization! In *MESSIAH* I simply examined the future events concerning Russia in light of the Bible's prophecies about Magog from Ezekiel 38 and 39. The prophet spoke about a confederacy of nations from the area of the old Soviet Union joining with the Arab nations in a military alliance against Israel in the last days. Instead of describing the huge geographic area of the Soviet Union with one name, the prophet Ezekiel (38:6) described an alliance of nations. "Magog" would join with "Gomer and all its troops; the house of Togarmah from the far north, and all its troops and many people are with you" in the coming invasion of Israel. The prophet also declared that "every man's sword will be against his brother" (Ezekiel 38:21). This prophecy, combined with intelligence reports, suggested to me that the USSR might break up into its fifteen republics prior to its invasion of Israel.

The Communist Party is supposed to be out of business today, but only a fool would believe this. They simply changed the name of their party as they did in 1912, 1918, 1925 and 1952. When the Soviets claimed that they were now going to become democratic and freedom loving the western politicians and media believed the lie. Most of the communist bureaucrats and leaders of the republics of the Soviet Union remain in power. Very few lost their jobs. The military has not changed its leadership. Less than one hundred KGB officers, out of 250,000, lost their positions. It is worthwhile to remember the revealing words of Gorbachev in his 1987 book *Perestroika*, "We are not going to change Soviet power, of course, or abandon its fundamental principles, but we acknowledge the need for changes that will strengthen socialism." Remember that "socialism" means "communism" in Gorbachev's vocabulary. He promised that these changes and reforms will only lead to a stronger communism without changes in Soviet power or the abandoning of fundamental marxist objectives. Those fundamental principles include the destruction of America, western democracy, and your freedoms as a citizen. The word *socialist* sounds far less threatening to the West than the word *communist*, but in the end, the loss of freedom will be the same.

THE KGB AND THE COMMUNIST PARTY

The media tells us that the KGB and the Communist Party has disappeared forever. Nothing could be farther from the truth. The communists in Russia and Eastern Europe have gone underground as they planned in the final stage of their deception campaign. As proof that the communists have not disappeared, consider these facts. Of the twenty million members of the communist party that ran every single area of the Soviet Union, intelligence sources claim that only ten thousand lost their jobs. If the Communist Party had truly lost its power we would see the worst bloodbath of righteous vengeance in history. For seven decades the communists and KGB murdered over sixty million of their own citizens. Sixty million victims! The mind can scarcely conceive of human butchery on so vast a scale over seven long decades. There are few families in Russia that have not lost a brother, mother or father to communist concentration camps and firing squads. Human nature and history suggest that many of these victims would want revenge, or at least demand justice. Why have there been no trials, investigations, or arrests of the thousands of well-known leaders, spies, informers, prison guards, torturers and executioners? The KGB archives alone contain over fifteen miles of files documenting their unspeakable crimes. However, in July 1993 the Russian Supreme Soviet and Yeltsin agreed to seal the KGB archives for at least twenty years to protect their friends.

After the collapse of Germany's Nazi party at the end of World War II, there were thousands of arrests and trials of the people who had carried out Hitler's program of genocide. Yet in Russia and Eastern Europe today, there is a deafening silence. No one is placing blame, there are no calls for trials or justice. Why has there been no demand for "Nuremberg Trials" for the communist slave masters of Eastern Europe and the former Soviet Union? The answer is that the people living in these countries are not deceived by the propaganda. They know that the huge communist bureaucracy of spies, secret police, and the military are still there, waiting in the shadows. They know that it would be suicidal to demand justice. They realize from brutal experience that the Russian bear is not dead, it is just sleeping. The bear is only pretending to be dead, lying still, waiting for the unsuspecting hunter to come within range of its deadly paws.

The twelve former republics of the Soviet Union are now led by former communists. The leadership and bureaucracies of each of these successor governments have worked for decades as faithful communist party members. If you think that all of these people simultaneously experienced a genuine political conversion to democracy, you are dreaming. Russian President Boris Yeltsin is now widely credited in the western media as "a staunch anti-communist, a democrat, a lover of freedom." Consider the facts. Yeltsin officially joined the Soviet Communist Party of the USSR in 1961 and was rapidly groomed to join the Central Committee. In 1985 he became general secretary of the Moscow City Communist Party Committee, the largest in the USSR with 1.2 million members. No one could rise this high in the Soviet Communist Party unless their commitment to communism was absolute. Each leader is subject to rigorous KGB surveillance and political indoctrination throughout their political career.

For centuries the Russian empire and the USSR was dominated by the huge Russian republic. After the official breakup of the USSR the new Commonwealth of Independent States is still completely dominated by Russia. In May of 1992 the Russian Parliament annulled the "gift" of Crimea that was made to the Ukraine in 1954. Back then, it was a phony ceremonial act. But today, with the official independence of the Ukraine, the Russians have demanded the return of their vital Crimean outpost. The Soviet Black Sea Fleet has returned to the full control of Mother Russia. As Azerbaijan and Armenia continue their military struggle, this could trigger a wider civil war in Central Asia. In recent months the independent republics of the C.I.S. have submitted to the complete economic

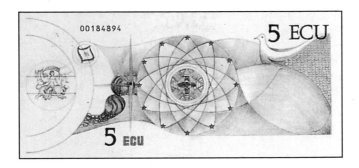

European Currency Unit
With the symbol of a woman riding a bull: "I saw a woman sitting on a scarlet beast." Rev. 17:3

The Stamp of the European Parliament
With the symbol of Europa and Zeus, the bull

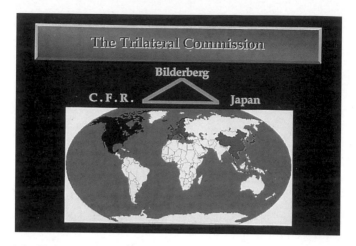

The Trilateral Commission
Dividing the planet for world government

Grant Jeffrey
Our TV program, *Appointment with Destiny*, seen on 300 stations across North America

Grant and Kaye Jeffrey
Visiting Capernaum,
where Jesus lived and
taught

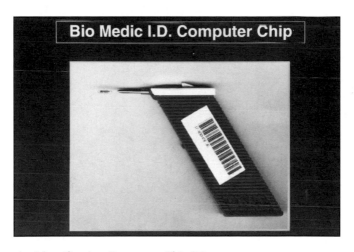

An Identification Computer Chip Dispenser
This implants a miniature chip beneath the skin of your pet

The Rebuilt City of Babylon
Over $800 million spent to date by Iraq

The Rebuilt Ishtar Gate in Babylon
Daniel and the Jewish captives were led through this gate
twenty-five centuries ago

control of the Russian Central Bank and currency control. In addition, they have signed a new economic and military union treaty committing themselves to act as one— the "one" being "Russia" of course. In addition the KGB and the Red Army operate throughout each of the republics of the C.I.S. as though nothing has changed since the days of the Soviet Union.

THE DISARMING OF THE WEST

We are constantly told by our leaders and the media that the U.S.A. is the world's only remaining superpower. As illustrated by the evidence in this chapter, that is a blatant lie. Why would the Russians pretend to be so weak and the West so strong? Everywhere you read the propaganda that Russia is defenseless and could not possibly launch an attack on any other nation. This is a total lie, but it has successfully eroded political support in America and Europe for an adequate defense. America is disarming as our politicians compete to spend the "peace dividend." The tragedy of democracy is that it seldom has the foresight or strength of character to pay the price of eternal vigilance against a long-term adversary. In World War II the Atlantic and Pacific Oceans protected North America during those crucial months needed to train a huge army and build up a formidable military machine. Unfortunately, today we live in an age of intercontinental missiles and nuclear submarines. When the struggle begins we will not have the luxury of a period of grace to rearm our military and catch up to our massively armed adversary.

WESTERN AID TO RUSSIA

Although the Russians and the C.I.S. continue to arm for war against us, the West is providing them with $200 billion in aid and advanced western technology. Russia and the C.I.S. republics recently joined the International Monetary Fund and World Bank enabling them to qualify for massive loans on attractive terms. The nations of the West are unable to provide food, clothing and basic medical services for our poor and homeless citizens. Why do our leaders pour billions of taxpayer's funds into our enemies while Russia still spies on us and spend enormous sums on armaments?

THE GREAT RUSSIAN DISARMAMENT FRAUD

What about disarmament? Aren't the Russians disarming? The simple answer is No. Despite all of the disarmament talks, treaties and the actual disarming of the West, the former Soviet forces have not disarmed at all. The only actions taken thus far have been cosmetic. Despite all the talk of disarmament, the C.I.S. has the largest military machine in human history. The army contains over five million troops, plus one million special KGB interior ministry troops and border guards. In addition they trained 250,000 commandoes known as Spetznaz forces that specialize in infiltration, sabotage, and assassination of political, military, and intelligence forces. Their air force and navy massively exceed America's armed forces. To date there has been no dismantling of Soviet military forces. In fact, the Russian government recently withdrew the draft exemption from approximately five million students. This surprising action makes these military-age students available to be drafted into the armed forces. After promising the West that they would cut their army in half Yeltsin has now admitted there will be no reductions in size. Why would Russia need this huge additional manpower if they truly want peace? President Yeltsin recently hired 150,000 additional special contract soldiers with higher pay for dangerous service fighting in the civil wars in the former Soviet Muslim republics.

Despite massive American disarmament and reductions of forces, no Soviet divisions or units have been disbanded. The Russians completed the world's most advanced civil defense system designed to protect most of their population and industry. They just finished seventy-five enormous underground civil defense shelters deep beneath Moscow, each one larger than five city blocks. America has virtually no civilian defense bomb shelters.

The old U.S. fallout shelters from the 1950s are almost useless as protection against the new extremely accurate Russian nuclear warheads. Even the special nuclear shelter for Congress is about to be decommissioned because our naive politicians believe the Cold War is over. Over six hundred huge Russian arms factories are running non-stop shifts despite the talk of disarmament. When the U.S. president challenged President Yeltsin about this, he claimed their unemployment problem forced them to keep the factories producing weapons for sale to other countries. *Time* magazine revealed recently that the C.I.S. still spends over 42 percent of its gross national product (G.N.P.) on their military compared to some 5 percent for America. The U.S. Congress plans to reduce America's military spending to less than 4 percent of G.N.P.

When Gorbachev became the leader of the USSR in 1985 the Soviets had a huge lead on America in every single area of weapons and military manpower. Gorbachev and Yeltsin have now had eight years to demonstrate their true commitment to disarmament and peace. What has occurred under their political control? To illustrate that Russia has continued to arm for war, consider these weapons production figures.

WEAPONS PRODUCTION COMPARISON FROM 1985 TO 1991

Weapon	Russia	America	Ratio
I.C.B.M.s	715	68	10 to 1
Tanks	16,300	4,891	3 to 1
Armored Vehicles	28,800	5,375	5 to 1
Bombers	450	104	4 to 1
Submarines	54	24	2 to 1
Sub-launched Missiles	490	205	2 to 1

Source: U.S. Defense Intelligence Agency

The Kremlin is forging ahead with a unprecedented conventional and strategic weapons build-up despite its worsening economic situation. They recently installed eighteen new nuclear missile railway launchers for their SS-24 missiles. This is the same type of MX missile system turned down by Congress because America could not afford it. The U.S.A. has determined that our satellites cannot locate these mobile rail missile launchers as they move along eighty thousand miles of railway track. A U.S. official commented: "They operate like submarines . . . they're the ultimate strategic stealth weapon." Each of the ten warheads on the SS-24s can deliver a one-hundred kiloton bomb up to sixty-two hundred miles—easily within range of America when fired over the polar ice cap. The Russian submarines are now engaging in extremely aggressive naval maneuvers against American submarines underneath the Arctic ice cap.

Although Russia is begging the West for vast amounts of food aid and billions in financial assistance, they continue to produce six new highly advanced nuclear ballistic submarines every year, costing over three billion dollars each. Russian officials acknowledged that they still retain nuclear weapons in Eastern Germany along with almost 200,000 troops. It is astonishing that Russia is allowed to station a huge army complete with nuclear weapons inside a European NATO country. Amazingly, Germany is now paying the full cost of food, gas, and upkeep of Russian troops still occupying the eastern portion of their country. The Red Army has declared they have no intention of leaving Germany until at least 1995. As agreed in the INF Treaty of 1988 the U.S.A. destroyed 100 percent of its European-based intermediate range missiles. However, Russia kept 93 percent of her missiles targeted on Western Europe. It has since deployed many additional SS-24 and SS-24 road and rail mobile missiles.

The 1991 Conventional Forces Europe Treaty required Russia and the West to destroy huge amounts of sophisticated weaponry in Central Europe. Three weeks before the November 1991 implementation date, the Soviets moved seventy thousand pieces of equipment (i.e., tanks, planes, armored vehicles, and artillery) east of the Ural Mountains. Since the treaty only covers Central Europe, they simply moved the equipment outside the defined area so they can move it back in a few days if war breaks out. Gorbachev lied and cheated regarding the CFE treaty before the ink was even dry on the document.

In normal times the West would have responded to this outright deception by canceling the treaty. However, our spineless New World Order leaders forgave the Russians their deception and refused to publicize Russia's blatant cheating. We continued to destroy our western weapons as though everything was fine.

The Red Army is more than four times larger than U.S. military forces and still operates throughout each of the former republics of the Soviet Union. If anyone doubts the real intentions of the Red Army, consider the following facts reported in *The State*, March 16, 1993. When Germany was re-united a number of Soviet military documents and bases fell into western hands in former East Germany. U.S. and West German intelligence discovered massive planning and preparations had been made to invade Western Europe. The Russians had prepared huge quantities of Russian language street signs for western cities, minted massive amounts of currency for the Soviet occupation government, and produced specialized equipment to alter their trains to run on the different gauge tracks in Western Europe. Enormous underground storage facilities contained military assault equipment and huge stocks of ammunition for the invasion. Medals were already minted to award soldiers who performed with valor in conquering the West. "We have found that the National People's Army [East Germany] made every necessary preparation to conquer and occupy the West and especially, West Germany," according to Vice Admiral Ulrich Weisser of the German Bundeswehr (armed forces).

The Russian Parliament approved a 20 percent increase in the KGB and military budget for the next twelve months. The KGB employs more than one million spies and border troops together with five million secret informers. The Russian intelligence assault on western defense targets has accelerated with a huge increase in KGB agents arrested by the FBI last year while trying to steal American defense secrets. They talk peace but they prepare for war. Lenin defined the communist interpretation of disarmament in 1921, "They [the West] disarm—we arm."

Intelligence studies indicate that the Russian Strategic Rocket Forces have purposely erased the serial numbers and other identifying factory marks from 654 SS-20 missiles to prevent American inspectors from determining the actual number destroyed. A 1991 White House study called the "Soviet Non-Compliance with Arms Control Agreements" admits that the Soviets secretly concealed their SS-23 missiles in East Germany, Czechoslovakia and Bulgaria after they guaranteed their destruction. Gorbachev repeatedly lied about the size of their nuclear arsenal. A few months ago intelligence confirmed that the Russians have 45,000 nuclear warheads, not the 27,000 they claimed.

THE SEARCH FOR RED GOLD

The Russian state prosecutor's office released reports of its investigation into the massive disappearance of Soviet gold reserves and billions in western hard currency from the Soviet Union's State Bank. The investigators discovered Gorbachev and his associates established 7200 secret bank accounts in foreign countries, including Switzerland and Panama. These illegal accounts were set up by the communist party for the illegal private benefit of their top officials. Over $174 billion in hard currency was given to the USSR for food aid. However, it was diverted and has now disappeared into these illegal foreign accounts. Who authorized these illegal undertakings? *Time* magazine's Man of the Year—Mikhail Gorbachev.

In addition to this theft, investigators discovered that thirty-five hundred tons of Soviet gold has vanished. The Russian prosecutor revealed that the Soviet gold reserve is practically empty because the former communist leaders authorized the secret sale of Soviet gold through Switzerland and South Africa. Their purpose was to provide enormous amounts of secret funds for the private use of members of the communist elite. "Soviet gold reserves have dwindled away to almost nothing (240 tons)," according to *The Financial Post* on November 26, 1991. The prosecutor's office revealed that these secret and illegal sales were signed for by top party officials including Secretary-General Mikhail Gorbachev. These and many other revelations of Soviet illegal activities are being uncovered by competing factions in the ongoing struggle for leadership and position in the restructured C.I.S.

MIKHAIL GORBACHEV—THE MAN OF MYSTERY

Despite his rhetoric about democracy, glasnost and perestroika, former President Mikhail Gorbachev is an unrepentant Marxist-communist. He was trained as a lawyer in the Soviet Union to work for the KGB. For years he was groomed as heir-apparent by his mentor Yuri Andropov, the head of the KGB. Soviet disinformation propaganda falsely presented Gorbachev as a "true reformer and lover of freedom." In his revealing book *Perestroika*, Gorbachev called for the reform of the Soviet Union on the basis of Marxist-communism. He only officially abandoned the Communist Party when it seemed expedient to become the "unelected" president of the Soviet Union. As a committed communist he never stood for election in his life. Pity the man like Mikhail Gorbachev who believes in communism—he believes in a philosophy that does not believe in him.

Despite his personal history of repression and corruption, Gorbachev appealed to the media and public in the West that were desperately hoping for a reform-minded Soviet leader. He virtually destroyed the economy of his country with his half-hearted reform measures, refusing to allow private property rights or the independence of the various republics. Gorbachev is doing everything in his power to become an international statesman and unabashed spokesman for the New World Order. Everywhere you look there are articles, media interviews, speeches and reports of meetings between Gorbachev and other world leaders. Recently, Gorbachev appeared on the CNN Larry King show to promote the New World Order. He is being groomed for something else. Newspaper reports claim that western industrialists, including David Rockefeller, have established a peace and security foundation in Moscow endowed with several hundred million dollars to be directed by Gorbachev. In addition, Gorbachev was appointed the chairman of the Green Cross, a

New World Order think tank for global environmental issues.

GORBACHEV AND THE VATICAN

As indicated in the chapter on the coming inquisition Mikhail Gorbachev communicated with Pope John Paul II for many years in their secret coordination of the political events in Eastern Europe. Malachi Martin, the Catholic writer of *The Keys of The Blood*, completed extensive research on Gorbachev and John Paul II's extraordinary alliance leading to a New World Order. He says, "The prospects for Mr. Gorbachev in the New World Order are very bright. Once Russian and the members of the Commonwealth of Independent States join the EC, there will be a need for a new leader—a moderate—popular with both sides. The headquarters for the New World Order will not be Strasbourg or Brussels, but a new thing called the CSCE, the Council for Security Cooperation of Europe, a 35 member organization. It will need a new dynamic head acceptable to both sides. Probably, Mr. Gorbachev will be that head, and thus enter as the leader of the New World Order, unless there is an accident of history." This is a fascinating theory but not very probable. The Antichrist who will lead the revived Roman Empire will almost certainly be Jewish to make the claim that he is the messiah. Daniel prophesied that he will arise from the area of the Roman Empire. However Gorbachev may play a major role in the formation of the New World Order, possibly with the United Nations.

A FINAL WARNING TO THE WEST

General Sir Walter Walker, the former NATO Commander-in-Chief, recently issued one of the most important warnings ever given to the West. In an article in the October 1991 issue of the excellent paper, the *McAlvany Intelligence Advisor*, General Walker warned, "We are now in a period of the greatest strategic deception, perhaps in all history, that I feel I should not allow this occasion to pass without warning you of the future that lies ahead in the next decade. I say most emphatically that the Cold War is not yet over, but only in a state of re-mission ... the Soviet Union is still devoting a vast pro-portion of its resources to sustain a military machine capable of threatening the west. ... The Soviet military threat has not evaporated. The neutralization of NATO has long been one of the Soviet's prime glasnost deception goals ... I leave you with the stark fact that unless we stand fast and stop the rot, the demonstrable truth is that, contrary to the Kremlin's self-serving pose of humility, the Soviet Union is not 'on the verge of collapse.' Western de-fense, on the other hand, is."

At this point you may be shaking your head and wondering: if all that I have written is true, why in the world are America and other western governments dis-arming? The evidence provided in this chapter is true and verifiable. The United States, led by President Clinton, and formerly by President Bush, who was director of the CIA for years, are fully aware of these facts and much more. Why then have they failed to warn the public of the terrible danger? The answer is that most western leaders are persuaded that their vision of a New World Order with a peaceful merger between Russia and the West is in-evitable. This globalist vision presupposes an end to the Cold War and a merging of Russia and America leading to a One World Government. They feel their secret deals with the Communists will protect the West from Russia's overwhelming military power. However, it is quite possi-ble that communist powers fully intend to betray their western financial and political New World Order partners at the last minute. They could easily use the KGB and their overwhelming military power to establish their own version of a world government—a true communist double-cross victory that Lenin always planned. The other reason western leaders fail to respond is that they cannot bring themselves to admit the horrible truth that they have been deceived. They have placed western democracy in its most dangerous position since the darkest days of World War II when Hitler's armies conquered all of Eu-rope. Sometimes the fact that you have been deceived is so horrible that the mind refuses to acknowledge the true danger.

The devastating truth is that Russia and her allies are completing the most overwhelming military build-up in history to place themselves in a position to put a gun to the head of the West. On that day, in one scenario, they could launch a swift attack with Spetznaz commando troops and submarine-launched nuclear missiles to decapitate the military command-and-control functions of our greatly reduced western armed forces. A phone call from Moscow could then inform the White House that we either surrender to the Russian threat or face the annihilation of our cities, towns, and villages. With our weakened military situation our only credible military response would be to launch our remaining nuclear weapons at Russia. This would guarantee a second Russian missile strike that would wipe out a majority of the unprotected American population. Unlike the huge civil defense system protecting the Russian leadership and population, Americans today are virtually without a civil defense. The U.S. government has resisted creating a proper civil defense system for the last forty years. In addition, Congress refused to develop a strategic defense program that could stop incoming missiles. The Russians have produced eight thousand anti-ballistic missiles while the U.S. has none. Without civil defense, the estimated casualties in the event of an all-out attack would exceed two hundred million dead Americans.

THE RUSSIAN STRATEGY—TO WIN WITHOUT NUCLEAR WAR

The Russian strategy was always to win without having to fight a thermonuclear war. They do not want to destroy their own country. Russia endured the twenty-five million casualties during the devastation of World War II. Nor do they want to inherit the burning radioactive cinders of a destroyed America. Their goal is to achieve their long-sought victory without fighting a nuclear war. As Sun Tzu declared in the introduction to *The Art of War*: "To subdue the enemy without fighting is the height of skill for a general." It is quite possible that an American president would be forced to surrender to the communists at the point of the first Russian missile strike. He might surrender before the first strike if he was convinced that western military weakness made practical resistance impossible.

Personally I do not believe that Russia will succeed in fulfilling their military deception strategy as I have outlined above. This is not because the West will awaken and re-arm to stand against the Russians. The reason is found in the ancient prophecies of the Bible, that have never yet failed. The Scriptures indicate that Russia and her allies will fail in their plan to conquer the democracies. The Scriptures do not prophecy about a Russian worldwide empire. If Russia succeeded in destroying the West it would violate the prophecies of the Bible that declare that no other power will succeed in establishing a world empire except the revival of the Roman Empire in Europe.

VLADIMIR ZHIRINOVSKY AND THE RISE OF FASCISM

The specter of Russian fascism is rising within the former Soviet Union. This resurgence of imperialism is led by Vladimir Zhirinovsky, the dangerous new leader of the Liberal Democrat Party. This man appeared out of nowhere to win six million votes in the 1991 Presidential election, coming in third behind Yeltsin. After the election he declared, "When I come to power, I will be a dictator. Russia needs a dictator." Zhirinovsky's slogan "No democracy without violence" warns us of terrible days ahead for Russia. In the parliamentary elections of December 1993, to the surprise of everyone, Zhirinovsky won the highest number of seats in the Russian Duma and the balance of power. In only two years, Zhirinovsky may become the president of a resurgent Russian Empire intent on conquering its neighbors. He stunned audiences on a German radio program threatening them with nuclear destruction if Germany interfered in Russian affairs. Later he warned Japan, "We will create new Hiroshimas and Nagasakis. I will not hesitate to use nuclear weapons."

His program calls for re-militarizing Russia and a massive increase in foreign arms sales. Who is he? Who is secretly supporting his plan to rule Russia?

Despite his strange comments many Russians find his tough and belligerent approach attractive. His irresponsible statement—"Vote for me and I will give you everything you want"—appeals to many disillusioned voters. In addition he promises to restore Russian pride and power. While many dismiss Zhirinovsky as a buffoon, he is quite intelligent, speaking Turkish, English, French and German. Zhirinovsky worked for the KGB since he was nineteen, attending studies at the oriental language institute of Moscow University, a school open only to KGB agents. He has attacked Zionism and Israel blaming Jews for both World Wars while calling for the firing of Jewish television announcers. Despite his open anti-semitism and calls for ethnic cleansing, Zhirinovsky's deceased father was a Jew. Two Israeli officials confirmed that in 1983 he applied to enter Israel under the Law of Return as a Jew. He was an official in a Jewish cultural organization in Moscow in 1987.

His Liberal Democratic Party is neither liberal or democratic. It is an extremely nationalistic, fascist, imperialistic and Neo-Nazi party. Zhirinovsky proposes to conquer Central Asia, the Middle East, and the Persian Gulf. He has threatened Japan, Germany, and Lithuania with nuclear devastation. Astonishingly he warns about a new Russian machine gun "that will establish order in any place." Recently he promised to expand the Russian Empire toward the Indian Ocean and Mediterranean. In addition he promises to execute leaders of organized crime on the spot. He is a skilled political orator promising the voters whatever they want to hear.

His 142 page autobiographical book *The Last March to the South*, released December 26, 1993, lays out Zhirinovsky's plans to conquer the former Soviet Republics, Turkey, Iran, India, Finland, Eastern Europe, the Baltic Republics, and the Middle East. It pictures Russia as a kind of white knight saving "the south" while conquering the territories from the Middle East to the Indian Ocean. "From Constantinople to Kabul . . . to the shores of the Indian Ocean everyone will speak Russian." He wants to recreate the Czarist Russian Empire occupying Poland, Finland, and incredibly, Alaska. The *Dallas Morning News* on December 14, 1993, reported that he warned of future conflicts with Iraq, Azerbaijan, Armenia, and Pakistan that "will make a hell out of these regions, with wars raging for 10–15 years ... Cities and roads will be destroyed, epidemics will explode, millions will die and neither America nor the United Nations will be able to do anything about it. The world community will beg Russia to save what remains of those peoples in Central Asia, the Middle East and the Indian Ocean. We will be obliged to send our boys there. Our army will then appear on the coast of the Indian Ocean."

Amazingly his book also details the rejection he felt as a child naming the boys who tormented him. He admits his sexual failures and claims that no one cared, forcing him to turn to vodka and politics. *Time* magazine reported on December 27, 1993 that Zhirinovsky may be a homosexual. When the German government refused to allow him to visit he threatened to unleash "a Chernobyl in Germany." As the editor of the Jewish Gazette wrote, "The grounds for alarm have already passed, the grounds for panic have begun!" He threatened NATO with a Russian secret super-weapon known as the "Elipton," which he claimed is more powerful than a hydrogen bomb and "is capable of destroying the West." He may be referring to a secret Russian weapon, a Particle Beam Weapon, that can vaporize a target from space.

Deputy Prime Minister Chubais warned that Zhirinovsky's policies would lead to disaster. "If we try to fulfill his policies, there will be World War III." In a future conflict between Yeltsin and Zhirinovsky, the Russian military might support Zhirinovsky. It is chilling to realize that Zhirinovsky won over 74 percent of the vote in most of the army including the two army divisions that Yeltsin used to attack the Parliament Building. Over 93 percent of the Russian Strategic Missile Forces support Zhirinovsky. While he can disrupt Parliament, the real danger will come in a future crisis if Zhirinovsky calls on the army to support him.

Oleg Gordievsky, a former senior Soviet intelligence officer, told the *European* that Zhirinovsky was recruited by the KGB while working as an interpreter for the Soviet Embassy in Turkey. Gordievsky added, "the Liberal Democratic Party was created by the Fifth Chief Directorate of the KGB in the last years of Gorbachev's perestroika to split the growing democratic forces." His sinister presidential running mate, Andre Zavidia, purchased a nationalistic newspaper, the *Sovietkaya Rossiya* (Soviet Russia), with a mysterious 3 million rouble loan from the Communist Party as revealed by secret party archives. When Zhirinovsky's Liberal Democratic Party was launched in 1990 the official Soviet newspaper *Pravda* carried the story on the front page, indicating that the party was secretly supported by the Communist Party and the KGB. During the 1993 Parliamentary elections the Communist Central Committee gave Zhirinovsky 70 million roubles to purchase massive television and radio coverage nationwide.

President Yeltsin won a clear majority to institute his new Russian constitution giving him sweeping powers over Parliament to rule the country in its difficult crisis. These dictatorial constitutional powers could prove to be a time bomb waiting to explode two years from now. Yeltsin has declared that he will not run again. However there is no obvious successor to continue Yeltsin's reform program. If Zhirinovsky wins the 1996 election the world will face an incredibly dangerous and nuclear armed "Hitler." The prophet Ezekiel warned that an enormous Russian-Arab military alliance would arise in the last days to launch a massive invasion of Israel. The Bible calls the leader of this great confederacy "Gog" and names his country "Magog." In the next chapter we will explore the fascinating prophecies about the great War of Gog and Magog that will set the stage for the rise of Satan's Prince of Darkness to rule the whole earth.

The Word of God does not leave us in darkness concerning the role of Russia in end time events. Twenty-five centuries ago the prophet Ezekiel declared that Russia and its allies will be destroyed by the supernatural power of God when they invade Israel in the last days. In the next chapter we will examine the prophecies that reveal the incredible destiny awaiting Russia and her allies. Rather than attack America or Europe directly, the Bible's prophecies indicate that Russia will join with her Arab allies in a strategic invasion of the Middle East to alter the balance of power. The armies of Russia and her huge confederacy will be destroyed by the hand of God when they attack the Chosen People on the mountains of Israel.

12

The Coming Russian Invasion of the Middle East

"Thus says the Lord God: 'Behold, I am against you, O Gog, the prince of Rosh, Meshech, and Tubal ... In the latter years you will come into the land of those brought back from the sword and gathered from many people on the mountains of Israel, which had long been desolate; they were brought out of the nations, and now all of them dwell safely. You will ascend, coming like a storm, covering the land like a cloud, you and all your troops and many peoples with you.... Then you will come from your place out of the far north, you and many peoples with you, all of them riding on horses, a great company and a mighty army' " (Ezekiel 38:3,8,9,15).

THE MOTIVE FOR THE WAR OF GOG AND MAGOG

From the beginning of history the narrow strip of land along the Mediterranean known as Palestine has been a vital geostrategic prize for kings and emperors who wanted to dominate the world. The empires of Egypt, Assyria, Babylon, Media-Persia, Greece, and Rome have each fought in their turn to capture the Holy Land as a key step in their plans for world conquest. The Bible prophesied that this impending attack on Israel by Russia and the Arab nations would take place after the exiles have returned to rebuild the Promised Land.

Russia's motivation, of course, is to gain control of the Middle East, which they cannot do as long as Israel remains an independent and powerful military force. If Russia can occupy the Middle East she will control over 65 percent of the world's oil. Despite the experience of past Arab oil embargoes, Europe and Japan remain quite vulnerable with less than one-hundred days supply of oil in their strategic reserves. If Russia were to cut off their oil supplies, and threatened an overwhelming military invasion, it would cause Europe and Japan to capitulate to Russian demands. Russia and her allies could achieve their goal of world domination without risking a thermonuclear war that would inevitably follow a direct military invasion of Western Europe. The Arab states are motivated toward this invasion by their overwhelming hatred of the Jews. The Arabs have been frustrated in their attacks on Israel by their inability to conquer the brilliant, well-motivated and technically advanced Israeli Defense Forces. The Arabs and Russians learned some costly lessons in the four previous Arab-Israeli wars and the recent War in the Gulf. They now know that their only chance to defeat Israel's well-trained, high tech western army is to combine their huge Arab armies with well trained Russian soldiers and generals wielding high-tech Soviet weapons. The Arab states have accumulated hundreds of billions of petrodollars which they will enthusiastically commit to capture Jerusalem and Palestine from the Jews. The Russians and their C.I.S. republics still possess the most powerful army in the world and an array of nuclear, conventional, biological, and chemical weapons.

Is Russia still powerful enough to lead an invasion of Israel in light of their disastrous economy? The truth is that Russia is not in quite as bad economic shape as they pretend. While the unfortunate Russian citizens must stand in line for hours for bread and other goods, that is more a commentary on their disastrous distribution system and widespread corruption than an indication of real starvation. Russians have stood in line for food during the last seventy years of inefficient communist administration. Russia was able to field a tough army of over ten million soldiers during World War II despite their ruined economy and famine conditions. They defeated the best armies of Hitler's Germany at a time when western governments predicted that Russian troops must retreat in disarray. The Russian soldiers are incredibly well disciplined due to their harsh training and draconian punishments for the slightest disobedience. If Russian generals order their troops to march against another country, they will. As detailed in the last chapter, the new C.I.S. possesses the most powerful military force in history. Their military capability is more than adequate to accomplish the invasion of the Middle East as described by the prophet Ezekiel.

Recent events in the Middle East and Russia have led some prophecy students to doubt that Russia will attack Israel. However, regardless of the confusing events and signals emanating from Russia, the Bible's prophecy will be fulfilled in these last days. After almost thirty years of studying prophecy I remain convinced that Ezekiel 38 and 39 will be literally fulfilled in our lifetime. Recent events suggest that this conflict may be very close. Twenty-five centuries ago, God promised that He would destroy the massive invading armies of Russia and her allies—Eastern Europe, Iran, Sudan, Ethiopia, Libya and other Arab nations—on the mountains of Israel.

THE ISLAMIC NUCLEAR THREAT

Since the break up of the Soviet Union, the Arab and Islamic nations—including Iraq, Iran, and Libya—have offered the six former Muslim Soviet Republics billions of dollars in aid in return for advanced Russian weaponry, including tactical nuclear weapons. Kazakhstan, an independent Sunni Muslim state, is now the world's third largest nuclear power. It has long-range nuclear missiles capable of devastating cities in Europe, Israel, China, or America. The Islamic states of Iran, Pakistan, the Arab nations and the six southern republics of the C.I.S., Kazakhstan, Azerbaijan, et cetera, have now joined a new Muslim Common Market and Islamic League. Despite many other problems, their initial conference focused on how they could help their Muslim brothers defeat their mutual enemy Israel.

The *Intelligence Digest* from Britain released a report that military authorities in Russia and the C.I.S. concluded a secret treaty with Muslim fundamentalist forces throughout the Middle East to join in a decisive invasion of Israel between 1995 and 1999. This commitment to the Arabs was in return for help in suppressing rebellion in the Muslim ethnic republics of the C.I.S. and for guaranteeing Russian access to Persian Gulf oil. Russia has just built an enormous T-72 heavy tank factory in Iran to supply their most advanced tank technology to these enemies of Israel. In addition the Iranians purchased two dozen advanced MIG-29 fighter planes and are negotiating for the newest MIG-30 planes. Iran has promised to supply these planes to the Arab front line states surrounding Israel in the next conflict. .

For years Israel and the western intelligence services have worried that the Islamic countries would use their vast financial resources to develop a nuclear capability to threaten their enemies. The Islamic nuclear bomb is now here. The Russian Secret Service recently confirmed CIA reports about missing Russian nuclear weapons. It was revealed that three nuclear warheads were "taken" from a Ukrainian special nuclear weapons depot by a "well trained commando unit." As the situation in the southern Muslim republics deteriorates into civil war we may witness the world's first nuclear conflict breaking out there. The ethnic and national hatreds in Eastern Europe and the southern C.I.S. republics could easily spill over into massive civil wars. A huge number of civilians received military training in the past during compulsory army service. In addition, enormous armories of sophisticated weapons are stored throughout these areas that could provide the armaments to fuel a dozen civil wars like the one in Yugoslavia. Investigations also confirmed that Kazakhstan recently secretly sold four nuclear warheads and their long range missile systems to Iran. These nuclear missile warheads have a sophisticated security code system that guarded the arming sequence. Iranian engineers and mathematicians are using their recently purchased western supercomputers to break the cipher codes to allow them to re-arm and re-target these thermonuclear warheads for a long-range missile attack on Israel or the West.

Intelligence reports warn that Russian KGB nuclear security officers have offered to sell tactical nuclear bombs, small enough to fit in a duffel bag, to Arab countries for $20 million each. At these prices, unstable Arab regimes or terrorist organizations such as the PLO, Hamas, or the I.R.A. could become a "nuclear power." These terrorist groups have proven their utter disregard for human life by bombing stores and planes containing hundreds of innocent victims. The acquisition of nuclear, chemical or biological weapons will give these radical groups the ability to terrorize whole cities and countries for financial gain or to force their political demands. The break-up of the Soviet Union has destroyed the former extremely tight security over the USSR's forty-five thousand nuclear warheads and other deadly military technology, including chemical and biological weapons.

A Possible Scenario for the War of Gog and Magog

This century has witnessed a tragic series of wars in the Middle East between Israel and her neighbors. The Arab nations refuse to accept the fact that the Jews have returned to establish their permanent homeland in the Promised Land. In my book *MESSIAH* I explored the background to the competing historical claims by the Palestinians and the Jews to this small strip of desert. For the last two years the eyes of the world have been on the continuing peace conferences between Israel and her enemies under the joint sponsorship of Russia and America. Israel offered twenty-five separate areas of autonomy, including agriculture and police powers, to the Palestinians in the West Bank and Gaza. The PLO have finally accepted Israel's offer of limited autonomy in the territories but they declare to other Arabs they will not be happy until Israel is pushed into the sea. Many commentators suggest that the Palestinian situation is the main obstacle to peace in the Middle East. However, the Arab states were committed to Israel's destruction long before Israel's capture of the West Bank and Gaza during the 1967 Six Day War and the creation of the "Palestinian problem." Israel cannot negotiate away her right to exist as a nation. Yet nothing less will satisfy the Arab regimes. If the PLO succeeds in establishing their new state in the West Bank and Gaza they will then launch a renewed call for the ultimate Jihad—a holy war to destroy Israel forever. It is hard to visualize any lasting peace coming out of these Rabin—Arafat negotiations until the Arabs accept that Israel has a right to live together in peace with them in the Middle East.

THE IDENTIFICATION OF MAGOG AS RUSSIA

Many biblical scholars agree with the identification of Magog as the ancient Scythians, the Russians. While there are a number of modern scholars who disagree with this identification of Russia, most of them also reject the interpretation that the prophecy refers to a real future battle. Those who reject the identification of Magog with Russia tend to view this prophecy and many others in a purely symbolical light. They usually believe that the prophecies refer merely to a symbolic war between the forces of good and evil rather than a real future military battle in the Middle East. The prophet Ezekiel listed the names of the ancient tribes descended from the sons and grandsons of Noah (Genesis 10). These ancient descendants of Noah settled into the areas now occupied by the modern nations of Eastern Europe, the Muslim republics of the C.I.S., Iran, Iraq, Saudi Arabia, Syria, Libya, Sudan, and Ethiopia. By naming the ancient tribes, the prophet identified for all time the correct geographical area. The name "Gog" is a prophetic name applied by the Bible to the leader of Magog, the nation of Russia.

Over two dozen Jewish and Christian scholars and writers identify Magog as Russia. Flavius Josephus, writing in the first century, claimed Magog was connected to the Scythian people who lived north of the Black Sea. As

G. Rawlinson wrote in his *Five Great Monarchies* (Assyria: Chap. 9, footnote): "The Scythians proper of Herodotus and Hippocrates extended from the Danube and the Carpathians on the one side, to the Tanais or Don upon the other." This geographic area of the Scythians is the land of ancient southern Russia. The prophet Ezekiel used the ancient tribal name Magog (from Genesis 10:2) to identify the geographical location where the leadership of the prophesied invasion would originate. The well respected scholar of biblical languages, Gesenius, in his definitive *Hebrew and Chaldee Lexicon* identified Magog as follows: "A region, and a great and powerful people of the same name, inhabiting the extreme recesses of the north, who are at some time to invade the Holy Land (Ezek. Chap. 38,39) We are to understand just the same nations as the Greeks comprised under the name of Scythians (Joseph. Arch. 1.6,–1)." Gesenius refers to "Magog" as a real nation and as a people who will actually invade the Holy Land in the future. Also Gesenius's comment on "Gog" treats him as a real "prince of the land of Magog . . . also of Rossi, Moschi, and Tibareni, who is to come with great forces from the extreme north (38:15; 39:2), after the Exile (38:8,12) to invade the holy land, and to perish there, as prophesied by Ezekiel."

The nation Ezekiel called "Magog" must be a great northern nation capable of fulfilling the prophet's words, "Prepare yourself and be ready, you and all your companies that are gathered about you; and be a guard for them" (Ezekiel 38:7). In addition to these reasons for identifying Russia as Magog, the prophet refers to Magog as coming from the "far north." He said, "Then you will come from your place out of the far north, you and many peoples with you, all of them riding on horses, a great company and a mighty army" (Ezekiel 38:15). Aside from Russia, it would be difficult to name any other nation to the far north of Israel that is capable of leading a huge confederacy of nations from Africa, Asia, Eastern Europe, and the Middle East against Israel. Furthermore, Russia is the arms supplier to every one of these nations. They all use Russian AK-47 rifles, T-72 tanks, missiles, and personnel carriers. For the last four decades Russia has trained the military officers and intelligence staff of all of the nations listed in Ezekiel's prophecy. The phrase "Prepare yourself" and "be a guard for them" may indicate Russia's future role in providing arms and military leadership to the huge confederacy of nations.

THE REBIRTH OF ISRAEL IN THE VALLEY OF DRY BONES

The fury of God against Gog and Magog will be demonstrated through the supernatural destruction of their armies when they try to destroy His Chosen People. In Ezekiel 37, the prophet described his vision of the valley of dry bones. The prophet was taken in vision into a valley full of the bones representing millions of Jews killed during twenty centuries of persecution and cruel exile. Yet God showed Ezekiel that He would still have mercy on His people. God's covenants cannot be broken. God told Ezekiel, "Prophesy to these bones, and say to them, 'O dry bones, hear the word of the Lord!' " (Ezekiel 37:4). Then the Lord promised to resurrect the nation of Israel. "Thus says the Lord God to these bones: 'Surely I will cause breath to enter into you, and you shall live' " (Ezekiel 37:5). No other nation in history that has ceased to exist for centuries has ever been resurrected as a nation state. Yet God promised He would raise Israel out of the graveyard of the nations.

In one of the most extraordinary miracles of all time, the nation Israel was reborn during the dramatic events on May 14 and 15, 1948. Despite enormous opposition, Israel now takes its place in the councils of the nations. "So I prophesied as He commanded me, and breath came into them, and they lived, and stood upon their feet, an exceedingly great army" (Ezekiel 37:10). In a remarkable fulfillment of the prophet's words, Israel is now the third most powerful military force in the world. Immediately after his prophecy of Israel's rebirth, Ezekiel was given a vision (recorded in Ezekiel 38 and 39) about an enormous confederacy of nations, led by Magog from the extreme north, that would attack Israel after the Jewish exiles had returned to the Promised Land. The following prophecy was addressed to Gog, the leader of Magog (Russia): "After many days you will be visited. In the latter years you will come into the land of those brought back from the sword and gathered from many people on the mountains of Israel, which had long been desolate; they were brought out of the nations, and now all of them dwell safely" (Ezekiel 38:8).

The Jewish sages believed the War of Gog and Magog (Ezekiel 38 and 39) will be one of the key events to usher in the Messianic era (*Avodah Zara* 3b). In *Yerushalmi, Shabbat* 1:3 the rabbis describe Elijah's preparing the hearts of the Jews prior to Magog's invasion.

THE RUSSIAN BEAR'S LAST ATTACK

"And it will come to pass at the same time, when Gog comes against the land of Israel," says the Lord God, "that My fury will show in My face. For in My jealousy and in the fire of My wrath I have spoken: 'Surely in that day there shall be a great earthquake in the land of Israel . . .' "I will call for a sword against Gog throughout all My mountains," says the Lord God. "Every man's sword will be against his brother" (Ezekiel 38:18,19,21).

Apart from the strategic and economic motivations mentioned earlier, the real reason the leader of Russia will attack Israel is because God will put the thought into his mind. The only other occasion in the Bible where we find God overriding a man's mind is recorded in the history of the Exodus. God forced Pharaoh to refuse to let the Israelites go so that He could demonstrate for all time His great power to deliver His people from slavery. In a similar manner, God has determined to reveal His power to deliver His Chosen People from their enemies by destroying the Russian and Arab armies as they attempt to annihilate the people of Israel. It will not be Israel's army nor America that saves the nation in her greatest hour of need. God will intervene supernaturally as He did during the days of Moses. After saving Israel, God will judge Russia and her allies for the sixty million innocent people the communists imprisoned and killed for the last seven decades. Researchers claim that over fifteen million Christians and five million Jews died in the concentration camps of Russia since 1917.

The Lord will unleash the greatest earthquake in history in response to the attack of the Russian and Arab armies. Though centered on the mountains of Israel, God declares that "all men who are on the face of the earth shall shake at My presence. The mountains shall be thrown down, the steep places shall fall, and every wall shall fall to the ground" (Ezekiel 38:20). God will cause confusion between the various military units in Magog's armies: " 'I will call for a sword against Gog throughout all My mountains,' says the Lord God. 'Every man's sword will be against his brother' " (Ezekiel 38:21). Several times in biblical history God has confused enemy armies so that they mistakenly attacked their own armies. The prophet also revealed that God will "send fire on Magog and on those who live in security in the coastlands" (Ezekiel 39:6).

Ezekiel prophesied (38:22) that "pestilence and bloodshed" and "flooding rain, great hailstones, fire, and brimstone" will display God's vengeance on the enemies of Israel. These divine weapons will produce the greatest military disaster in history with some 85 percent of the enemy's soldiers left dead on the field of battle (Ezekiel 39:12). The numbers will be so overwhelming that it will take seven months for Israel to bury the dead soldiers in a valley east of the Dead Sea in Jordan. It is called "Hamon Gog," the "valley of the multitude of Russia." The Bible declares that their weapons and fuel won't be wasted. "Then those who dwell in the cities of Israel will go out and set on fire and burn the weapons, . . . they will make fires with them for seven years" (Ezekiel 39:9). Some Russian weapons are made of lignostone, a combustible material. Also, the Red Army transports enormous quantities of fuel in portable and inflatable fuel dumps. Possibly the prophet saw these military fuel dumps, as well as weapons, being used for fire by Israelis for seven years.

Some may ask why God would judge Russia when His Holy Spirit is moving so powerfully throughout that land since it has opened up to the free proclamation of the gospel. I rejoice that Russia has allowed the Bible to be distributed to the hundreds of millions of citizens who were cut off from freedom of worship for seven decades. God loves the Russian people and the Arabs as much as He loves anyone. However, as indicated in the last chapter, the leadership of the Communist Party, the military-industrial complex and the KGB remain committed to the destruction of the West and the enslavement of our people. For seventy years these groups persecuted the Russian Christians and Jews killing millions in concentration camps. When Russia and her allies launch their invasion of Israel these evil groups will be destroyed by God.

We live in the most materialistic and atheistic generation in history. However, this supernatural intervention of God will shatter the complacency of billions of men and women. When God defeats this awesome invasion force with the greatest display of miraculous power in history many will turn and repent of their sinful rebellion and unbelief. "I will set My glory among the nations; all the nations shall see My judgment which I have executed, and My hand which I have laid on them. So the house of Israel shall know that I am the Lord their God from that day forward" (Ezekiel 39:21,22).

When the Gentile nations see the devastation of the Russian and Arab armies they will know that God is the Lord of Israel. The Jews in Israel will also know that it is God who saved them from certain destruction at the hands of their enemies. When the War of Gog and Magog concludes, the stage will be set for the rebuilding of the Temple in Jerusalem and the rise of the Antichrist in Europe. The defeat of the Arab armies will make it possible for Israel to rebuild the Temple. Russia and her Eastern European allies will be militarily destroyed. This elimination of Russia as a military superpower will create a power vacuum that will be filled by the rising colossus of a reunited Europe under the dynamic leadership of the coming Prince of Darkness.

THE TIME OF THE WAR OF GOG
AND MAGOG

A final question concerns the timing of this future War of Gog and Magog. Some writers conclude that the battle will occur during the seven-year treaty period leading up to the Battle of Armageddon. After years of study I am convinced that the burden of evidence points to this War of Magog happening in the near future, prior to the Antichrist making his seven-year treaty with Israel. Ezekiel 38 and 39 give the most detailed description of a future war found in Scripture. The prophet describes in great detail the weapons used, the nations on each side, the sequence of the battle, and the supernatural destruction of Israel's enemies by God. However, there is no mention of the Antichrist or his seven-year treaty to protect Israel. If this battle takes place within the seven-year treaty period leading to Armageddon you would expect the prophet to refer to either (1) the Antichrist defending Israel against this attack, or (2) to his betrayal of Israel by refusing to protect them as he agreed in his treaty. Ezekiel's prophecy about the War of Magog is silent about the Antichrist or the Messiah although they are the central figures in the period leading to the Battle of Armageddon. This silence of Ezekiel convinces me that the War of Gog and Magog will occur at some point in time prior to the Antichrist arising to conclude his fateful seven-year treaty with the Jews.

Some have suggested that the prophet's description (Ezekiel 38:8) that Israel will "dwell safely" could only occur after the Antichrist signs his treaty to guarantee their security. Ezekiel declared: "After many days you will be visited. In the latter years you will come into the land of those brought back from the sword and gathered from many people on the mountains of Israel, which had long been desolate; they were brought out of the nations, and now all of them dwell safely." Does this phrase "dwell safely" mean that Israel has found true lasting peace with her neighbors? In the light of the grim history of the Middle East during this century it is unlikely that Israel will disarm to any degree before the Messiah returns. Israel will remain an armed camp surrounded by enemies committed to her destruction until God changes the hearts of mankind. The phrase "dwell safely" may simply indicate that Israel will be living in an expectation that they will not be attacked at that time, perhaps because of the recent peace agreement with the PLO.

However, the study of Bible prophecy provides some insight into the ongoing peace negotiations. Ezekiel predicted that a future military leader of this Russian-Arab alliance will say "I will go up against a land of unwalled villages; I will go to a peaceful people, who dwell safely, all of them dwelling without walls, and having neither bars nor gates." For the last forty-five years Israel has not lived in "safety." However, this recent peace accord may create a false sense of security and safety over the next few years that will allow Israel to relax its defenses and "dwell safely." This peace agreement may set the stage for the fulfillment of the great War of Gog and Magog. These awesome prophetic events will prepare the way for the rise of Antichrist and his signing of a seven-year treaty with Israel. This will commence a seven-year countdown to the return of Christ and His saints at the Battle of Armageddon to establish His millennial kingdom. These exciting events in the Middle East encourage us as Christians to live in constant expectation of the glorious rapture of the Church to meet our Lord. Jesus said, "When these things begin to happen, look up and lift up your heads because your redemption draws near" (Luke 21:28).

Jeremiah (6:14) warned that in the last days men would say " 'Peace, peace!' When there is no peace." Our world will not know real peace until Jesus Christ, the Prince of Peace comes. In light of these facts it will be some time before true peace will exist between Israel and the Palestinians. According to the Bible, real peace will only come to the Middle East when Jesus Christ, the Prince of Peace, changes the hearts of both the Arabs and the Jews. Then both peoples will dwell as brothers in true peace forever under the rule of their Messiah.

The prophet explains God's motive in using His supernatural power to defeat these Russian-Arab armies. "Thus I will magnify Myself and sanctify Myself, and I will be known in the eyes of many nations. Then they shall know that I am the Lord" (Ezekiel 38:23). When the miraculous battle is over, the nations and Israel will both know that it was God alone who saved the Jews from certain destruction. There will be few atheists, if any, left in the world after this. This miraculous deliverance of Israel will set the stage for the Great Tribulation and the coming Messiah. With Russia defeated, Europe will complete its unification plans. With the defeat of the Arab armies, Israel will finally be able to build the Third Temple in the area north of the Dome of the Rock. The coming War of Gog and Magog is the key future event that will prepare the way for the completion of God's prophetic program to establish His Messianic Kingdom.

13

Will the Church Face the Antichrist?

"For the Lord Himself will descend from heaven with a shout, with the voice of an archangel, and with the trumpet of God. And the dead in Christ will rise first. Then we who are alive and remain shall be caught up together with them in the clouds to meet the Lord in the air. And thus we shall always be with the Lord" (1 Thessalonians 4:16, 17).

The promise of the Rapture is the blessed hope and joy of the Church. The Apostle Paul described the event: "For the Lord Himself will descend from heaven with a shout, with the voice of an archangel, and with the trumpet of God. And the dead in Christ will rise first. Then we who are alive and remain shall be caught up together with them in the clouds to meet the Lord in the air. And thus we will always be with the Lord" (1 Thessalonians 4:16, 17).

The Bible teaches that Christ will return to rapture His saints to heaven. But the questions are always asked, When will it happen? Before the Tribulation? During the Tribulation? Or, at Armageddon? Will we face the wrath of God and the horrors of persecution under the rule of the Prince of Darkness, the Antichrist?

JESUS PROMISED TO RAPTURE HIS CHURCH

The first hint of the Rapture of the saints is found hidden in the wonderful promise Jesus gave to Martha about the resurrection of Lazarus. When Jesus promised that His friend Lazarus would rise from the dead, Martha responded with the statement, "I know that he will rise again in the resurrection at the last day" (John 11:24). Jesus then said, "I am the resurrection and the life. He who believes in Me, though he may die, he shall live. And whoever lives and believes in Me shall never die. Do you believe this?" When many Christians read this passage they assume that Jesus was simply repeating His assurance about the resurrection of departed believers. However, a closer examination of His words shows that Jesus revealed something entirely new that the Scriptures had never promised before. When Christ made the first part of His statement, "He who believes in Me, though he may die, he shall live" He repeated the well known biblical truth that God will raise all righteous believers at the final resurrection. However, in the second part of His statement, Jesus provided a startling new revelation about the resurrection. Jesus promised, "And whoever *lives* and believes in Me shall never die." This revelation was so earthshaking that Jesus asked Martha, "Do you believe this?"

Unfortunately, many readers of the Gospel of John have ignored the specific revelation about the Rapture contained in these words of Jesus. Christ promised that the saints who "believe in Me" who are living when He returns "shall never die." Obviously there will be a generation of Christians who will be alive when He appears in the clouds at the Rapture. Jesus is clearly speaking about physical death, not spiritual death. Prior to this teaching of Jesus, the Scriptures focused solely on the destiny of the departed saints to rise "from death to life eternal." In His conversation with Martha, Jesus began by confirming that the departed saints will be resurrected at the last day. Then Christ startled Martha by promising something entirely new. He prophesied that there will be living saints who "believe in Me" at the time of His return who "will never die." Those Christians living when Jesus returns will be the first generation of saints that will never experience death. Their unique destiny is that they will pass from "life to life eternal."

THE TRUE PURPOSE OF THE RAPTURE

Paul spoke of the Rapture in 1 Thessalonians 4:17. He said, "Then we which are alive and remain shall be caught up together with them in the clouds, to meet the Lord in the air. And thus we shall always be with the Lord." The Greek word *harpazo* which is translated "caught up" was rendered as *rapere*, "caught away," in Jerome's Latin translation from the fifty century of our era. Thus our modern translation translates the word as "Rapture," from Jerome. For over a thousand years Jerome's translation was the most influential in Christendom. In the *Interlinear Greek Translation* it appears as follows: ". . . shall be seized in clouds to a meeting of the Lord in the air; and so always with the Lord shall be." When opponents of the doctrine of the Rapture claim that the word "rapture" is not in the Bible, they are playing word games. In effect, they are claiming that the English word "rapture" is not found in the Greek New Testament. No English words appear in the original Greek New Testament. However, the real question is: Do the words of Scripture teach that the Lord will "catch away" the saints found in scripture. The answer is Yes! The doctrine of the rapture is taught clearly in several passages in the New Testament and is illustrated in the Old Testament by the rapture of both Enoch and Elijah.

It is important to realize that this Greek word *harpazo* (to strip, spoil or snatch away), translated "caught up," appears in several other verses in the New Testament. In each instance the word *harpazo* denotes a supernatural "catching away" of someone to heaven. The three additional references using the phrase "caught up" are the following: "I know a man in Christ who fourteen years ago—whether in the body I do not know, or whether out of the body I do not know, God knows— how he was *caught up* into Paradise" (2 Corinthians

12:2). "How that he was *caught up* into Paradise and heard inexpressible words, which it is not lawful for a man to utter" (2 Corinthians 12:4). "And she bore a male Child who was to rule all nations with a rod of iron. And her Child was *caught up* to God and to His throne" (Revelation 12:5).

Another reference to *harpazo* appears in the book of Acts where Philip is "caught away" after he converts the Ethiopian treasurer. In this passage, Philip is "raptured" away from where he stood by the supernatural power of God. "Now when they were come up out of the water, the Spirit of the Lord *caught* Philip *away* so that the eunuch saw him no more: and he went on his way rejoicing" (Act 8:39).

The real purpose of the Rapture is to gather together and "translate" all the members of the Church, living and departed, into their new resurrection bodies to live with Christ forever. If we are to rule with Christ on the earth and enjoy all that God has prepared for us in heaven we must have a resurrection body. When a Christian dies his soul is transferred instantly to heaven in the spirit while his body is said to "rest" in the ground. Jesus told the thief on the Cross, "Today you will be with me in Paradise" (Luke 23:43). When Paul talked about being "absent from the body and to be present with the Lord" (2 Corinthians 2:58), he confirmed that, at death, our spirits go immediately to heaven. The moment a Christian dies, their spirit is taken to heaven where they will dwell with Christ and the other departed saints until the Rapture when they will receive their new spiritual bodies. The apostle Paul and hundreds of millions of departed saints are in heaven today in their spirit without their bodies. They eagerly await the day of the Rapture so that they can receive their glorious resurrection bodies. As Paul tells us in Romans 8:22,23: "For we know that the whole creation groans and labors with birth pangs until now. And not only they, but we also who have the firstfruits of the Spirit, even we ourselves groan within ourselves, eagerly waiting for the adoption, the redemption of our body." Finally, in their new resurrection bodies, they will enjoy the Marriage Supper of the Lamb. Then, in their glorious new bodies, the saints will "rule and reign" with Christ on earth forever.

At the moment of the Rapture all Christians, including the living saints as well as the departed saints whose souls are in heaven, will instantly receive their new spiritual resurrection body. This body will be identical in nature to the body of Christ after He rose from the dead two thousand years ago. Philippians 3:21 tells us that Christ "will transform our lowly body that it may be conformed to His glorious body, according to the working by which He is able even to subdue all things to Himself." Until the Rapture the life of a departed saint is somewhat limited in heaven because he cannot participate in actions that require a physical presence. At the glorious moment of the Rapture all members of Christ's true Church, living and dead, will be instantly transformed into their spiritual bodies that will be immortal, indestructible, and able to travel at the speed of thought, just as Jesus did after His resurrection.

Who Will be Present at the Rapture?

When Christ descends from heaven to meet the raptured Christians, the spirits of all of the departed saints will descend in the clouds with Him to be joined to their new resurrection bodies that will rise to meet them. As Paul assured us, "For if we believe that Jesus died and rose again, even so God will bring with Him those who sleep in Jesus" (1 Thessalonians 4:14). This passage assures us that all departed saints will participate in the glorious Rapture of the Church. Some writers have asserted that only the most holy of Christians will be raptured. However, the clear teaching of Scripture is that all believers, regardless of their degree of personal holiness, will join in that glorious transformation. In 1 Thessalonians 4:14 Paul declares that all departed saints will return at the Rapture with Christ. "For if we believe that Jesus died and rose again, even so God will bring with Him those who sleep in Jesus." Since "those who sleep in Jesus" includes departed Christians of varying levels of personal holiness it is obvious that our participation in the Rapture does not depend on our degree of personal sanctification. After all, we have no righteousness of our own, only the "righteousness of God" in Christ (2 Corinthians 5:21). If we are truly "born again" we will receive our resurrection body at the Rapture with the rest of the millions of Christian saints who have followed Jesus during the last two thousand years. The Lord will reward individual saints for their personal walk with Christ by giving rewards and crowns at the judgment seat of Christ following the Rapture.

THE TIMING OF THE RAPTURE

Additional details of this wonderful promise to the Church were revealed through the inspired writings of the Apostle Paul. "Behold, I tell you a mystery: We shall not all sleep, but we shall all be changed; in a moment, in the twinkling of an eye, at the last trumpet. For the trumpet will sound, and the dead will be raised incorruptible, and we shall be changed" (1 Corinthians 15:51,52). In this passage Paul reveals details of the sequence of events at the glorious Rapture. Notice that Paul first tells us that, "Behold, I tell you a mystery" which alerts us to the fact that his message will teach us something never revealed before. The details of the Rapture remained a "mystery" until God permitted Paul to reveal them. The apostle tells us that many Christians will not die (sleep) because they will still be alive when Christ returns.

Note that Paul included himself when he used the word "we": "We shall not all sleep, but we shall all be changed." It is obvious that he truly hoped the Rapture would occur while he was alive. This statement, together with Paul's constant exhortations to "be watchful," confirms that he hoped that the Rapture would occur during his lifetime. Paul believed that the Rapture was imminent. This statement does not indicate that Paul believed that Christ had to return while he remained alive but, rather, that Christ could return without warning at any moment. Paul knew that Christ could delay His return for thousands of years, but he also knew that He might return to rapture His saints at any time, from the days of the early Church until today. Paul's hope to participate in the Rapture indicates that Christ's return for His Church is imminent. The *Funk & Wagnalls Standard Dictionary* defines "imminent" as follows: "about to happen; impending; overhanging as if about to fall; threatening; signifies liable to happen at once, as some calamity, dangerous and close at hand." Throughout the New Testament the passages dealing with the return of Christ express the need for watchfulness in light of His imminent return. While Paul longed for the Rapture and commanded us to "wait for His Son from heaven" he never declared that the resurrection must occur within his lifetime. We should emulate Paul's attitude of watching expectantly for the Lord's return but refuse to set a date for it.

There will be no warning signs for the Rapture. No one can tell us the time of the Rapture until it occurs. Attempts to calculate the exact timing are doomed to failure and are in direct disobedience to the words of Christ. When the Lord has drawn a veil over the timing of this event, we should not try to lift the veil. The Rapture itself is a first stage of the second coming of Christ that will ultimately end with His revelation in glory at Armageddon. In fact, the prophets reveal that dozens of separate events will occur during final countdown to the second stage of His return. During the seven-year tribulation period a whole series of prophecies must be fulfilled leading inexorably to the final conflict at Armageddon. On the other hand, the Rapture itself could have occurred at any time from the days of Paul until today. It is truly imminent and can happen without warning. In other words, there are no prophecies that need to be fulfilled before the Rapture of the saints. The Rapture is the first in a long series of prophesied events that will culminate in Christ's return "with his saints" at Armageddon.

Some writers find it strange that the Second Coming should include several distinct events beginning with the Rapture and then, several years later, the Revelation when Christ returns with His saints at Armageddon. However, the many events that occurred during the First Advent of Christ occurred over thirty-three and a half years. The First Advent involved many different events including

Christ's birth, His coming to the Temple, baptism, miracles, crucifixion, and resurrection. However, we refer to all these events as the First Coming or Advent of Christ. Therefore, it should not surprise us that the events of the Second Advent also take place over a seven-year period with several distinct events occurring at different intervals.

The Confusion Between the Rapture and the Removal of Saints in Matthew 24

Much of the confusion in the minds of Christians about the timing of the Rapture has arisen from a misunderstanding of the words of Jesus Christ recorded in Matthew 24. "Then two men will be in the field: one will be taken and the other left. Two women will be grinding at the mill: one will be taken and the other left" (Matthew 24:40,41). Some have concluded that Matthew 24 teaches that the Rapture must occur at the time of Christ's return at Armageddon. This position is known as the post-tribulation Rapture, indicating that the Lord will not rapture His saints until the end of the seven-year tribulation period. Many writers identify this event where "one will be taken and the other left" with the Rapture, believing these two events are identical. Since this event in Matthew 24:40 clearly occurs at the end of the tribulation period when Christ will defeat the Antichrist, these writers naturally conclude that the Rapture will occur at Armageddon. After many years of study I am convinced that the Rapture will occur prior to the seven-year tribulation period, allowing the Church to escape the wrath of God.

The details of the Rapture of the Church were not revealed in Matthew 24 in Christ's prophecy to His Jewish disciples. At the time of our Lord's conversation with His disciples, the Church did not yet exist. The apostle Paul declared that the Church was a mystery which God did not reveal until after the death and resurrection of Christ. "The mystery which has been hidden from ages and from generations, but now has been revealed to His saints." The Church was not revealed until the coming of the

Holy Spirit at the Feast of Pentecost fifty days after Christ rose from the grave. This occurred almost two months after Christ's prophetic discourse recorded in Matthew 24. The Church and its prophetic destiny was not the focus of that passage. His Jewish disciples had asked the Lord for the signs leading to His return. In Matthew 24 Christ answered their question by revealing the specific prophetic events in the last generation that will lead to Israel's final deliverance at His return.

While both events involve a supernatural deliverance of a group of saints by the power of God, a closer examination reveals that these two events differ in every other particular. Two different groups of saints are involved with two different destinies. In addition, several years will intervene between these two events. One of the clearest differences is that the Rapture passages declare that the "dead in Christ will rise first" (1 Thessalonians 4:16), and, "The dead will be raised incorruptible, and we shall be changed" (1 Corinthians 15:52). Paul is telling us that the dead saints will receive their resurrection bodies first, then the living saints. This is quite different from what Jesus revealed to His disciples on the Mount of Olives. Christ did not tell His disciples about the "translation" of the Christian saints, giving them new resurrection bodies. Matthew 24 deals only with the physical removal of living saints to safety. There is no mention of the "dead" or those who "sleep" because Christ was teaching about the supernatural deliverance of "living" Tribulation saints, both Jews and Gentiles, which takes place during the terrible events leading up to Armageddon. These saints will become followers of Christ during the horrors of the tribulation period as a result of the witness of the two witnesses, the 144,000 and the three angels who will warn of the coming judgment. Jesus promised them that "he who endures to the end shall be saved." Christ told His disciples that He would send His angels to remove these living Tribulation saints from the wrath of God poured out at Armageddon.

Matthew 24:31 tells how God will remove the living tribulation saints, Jews and Gentiles, from immediate danger of physical death: "He will send His angels with a great sound of a trumpet, and they will gather together His elect from the four winds, from one end of heaven to the other." Only living believers will need angels to physically protect them; dead saints do not need this protection. Some writers have suggested that those removed by the angels are unbelievers being taken to judgment. However, the clear declaration of this passage is that the angels "will gather together His elect." Therefore we must conclude that those who are "gathered" are followers of Christ.

The Rapture of the saints which Paul speaks of in 1 Corinthians 15:51,52 and 1 Thessalonians 4:16,17 will provide a new resurrection body to every saint, dead and alive. Mortal and corruptible bodies of living and dead believers will be transformed into immortal and incorruptible spiritual bodies as they meet Christ in the air and ascend to heaven. Angels are not mentioned in the Rapture passages. My conclusion is that Matthew 24:40 refers to a totally different event than the Rapture. Therefore, we must seek the timing of the translation of the saints in other biblical passages.

THE PURPOSE OF THE GREAT TRIBULATION

The Tribulation will be the greatest crisis in the history of mankind. It was prophesied by the Old Testament prophets long before the revelation of the mystery of the Church. The entire focus of Old and New Testament prophecies about this terrible period deals with God's judgment of Israel and the Gentile nations. The Church is not mentioned specifically in these detailed prophecies about the Great Tribulation. When the Scriptures speak of "saints" or "the elect" being persecuted during the Tribulation period a close examination of the passages reveals that they refer to Jewish or Gentile believers who will become followers of God following the Rapture of the Church.

One of the purposes of the Tribulation during Daniel's Seventieth Week is to demonstrate Satan's evil intention to destroy mankind. The prophet Jeremiah calls it "the time of Jacob's trouble" because it will be a time of refining and purifying for God's Chosen People. In addition, God will pour out His wrath on the sinful Gentiles of that day who will joyfully worship the Antichrist and kill the tribulation saints. During this terrible time of persecution following the Rapture of the Church, God will turn to Israel and call out 144,000 Jews as "a light unto the Gentiles." Though this will be the most horrifying time of judgment in history, hundreds of millions of men and women from every nation will respond to the preaching of the "gospel of the kingdom" and will turn from their sinful rebellion against God. In Revelation 7:9 John tells us of "a great multitude which no one could number of all nations, tribes, peoples, and tongues." Later the angel tells John that "these are the ones which came out of great tribulation, and washed their robes and made them white in the blood of the Lamb" (Revelation 7:14). The Tribulation will produce the greatest harvest of souls in history but it will be a harvest of blood. The vast majority of those who accept Christ during the Tribulation will become martyrs when they reject the false worship of the Babylonian church or the Mark of the Beast. It is probable that only a small remnant will survive till Armageddon to be supernaturally delivered by the angels when "one will be taken and the other left."

Jesus prophesied to His disciples that the "gospel of the kingdom shall be preached in all the world for a witness unto all nations; and then shall the end come" (Matthew 24:15, KJV). This "gospel of the kingdom" is different from the gospel of the Church that is now preached by Christians today. Today we invite people to accept Christ as their Savior, to obey Him and to join with other believers in the local church. The "gospel of the kingdom" will be the same as the kingdom gospel preached by Jesus and John the Baptist prior to Christ's crucifixion. Their message was "Repent ye: for the kingdom of heaven is at hand . . . Prepare ye the way of the Lord, make His paths straight" (Matthew 3:2,3, KJV). As the supernatural judgments of God are poured out on the sinners during the Great Tribulation, millions will turn to God and refuse the Mark of the Beast. They will be martyred for their faith in Christ and will demonstrate their belief with their life's blood. In Revelation 6:9–11 John describes the fifth seal as the "souls of those who had been slain for the word of God and for the testimony which they held." These martyred saints are told to "rest a little while longer, until both the number of their fellow servants and their brethren, who would be killed as they were." These martyrs are tribulation saints, not Christians belonging to the Bride of Christ which will be raptured at some point prior to the Tribulation. One of the evidences for this conclusion is that these tribulation martyrs cry out for vengeance against their enemies just as the Old Testament saints often did. However, during the Age of Grace, Christians are forbidden to seek vengeance. As Paul tells us, "Beloved, do not avenge yourselves, but rather give place to wrath: for it is written, 'Vengeance is Mine, I will repay,' says the Lord" (Romans 12:19).

God deals quite differently with the Jews and the Gentiles during the last seven years of Tribulation leading up to Armageddon. It is obvious that God always dealt differently with the Jews and Gentiles throughout the Old Testament until Christ created the Church in which "there is neither Jew nor Greek" (Gentile). During the Church Age, the Age of Grace, the Bible declares that there is no difference in how God deals with the Jews and Gentiles. We are brothers in the faith. "There is neither Jew nor Greek [Gentile], there is neither slave nor free, there is neither male nor female; for you are all one in Christ Jesus" (Galatians 3:28). However, when the book of Revelation describes the tribulation period, God again clearly deals separately and differently with the Jews and the Gentiles. The Lord seals 144,000 Jewish witnesses and supernaturally protects Israel as she flees into the wilderness from the Antichrist. In Revelation 11 John described the Jewish worshipers in the rebuilt Temple during the Tribulation. God's separate dealing with Jews and Gentiles during the tribulation period is consistent with the position that the Christians will have been raptured to heaven at this point.

THE CHURCH WILL ESCAPE THE WRATH TO COME

Paul encouraged the Church "to wait for His Son from heaven, whom He raised from the dead, even Jesus who delivers us from the wrath to come" (1 Thessalonians 1:10). Throughout the Bible God has always poured out His wrath and judgments on the unrighteous, never on the righteous. While He often chastens His children to bring them back to Him, He never delivers His wrath on them. When the Lord came to earth to destroy the wicked city of Sodom, Abraham spoke of God's justice. "Far be it from You to do such a thing as this, to slay the righteous with the wicked, so that the righteous should be as the wicked; far be it from You! Shall not the Judge of all the earth do right?" (Genesis 18:25). Despite the appalling wickedness of the cities of Sodom and Gomorrah the Lord declared that He would not destroy them if there were even ten righteous people left in them.

From Genesis to Revelation the basic principle never changes. First the prophetic warning is given; the righteous are removed to safety; then the judgment and wrath of God are delivered on those who refuse to repent of their sinful rebellion. Noah and his family were removed to safety in the ark before the wrath of God delivered the Flood on mankind. Lot and his family were warned by the angel, "Hurry, escape there. For I cannot do anything [destroy Sodom] until you arrive there [the other city]" (Genesis 19:22). When God poured out His wrath and plagues on the evil Egyptians, even the Israelites' cattle escaped the plagues. If any doubt remained about this principle, God repeated His promise that the Church would escape His wrath. "For God did not appoint us to wrath, but to obtain salvation through our Lord Jesus Christ" (1 Thessalonians 5:9). There are two opposing destinies: the wrath of God on those who reject His mercy; salvation for those who accept Christ as their Savior. The Great Tribulation will witness the pouring out of the wrath of God upon sinful rebels and those who worship the Antichrist. There is no place or purpose for the Church on the earth during that terrible period. The

Church will be with Christ at the Marriage Supper of the Lamb in heaven during that time.

Some have suggested that the Church must go through the Great Tribulation to be purified and perfected for the Marriage Supper of the Lamb. This attitude misses an important biblical truth. We are not purified by tribulation. We are purified only when the blood of Jesus Christ is applied to our hearts by our accepting His forgiveness for our sins. There is no need for the Church to experience the tribulation period to prepare itself for heaven. The majority of Christians have died during the last two thousand years and are already in heaven. They will escape the Great Tribulation. Obviously, there was no need for them to experience this period of judgment. However, the fact that we are promised an escape from the Tribulation does not imply that Christians will escape "without persecution" to heaven. Millions of Christians in the past—and millions today in China and Africa—paid the heavy price of martyrdom for their faith in Christ. Studies indicate that over three hundred thousand Christians are still martyred each year. We are warned that we may experience tribulations and persecutions in this world. If the Lord delays His return much longer we may experience real persecution and tribulations in North America. However, these persecutions will not be the Great Tribulation. That is a special time when God will deal with Israel and the Gentile nations, not the Church.

THE MYSTERY OF THE CHURCH— A NEW CREATION

"Even the mystery which hath been hid from ages and from generations, but now is made manifest to his saints. To whom God would make known what is the riches of the glory of this mystery among the Gentiles; which is Christ in you, the hope of glory" (Colossians 1:26,27).

The teaching of the New Testament is clear that Christ created a "new" creation, a separate body or entity when He established the Church. Jesus said, "Upon this rock the faith that Peter had just expressed I will build my Church" (Matthew 16:18). Note that Jesus said that He "will build" my Church; not that He would continue to build or add to an existing group of saints. He refers to a future body of believers that would come into existence after the Holy Spirit baptized them with power at the Day of Pentecost. Paul declared, "For in (by) one spirit were all baptized into one body, whether Jews or Greeks, whether bond or free; and were all made to drink of one spirit" (I Corinthians 12:13). The baptism of the Holy Spirit is the divine act of God through which the believer is supernaturally adopted into the body of Christ, the Church. The New Testament clearly declares that a 'new thing' was created at Pentecost. Paul says that the Church was a "mystery" hid from the saints of the Old Testament.

PAUL'S TEACHING ABOUT THE RAPTURE AT THESSALONICA

Paul had earlier taught this Church in detail about Christ's Second Coming. However, since Paul left them someone came along and totally disturbed their tranquillity by convincing some of the believers that they had "missed" the Rapture of Christ. "Now, brethren, concerning the coming of our Lord Jesus Christ and our gathering together to Him, we ask you, not to be soon shaken in mind or troubled, either by spirit or by word or by letter, as if from us, as though the day of Christ (Lord) had come" (2 Thessalonians 2:1,2).

Consider this carefully, Paul obviously knew himself the sequence of events in regard to the Rapture and the Revelation of Christ at Armageddon. There are only two possibilities: First, that Paul had told them that the Church would live through seven years of Tribulation, the persecution of the Antichrist, the defiling of the Temple and that the Lord would only rapture the believers at Armageddon. The second possibility is that Paul had taught them that the hope and joy of the Church was the imminent Rapture of the Church that would deliver them from the Tribulation and "the wrath to come." The church at Thessalonica was disturbed by false reports that the

Rapture had already occurred and left them behind. How could the Church in Thessalonica believe that they had missed the Rapture? Could they believe that they had missed observing the Tribulation, the seven-year treaty with Israel, the defiling of the Temple by Antichrist and the Great Day of the Lord, followed by the Rapture, without them knowing about it and leaving them still on earth? This is virtually impossible.

However, consider that Paul had told them earlier that Rapture would occur imminently, without warning or outward signs, and that it would precede the Tribulation. If Paul taught an imminent Rapture you can understand how the Thessalonian church could be misled by someone claiming that other believers were raptured but they had been left behind. Their confusion and fear about "missing" the Rapture was only possible if Paul had taught an imminent Rapture without warning. Paul spoke of the Rapture as "our hope, or joy, or crown of rejoicing" (1 Thessalonians 2:19). This attitude is consistent with an expectation that the Church will be delivered from the coming wrath of God by escaping through the promised Rapture.

The Scripture clearly distinguishes between two different parts of Christ's Second Coming—His return in the air to rapture His saints to heaven and His return to the earth at Armageddon with His saints. A close examination of the Scriptures reveals a number of specific prophetic events that must occur before the return of Christ to establish His kingdom. These prophetic events include the partial return of the Jews to the Holy Land, the rebuilding of the Temple, a seven-year treaty between the Antichrist and the Jews and, finally, the Battle of Armageddon. However, Scriptures also abound with commands to the Church to expect Christ's return "at any moment." The only logical conclusion is the Rapture must occur without warning at some point in time before the events of the Tribulation period. It is logical to conclude that the Rapture will occur before the detailed series of prophesied events that commence with the Antichrist signing the seven-year treaty with Israel.

THE TRANSLATION OF THE 144,000 JEWISH WITNESSES

In Revelation 7:3 an angel is held back from pouring out the judgments of God until 144,000 Jewish Witnesses are sealed for supernatural protection. The angel says, "Do not harm the earth, the sea, or the trees till we have sealed the servants of our God on their foreheads. And I heard the number of those who were sealed. One hundred and forty-four thousand of all the tribes of the children of Israel were sealed" (Revelation 7:3,4). The detailed listing of 12,000 Jews from each of the twelve tribes clearly identifies these "servants of God" as Jews, not Christians. Why would God supernaturally protect 144,000 Jewish Witnesses while leaving hundreds of millions of Christians unprotected against the coming wrath of God? The answer is that there will be no need to protect the Christians. The Church will be raptured to heaven before the wrath of heaven is poured out on earth and will not need to be sealed for protection against God's judgment.

This conclusion is confirmed by the passage in Revelation 9:3,4. "Then out of the smoke of the bottomless pit locusts came upon the earth. And to them was given power, as the scorpions of the earth have power. They were commanded not to harm the grass of the earth, or any green thing, or any tree, but only those men who do not have the seal of God on their foreheads." Revelation 9:3,4. The prophet John tells us that these demonic locusts will torment all the men on the face of the earth except those 144,000 "servants of God" who "have the seal of God on their foreheads." The Bible affirms in this passage that during this five-month period of the Great Tribulation there will be only two distinct groups of people on the earth. First, the 144,000 Jewish Witnesses will be sealed for Divine protection. Secondly, the rest of sinful humanity who will be tormented by demons because they don't "have the seal of God on their foreheads." The hundreds of millions of Christians cannot belong to either of these two groups. The 144,000 are clearly composed of twelve thousand Jews from each of the twelve tribes of Israel. Those tormented by demonic locusts cannot be Christians because we have the Holy Spirit dwelling within us. The logical conclusion is that the Church is not sealed for protection because there is no need. The Christians will be raptured to heaven at some point prior to the Tribulation.

Note that Revelation 14:1–5 describes the 144,000 Jewish Witnesses on the heavenly Mount Zion. It declares they are "the hundred and forty-four thousand who were redeemed from the earth . . . These are the ones who follow the Lamb wherever He goes. These were redeemed from among men, being firstfruits to God and to the Lamb." (Revelation 14:3,4). This group of 144,000 Jewish followers of Jesus from each of the twelve tribes of Israel were described earlier on the earth being "sealed" to protect them from the judgments and wrath of God. How did they arrive in heaven as described in Revelation 14 as "firstfruits to God and the Lamb?" Obviously, at some point during the tribulation period, within Daniel's seventieth week of years (seven years,) God will supernaturally "translate" these 144,000 "firstfruits" home to heaven. The Bible clearly describes this particular group of 144,000 Jewish believers being "translated" to heaven at some point prior to the Battle of Armageddon. Since these 144,000 are translated before Armageddon, there is no fundamental reason preventing God from rapturing His Church from the "wrath of God" prior to Armageddon. The Bible describes several groups of saints as belonging to the "firstfruits" of the first resurrection to eternal life. When Christ rose from the dead "many" of the Old Testament saints rose also (Matthew 27:52,53). They are called "firstfruits" in 1 Corinthians 15:20,23. As James wrote, Christians also are "a kind of firstfruits of his creatures" (James 1:18).

THE RAPTURE QUESTION— THE DYNAMIC SPIRITUAL TENSION

In this generation Christians are called to live in a dynamic spiritual tension in light of the imminent return of Christ. The prophecies pointing to Christ's return are being fulfilled before our eyes every day. On the one hand we are called to spiritual vigilance in light of the Rapture.

Paul exhorted Christians to be "looking for the blessed hope and glorious appearing of our great God and Savior Jesus Christ" (Titus 2:13). We must live and witness to others as though Christ will come before tomorrow dawns. Yet, on the other hand, we must plan and work as though the Lord might delay His second coming for another hundred years. Christ's command is to "Occupy till I come" (Luke 19:13, *KJV*). Far from leading to escapism, the hope of the imminent return of Christ should motivate each Christian to a greater witness to his friends and loved ones. If we truly believe that our Messiah may come at any moment we will walk in purity before our holy God. The prophet John wrote, "Everyone who has this hope in Him purifies himself, just as He is pure" (1 John 3:3).

Whenever the Church has violated this spiritual balance it has departed from the clear teaching of the New Testament. Although all of the prophetic signs point to the coming of the Messiah in our generation we must acknowledge God's sovereignty. God controls the timing of His plan in response to man's actions. In the days of Jonah, the prophet warned the wicked city of Nineveh that God would destroy it in forty days. However, the great city responded to the prophetic warning and repented of its sin. As a result God delayed the threatened judgment of Nineveh for a hundred years until the next generation fell into great sin. God is sovereign. The Lord could delay his second coming if the world repented of its sinful rebellion. However, in light of the dozens of specific prophecies that are being fulfilled in our lifetime, we need to remember the words of Jesus Christ. "Now when these things begin to happen, look up and lift up your heads, because your redemption draws near" (Luke 21:28).

14

The Rise of the Prince of Darkness

The world is longing for real leadership. There is a dearth of strong statesmen throughout the Western world and our problems seem too complex for its present political leaders. The cry heard around the world is for a wise and righteous government. Many seek a messianic leader who will provide answers—a perfect setting for the emergence of the Prince of Darkness. Jesus warned His disciples that a growing number of false religious leaders would arise in the last days; He called them "false christs and false prophets" who would be so clever that many would be deceived: "For false christs and false prophets will arise and show great signs and wonders, so as to deceive, if possible, even the elect" (Matthew 24:24). Satan's counterfeit messiah, the Prince of Darkness, will be introduced to a world desperate for a new "caesar." Tragically, the nations will choose to follow Satan's candidate rather than worship the true Messiah.

THE FINAL EMPIRE

The prophet Daniel occupied a unique place in both history and prophecy. His fascinating career spanned the great empires of the ancient world. The empires of Assyria and Egypt preceded Daniel. Then he rose from being a slave to rule as prime minister of both Babylon and Media-Persia. Two additional world empires, Greece and Rome, rose to prominence after Daniel. In the two thousand years since the days of Rome no one has been able to create a true fifth world empire.

When Daniel interpreted Nebuchadnezzar's dream about the "great image," he prophesied about these four great world empires. At the height of their glory, each of these empires were ruled dictatorially by one man. King Nebuchadnezzar led the great Babylonian Empire to build the greatest city the world has ever witnessed. King Cyrus led the Media-Persian forces to victory over the Babylonians and generously decided to return the Jewish exiles. Alexander the Great, as a young man, took over the Macedonian Kingdom and conquered the known world from Libya to India. The Roman Empire was led by Julius Caesar and a series of successor emperors.

However, in Daniel's interpretation of the vision of the metallic image he saw that the stone kingdom, the coming Kingdom of Christ, will suddenly destroy these great empires. "Inasmuch as you saw that the stone was cut out of the mountain without hands, and that it broke in pieces the iron, the bronze, the clay, the silver, and the gold; the great God has made known to the king what will come to pass after this. The dream is certain, and its interpretation is sure" (Daniel 2:45).

This will occur during the generation when the ten nations of the Roman Empire come together. The stone will pulverize the metallic image and blows it to dust. However, note that Daniel prophesied that, in addition to the clay and iron of the ten toes, the gold, silver, and bronze are also turned to dust. This detail suggests that, in some manner, there will be a simultaneous revival of the Babylonian Empire (the gold head), the Media-Persian Empire (the silver chest), the Greek-Syrian Empire (the bronze thighs) together with the Revived Roman Empire (the ten toes of clay and iron). It is possible that the ultimate kingdom of the Antichrist will contain the geographical territory encompassing all four past empires. Today we witness the rebuilding of the city of Babylon by

Saddam Hussein, the nuclear arming of Iran (Medea-Persia) and the continued growth of the military power of Syria (the Greek Empire). The book of Revelation declares that God will call all nations into the place called Armageddon. The Lord still has an appointment with destiny with these ancient and modern nations.

THE PERSONALITY OF THE COMING PRINCE OF DARKNESS

"And in the latter time of their kingdom, when the transgressors have reached their fullness, a king shall arise, having fierce features, who understands sinister schemes. His power shall be mighty, but not by his own power; he shall destroy fearfully, and shall prosper and thrive; he shall destroy the mighty, and also the holy people" (Daniel 8:23,24).

The Antichrist will be a strong, brutal leader with striking features. Daniel warned that he will understand "sinister schemes," indicating his preference for occult powers and satanic treachery. His awesome power will come directly from Satan. The first prophecy in the Bible refers to the Antichrist as "the seed of Satan." After the temptation of Adam and Eve God addressed Satan saying, "I will put enmity between you and the woman, and between your seed and her Seed" (Genesis 3:15). The phrase "your seed" indicates that, in some mysterious way, the Antichrist will be the seed of Satan. Although he will be an evil man during his rise to power, he will not fully take his role as the Antichrist until Satan is cast out of heaven. From that moment he will sell his soul and be completely possessed by Satan. The prophet warned that his satanic power will allow him to "prosper and thrive" in his drive to gain total power over mankind. After he defiles the rebuilt Temple the Antichrist will do everything in his power to "destroy the mighty, and also the holy people." Revelation 12 tells us that God will supernaturally protect Israel and the Jewish remnant fleeing from his overwhelming persecution during the last three-and-a-half years leading to the Battle of Armageddon.

He is a Blasphemer

His language will be characterized by constant blasphemy against God during the final three-and-a-half years of his tyranny over mankind. Daniel and John both comment on his spirit of blasphemy, "He was given a mouth speaking great things and blasphemies" (Revelation 13:5). Since he is motivated and directed by Satan he will hate God with everything within him. "Then the king shall do according to his own will: he shall exalt and magnify himself above every god, shall speak blasphemies against the God of gods, and shall prosper till the wrath has been accomplished; for what has been determined shall be done. He shall regard neither the God of his fathers nor the desire of women, nor regard any god; for he shall magnify himself above them all" (Daniel 11:36,37). Daniel reveals that the Antichrist will not respect "the God of his fathers." This phrase, "the God of his fathers," is used solely of Jews, suggesting that he will be a Jew.

In addition to hating God, the Antichrist will exalt and "magnify himself above them all." He will display the same evil pride that resulted in the fall of his father, Lucifer, when he first tried to rebel against God. Daniel's statement that he will not regard "the desire of women" may indicate a sexual perversion or to homosexuality. However the phrase "the desire of women" may refer to his contempt for the secret desire of Jewish religious women to give birth to the Messiah.

He is the Lawless One

"And then the lawless one will be revealed, whom the Lord will consume with the breath of His mouth and destroy with the brightness of His coming" (2 Thessalonians 2:8). Antichrist is called the "lawless one" because he will rebel against the laws of man and God. Law is the characteristic that establishes civilization. We attempt to build our society based on laws, not men. However, Satan's Prince of Darkness will despise the law because he hates the law of God. In addition he will change the laws of the land and the festivals.

THE CAREER OF THE COMING PRINCE OF DARKNESS

The Bible clearly prophesies the reunification of Europe in the last days. This revival of the ancient Roman Empire, encompassing Europe and the Mediterranean nations, is a prerequisite for the rise of the Antichrist. According to Daniel 9:26: "The people of the prince who is to come shall destroy the city and the sanctuary." This "prince who is to come" will arise from the Roman people who destroyed Jerusalem and the Temple in A.D. 70. The prophet foretold the future revival of the Roman Empire as a federation of ten nations that will rise in the last days. Then "another" horn, representing the Antichrist, "shall rise after them . . . and shall subdue three kings." Daniel confirmed that this dictator will appear on the scene after the ten-nation confederacy exists. "The ten horns are ten kings who shall arise from this kingdom. And another shall rise after them; he shall be different from the first ones, and shall subdue three kings" (Daniel 7:24). Beginning with these first three nations he will take over the remaining seven nations and use the ten-nation confederacy as his power base to conquer the entire world. Later, the book of Revelation 13 reveals the Antichrist in full control of the ten nations. "Then I stood on the sand of the sea. And I saw a beast rising up out of the sea, having seven heads and ten horns, and on his horns ten crowns, and on his heads a blasphemous name" (Revelation 13:1). The seven heads may refer to the remaining seven subsidiary kings who survive after the Antichrist destroys the three kings of the three nations he conquers.

HIS MILITARY CAREER WILL BE OUTSTANDING

The Bible prophesied that the Antichrist will have great success in his military adventures until he is finally destroyed by Christ at Armageddon. His initial successes will be so overwhelming that the people of the world will acclaim him the Messiah. "So they worshiped the dragon who gave authority to the beast; and they worshiped the beast, saying, 'Who is like the beast? Who is able to make war with him?' And he was given a mouth speaking great things and blasphemies, and he was given authority to continue for forty-two months" (Revelation 13:4,5). The prophet John warned that rebellious sinners in that day will openly worship Satan, acknowledging the true source of Antichrist's power. This passage helps us to understand why the Lord's wrath will be poured out upon unrepentant sinners. The people will enthusiastically join in the worship of Satan and his Antichrist while marveling at his unique military victories, "Who is like the beast? Who is able to make war with him?" In the concluding chapters we will examine the final battle that will set the stage for the defeat of the Antichrist's forces in the Valley of Jezreel east of the ancient city of Megiddo.

HE WILL CHANGE THE LAWS AND THE TIMES

"He shall speak pompous words against the Most High, shall persecute the saints of the Most High, and shall intend to change times and law. Then the saints shall be given into his hand for a time and times and half a time" (Daniel 7:25). The Lord commanded Israel to keep Passover, the Sabbath and the other festivals "forever in their generations." The prophet Daniel tells us that the "prince who is to come" will try "to change times and law." In his arrogant religious pretensions the Antichrist will abolish the old biblical festivals and introduce new ones to establish his satanic worship system. However, although this will be a time of unparalleled terror for the tribulation saints, God promised that it will not continue forever. Daniel and Revelation both promised that the terror of the Antichrist will be limited to a period of "a time and times and half a time." To the Israelites a "time" meant a year, two "times" meant two years, and "half a time" meant half a year. Therefore, this prophecy parallels several others which declare that the Antichrist's period of total power over the saints will last only three-and-a-half years. In other passages this period is identified as 1260 days and 42 months. This limitation is part of God's mercy to the men forced to live in that horrible time known as "the time of Jacob's troubles." This is the reason Jesus said, "But he who endures to the end shall be saved" (Matthew 24:13). Christ revealed the reason the Great Tribulation will be limited in duration. "And unless those days were shortened, no flesh would be saved; but for the elect's sake those days will be shortened" (Matthew 24:22). The worldwide devastation caused by man's doomsday weapons, the terror of Satan, and the wrath of God will be so overwhelming that no one on earth would survive if Christ allowed the Great Tribulation to continue any longer.

Our world is already threatened daily by terrorists, criminals and unstable dictators with sophisticated equipment and devastating weapons. In the last two decades using the threat of a nuclear warhead, fifty-five serious attempts were made to extort millions of dollars from North America. With over forty five thousand nuclear warheads available in the former Soviet Union our police and intelligence agencies must take these threats seriously. The danger of nuclear warfare naturally requires serious planning for a post-attack government. As a result, legislators in the West have passed numerous laws providing almost dictatorial powers to our leaders in the event of a national emergency. In the United States, Britain, and Canada, executive orders allow the President or Prime Minister to declare a national emergency and take over all communications, agriculture, transportation, banking, and food distribution. The key point to remember is that these laws allow the leader of the moment to define whether or not a "national emergency" exists. There is no legal definition in these laws of what precisely constitutes a national emergency. However, these emergency laws could easily be used by the coming Prince of Darkness to establish his totalitarian government.

THE INTELLIGENCE AND POLICE NETWORK OF THE PRINCE

As mentioned in a previous chapter, the worldwide battle against international drug dealers and terrorists has forced governments to share privileged police intelligence files with other governments in an attempt to apprehend these fugitives from justice. However, the loss of privacy for the average citizen has been tremendous. Today any authorized national government agency can tap into the international intelligence and police computer information network to access the complete files on any citizen. They have total access to the criminal and immigration records of every American and Canadian citizen. Access to these files will someday make it relatively easy for the Antichrist's police to track down anyone who refuses to accept the Mark of the Beast system.

THE ECONOMIC SYSTEM OF THE ANTICHRIST

One of the most distinctive characteristics of this final generation is the astonishing rise in the wealth of the rich nations while the Third World becomes poorer each year. The book of Revelation reveals John's prophetic vision of this terrible disparity between the rich and poor in the years leading up to the Second Coming. The tragic combination of huge riches existing side-by-side with terrible famine is both a sad commentary on our times and a sign of the last days. In Revelation 6:5,6 John records his vision: "I looked, and behold, a black horse, and he who sat on it had a pair of scales in his hand. And I heard a voice in the midst of the four living creatures saying, "A quart of wheat for a denarius, and three quarts of barley for a denarius; and do not harm the oil and the wine." This vision of the third horseman of the Apocalypse shows a horseman with the "scales of famine." The phrase "a quart of wheat for a denarius and three quarts of barley for a denarius" reveals a brutal famine situation when the entire daily wages of a worker (a denarius) will buy a quart of wheat, only one day's food supply. However, the concluding statement "do not harm the oil and the wine" reveals that "oil and wine," the luxuries of the rich, will still be available despite the abject poverty of the poor.

The Coming Economic Boom

The rise in real wealth plus continuing inflation has produced over a million millionaires in the U.S.A. By 1989 more than twenty-one thousand Americans were worth more than $10 million each. In fact, it takes a net worth of at least $20 million to be considered truly rich in the 1990s. *Forbes* magazine lists the four hundred richest people in the world each year. The magazine estimates the average wealth of those four hundred amounts to a staggering $500 million each. Much of their wealth was earned in the frantic real estate and stock market boom during the last decade. Prior to his arrest, Michael Miliken allegedly acquired over $550 million in ill-gotten gains in a single year. "The rich get richer and the poor get poorer" is still true. While the richest Americans have continued to grow richer every year, the poor have watched their true take-home pay drop every year for the last decade.

Gold and Silver Will Be Worthless

James commented on this situation: "Come now, you rich, weep and howl for your miseries that are coming upon you! Your riches are corrupted, and your garments are moth-eaten. Your gold and silver are corroded, and their corrosion will be a witness against you and will eat your flesh like fire. You have heaped up treasure in the last days" (James 5:1–3). This prophecy indicates that gold and silver will cease to be the ultimate safety net for wealth as they have served so often in the past. It is possible that the Prince of Darkness will make possession of gold and silver illegal. This may form part of his plan to introduce a new monetary system that will assure his totalitarian control of society. The governments of the world hate gold and silver. During the 1930s the Roosevelt administration made gold bullion ownership illegal. It is probable that the new world government will outlaw gold and silver to force people to use the new cashless, electronic financial instruments. In the Great Tribulation only those who carry the Mark of the Beast will be able to buy or sell.

Jesus warned men "Do not lay up for yourselves treasures on earth, where moth and rust destroy and where thieves break in and steal" (Matthew 6:19). In His statement Christ warned men to carefully consider where we invest our treasures. It is only those things we have accomplished for God that will be waiting for us in heaven. Additionally, Christ's words remind us that earthly riches will have little value during the rule of the Antichrist. In that terrible period, Revelation prophesies that the great men and the rich men will "hide" themselves "in the caves and in the rocks of the mountains." They will cry out, "hide us from the face of Him that sits on the throne, and from the wrath of the Lamb! For the great day of His wrath is come; and who is able to stand?" (Revelation 6:15–17).

He Will Divide the Land for Gain

"He shall cause them to rule over many, and divide the land for gain" (Daniel 11:39). In his ingenious plans to reform the world's economy the Antichrist will win great popularity with his plans to redistribute the wealth of society. Early in this century the communists won initial popularity in their promises to divide the land of the rich to distribute it to the peasants. The rise of democratic socialism in Europe has prepared the masses for the promises of the coming world dictator to "divide the land for gain." A growing sense of entitlement in the citizens of the West is setting the stage for the economic system of the Antichrist.

The prophet Daniel says that the Prince of Darkness will amass great riches through his total domination of the economies of the nations under his control. His greed will surpass the bounds of previous historical experience. His military conquests will produce massive amounts of captured treasures. "He shall have power over the treasures of gold and silver, and over all the precious things of

Egypt; also the Libyans and Ethiopians shall follow at his heels" (Daniel 11:43). And, "Through his cunning he shall cause deceit to prosper under his hand; and he shall magnify himself in his heart. He shall destroy many in their prosperity" (Daniel 8:25).

The economic prosperity produced by the satanic cunning of the Antichrist will be short-lived. In the end, everything will turn to dust in his hands. James 5:1–3 elaborates on this prophecy: "Come now, you rich, weep and howl for your miseries that are coming upon you! Your riches are corrupted, and your garments are moth-eaten. Your gold and silver are corroded, and their corrosion will be a witness against you and will eat your flesh like fire. You have heaped up treasure in the last days."

THE ECONOMY AND THE WORLD BANKING SYSTEM

The world's most exclusive and private club of international power brokers meets secretly ten times a year in Basel, Switzerland. These men are the most powerful leaders in the world of international finance. They meet here to plan adjustments to the world's money supply, interest rates, and credit for all nations. The Bank of International Settlements (BIS) was established in 1930 to oversee World War I reparation payments from Germany. It quickly became the safest depository for the gold bullion of the various European banks. Since 1945 the BIS, which controls more than $40 billion in cash, has become the central clearing house for European currencies and gold bullion. Their elite membership is composed of the governors of the Federal Reserve Bank, the Bank of England, the Bank of Japan, the Swiss National Bank, and the German Bundesbank. Over 10 percent of the world's foreign exchange is controlled by this single institution. The BIS holds as much gold as Fort Knox. This small group of anonymous financial leaders use this staggering amount of wealth to trigger the recurring recessions, booms, and busts affecting the world economy. They are one of the little known, but very significant, international institutions that are preparing the integration of the world economy in preparation for the coming New World Order.

Another major financial institution, the European Bank for Reconstruction and Development in London, is led by Jacques Attali, an enormously powerful French banker. He has written fifteen books including his latest provocative thesis, *Millennium—Winners and Losers in the Coming World Order.* In his book Attali strongly argues that world power is shifting inexorably toward the new rising economic alliances. He says that "Europe and Japan may supplant the United States as the chief superpowers fighting for global economic supremacy." Attali claims the "two new powers—a European sphere stretching from London to Moscow and a Pacific sphere based in Tokyo but extending as far as New York—will contest for supremacy." He argues that we need a new vision of "global stewardship" and national political leaders who "have the courage to abandon traditional notions of national sovereignty." Jacques Attali is a member of the small elite club in Europe working to establish the New World Order in this decade. He argues that few countries will voluntarily surrender their sovereignty and transfer their power to a world government. In discussing the continuing international summits as an embryonic form of the coming world order he claims that the world government may be "imposed by committees of self-appointed experts or by obscure cabals." In other words, if the democracies do join the program toward planetary government, other forces will secretly force the transfer of sovereignty. Attali is a knowledgeable authority who is aware of the secret planning in the board rooms of the New World Order. He warns that a totalitarian world government is being imposed "by obscure cabals," the secret elite leadership, moving us inexorably toward the Fourth Reich of the Antichrist.

Revival of the Wealth of Ancient Babylon

Babylon was the world's first great military, political and financial power in the days of Nimrod, the son of Cush, the grandson of Noah. This geographical area has always been a center of opposition to God, beginning with Nimrod's pagan idolatry, the Tower of Babel, and the Babylonian Empire of Nebuchadnezzar. Its wealth was beyond anything the world has ever experienced before or since. The walls of Babylon were over thirty stories high and extended fifty-six miles in circumference. Gold and silver were common due to its enormous wealth.

The Bible foretold that Babylon would rise again in the last days to become a center of the Antichrist's satanic power in the Middle East. In Isaiah 14:25 the prophet described the defeat of the Antichrist under his prophetic title, "the Assyrian." Babylon occupied the same geographical territory as Assyria. Jeremiah 50 to 52 prophesied the military rise and fall of Babylon (Iraq). These prophecies about Saddam Hussein's military defeat were analyzed in my book *MESSIAH*. Jeremiah's vision was fulfilled during the incredible events of the war in the Gulf exactly as Jeremiah foretold twenty-five centuries ago. However, Jeremiah, Isaiah, and the book of Revelation together prophesy that the ancient city of Babylon will be rebuilt as one of the capitals of the Antichrist during the Great Tribulation. In my book *MESSIAH*, I include a diagram of the rebuilt city illustrating that Iraq has invested over $800 million in its rebuilding program. Hussein is building palaces and hotels next to the ancient ruins. In the next few years Babylon will be fully rebuilt as a commercial city according to Iraq's plans. One of my sources recently provided me with sixty amazing photos of the rebuilt walls, gates, and temples of this ancient city. Once the UN sanctions end, the awesome wealth from the Iraqi oil wells (over $100 million per day) could easily transform Babylon into a rich, commercial center once more. Saddam has allowed the resumption of an annual Babylonian Festival with 2500 international guests honoring the ancient pagan gods of Mesopotamia. President

Hussein is deeply involved in witchcraft and occult practices. During the war in the Gulf he brought pagan witch doctors from Africa to predict the future of the war. He has allowed several satanic groups to establish themselves in the city.

But Babylon will not survive. The prophet John had this to say about her destruction: "The merchants of these things, who became rich by her, will stand at a distance for fear of her torment, weeping and wailing. . . . And they threw dust on their heads and cried out, weeping and wailing, and saying, 'Alas, alas, that great city, in which all who had ships on the sea became rich by her wealth! For in one hour she is made desolate' " (Revelation 18:15,19).

Isaiah also tells of Babylon's final destruction by God during the Great Day of the Lord (Isaiah 13). He prophesied that the city will be supernaturally destroyed "as God overthrew Sodom and Gomorrah" and that fire and smoke will ascend forever. Strangely, the whole city of Babylon is built over a subterranean lake of oil and asphalt thousands of feet deep. Once ignited, Babylon will burn forever. The sight of the burning oil wells of Kuwait gave the world a preview of the towering inferno that will consume the wicked city of the Prince of Darkness when the Lord destroys it forever.

FAMINE AND ECONOMIC DISASTER

"For nation will rise against nation, and kingdom against kingdom. And there will be famines, pestilences, and earthquakes in various places" (Matthew 24:7). Jesus prophesied in Matthew 24 that widespread famine will characterize the world during the last days. Despite all our advances in agriculture and food growing techniques there are more than one billion people in famine conditions around the world today. According to the United Nations an additional billion are malnourished. In many countries of the Third World more than half the population is out of work. Rising levels of unemployment and bankruptcies in America, Japan, and Europe are destroying the economic dreams of many in the middle class. These desperate conditions are fueling a great desire for a new "caesar" who will promise solutions to these apparently intractable problems.

THE ROLE OF RELIGION IN THE COMING WORLD GOVERNMENT

The New Age Religion

The staggering growth of New Age religion is a fulfillment of prophecy. The Bible warned of apostasy, heresy, and growing idolatry in the last days. The New Age movement will prove a willing ally of the globalist plans for a one-world government. The oriental religious invasion of the West has succeeded beyond the wildest dreams of the gurus of the 1970s. From the halls of government to the board rooms of big business, new age technologies and philosophies now dominate training programs and decision-making processes. The underlying philosophy of the New Age movement is anti-family, anti-Christian, and anti-Jewish. They openly reject the Bible and Judeo-Christian morality. The attitude of the New Age movement is that anything goes from astrology to crystals as long as you don't claim that there is an ultimate standard of right and wrong such as is found in the Bible. The greatest sin in our New Age world is intolerance. It is noteworthy that pagan Rome also allowed anyone to believe anything as long as they didn't claim that their faith was exclusively correct.

Paganism held that all religious paths were equally valid. The pagans hated the Christians because their Bible declared that there was only one path to God, faith in Jesus Christ: "I am the way, the truth, and the life. No one comes to the Father except through Me" (John 14:6). This declaration of Jesus was offensive to the pagans who wanted to believe that all roads led to Rome.

Just as the pagans of the Roman Empire persecuted and martyred Christians for their faith in Christ, the New Age movement is gearing up for an all-out assault on

Christians of the West. In some of their literature they actually claim that the planet cannot evolve to its next stage of planetary evolution until the intolerant Christians are removed by God or the UFOs. This may be their explanation in the future after the Rapture occurs. The Bible describes Christian believers as the "salt of the earth" and states that our presence is preventing the rot from settling in. When the Rapture removes hundreds of millions of Christians from nations around the world, the moral rot will set in quickly. The loss of millions of Christians from key positions in the military, law enforcement, judiciary, education, and business may trigger the collapse of America from its position as a superpower.

THE FALSE CHURCH

During the final seven-year period leading to the Battle of Armageddon the Antichrist will try to dominate the entire world. Initially he will consolidate his political power base using his strategic alliance with the rising new religious power. The Antichrist and False Prophet will find willing allies in the false worldwide ecumenical church that will fill the void after the Rapture of the true Christians. After the Rapture the apostate religious leaders of the world will be in a state of shock. The Rapture may force them to invent some lie about what has happened to millions of Christians around the world. This ecumenical alliance will bring all of the religious powers of the world together under one head in Rome as John revealed in Revelation 17. For decades many ecumenical discussions have proceeded on the assumption that the Roman Catholic Church, led by the Pope, would occupy the leading position in this worldwide church. No other religious group has ever ventured to suggest themselves as an alternative leader instead of Rome. Although the ecumenical apostate church will involve many diverse religious groups, the largest organized group is obviously Rome.

In a fascinating revelation, Archbishop Runcie of the Church of England told *Time* magazine (October 16, 1989) that he had given a special ring to the Roman Pontiff. He explained that this ring was "an engagement ring" between him and Pope John Paul II as a promise of the coming union between the Church of England and the Church of Rome. These ecumenical groups have often complained that the only real obstacle to their religious union was the resistance of the evangelical conservative Christians. Once these Christians are removed supernaturally by the Rapture, there will be little resistance from any other group to this proposed union. Ultimately this false world religion will involve an alliance of the Roman Catholic Church, the Russian and Greek Orthodox Churches, various Protestant groups, and the New Age cult groups. Virtually all religiously minded people will enthusiastically join this false church in a tremendous alliance with the new political leader of the New World Order, the Antichrist.

The prophet John saw this future satanically inspired alliance of religion and politics as symbolized by the Babylon, "Mother of Harlots." As John prophetically looked down the centuries he saw this worldwide religious system supporting the Antichrist and the ten nations of his kingdom in their rise to power: "I saw a woman sitting upon a scarlet beast which was full of names of blasphemy, having seven heads and ten horns. The woman was arrayed in purple and scarlet, and adorned with gold and precious stones having in her hand a golden cup full of abominations and filthiness of her fornication. And on her forehead a name was written: MYSTERY, BABYLON THE GREAT, THE MOTHER OF HARLOTS AND ABOMINATIONS OF THE EARTH" (Revelation 17:3–5).

Note that John saw the end-time false religious system "sitting upon a scarlet beast." This indicates that the religious system will initially be lifted up and honored by the Antichrist's political allies. However, John reveals that this last day religious system will be characterized by apostasy and blasphemy. She will be known for her vast riches, yet her true secret nature is indicated by the prophet's words, "abominations and filthiness of her fornication." The Bible often uses the imagery of sexual unfaithfulness to signify spiritual apostasy. This false church will wallow in sensuality and will express the materialistic spirit of these last days. It will be known as "Mystery, Babylon the Great" because it will secretly embody the Babylonian religious mysteries that have characterized every man-made religion and cult since man's rebellion at the Tower of Babel.

PERSECUTION OF TRIBULATION SAINTS

The false church will enthusiastically join in the campaign to consolidate the Antichrist's New World Order. It will persecute and martyr all tribulation believers who follow the true Messiah. Millions will be martyred for their faith in Christ during this terrible period of persecution. They are described in Revelation 7:9: "I looked, and behold, a great multitude which no one could number, of all nations, tribes, peoples, and tongues, standing before the throne and before the Lamb, clothed with white robes, with palm branches in their hands." When John asked the angel who they were the answer was given as follows: "These are the ones who come out of the great tribulation, and washed their robes and made them white in the blood of the Lamb" (Revelation 7:14).

During the first three-and-a-half years of his seven-year treaty with Israel the Antichrist and his ten allied nations will cynically use the false church in their propaganda campaign to consolidate their political power. Once they acquire supreme power, they will no longer want to share it with this ecumenical church. The ten kings will turn and destroy her because they secretly hate the church. "And the ten horns which you saw on the beast, these will hate the harlot, make her desolate and naked, eat her flesh and burn her with fire" (Revelation 17:16). The Babylonian false church will oppress the tribulation saints during the first half of the seven-year period. In Revelation 17:6, John says, "I saw the woman, drunk with the blood of the saints and with the blood of the martyrs of Jesus." However, during the last three-and-a-half years after the Babylonian church is destroyed, the Antichrist and his False Prophet will persecute the tribulation saints until Christ saves them at His coming.

VARIOUS CHURCH VIEWS ON THE ANTICHRIST

The Antichrist is destined to rise in the last days as the great opponent of Israel, the tribulation saints and Jesus Christ. The early Christians understood from the prophecies of Daniel and Revelation that this fearful tyrant will appear in the last generation before Christ comes to set up His millennial kingdom. Hippolytus, a writer in the first centuries of the Church, expressed this view of the coming Antichrist. As recorded in *Fragments From Commentaries*, Hippolytus wrote, "When the times are fulfilled (6000 years) and the ten horns spring from the beast in the last (times), then Antichrist will appear among them." He also talked about the Antichrist stopping the daily sacrifice. "For when the threescore and two weeks are fulfilled, and Christ is come, and the Gospel is preached in every place, the times being then accomplished, there will remain only one week, the last, in which Elias will appear and Enoch, and in the midst of it the abomination of desolation will be manifested, viz. Antichrist, announcing desolation to the world. And when he comes the sacrifice and oblation will be removed . . ."

Some writers who dislike Bible prophecy claim that our belief in a future literal Antichrist and the Great Tribulation is a recent invention without precedent in the early Church. These writers are ignorant of the true belief of those early Christians who were taught by the disciples of Christ. Far from being a new invention, our literal interpretation follows the teachings of the apostolic Church. These quotations from Hippolytus and Irenaeus reveal the early Church believed in an individual Antichrist in a rebuilt Temple with restored animal sacrifice. They expected the fulfillment of Daniel's 70th Week of seven years in the last days. In addition they expected the two witnesses to appear before Christ returned to defeat Antichrist and establish His millennial kingdom approximately 6000 years from Adam.

In another passage Hippolytus wrote, "Thus, then, does the prophet set forth these things concerning the Antichrist, who shall be shameless, a war-maker, and despot, who, exalting himself above all kings and above every god, shall build the city of Jerusalem, and restore the Sanctuary. Him the impious will worship as God, and will bend to him the knee, thinking him to be the Christ. He shall cut off the two witnesses and forerunners of Christ, who proclaim his glorious kingdom from heaven, as it is said "And I will give (power) unto my two witnesses and they shall prophesy a thousand two hundred and threescore days, clothed in sackcloth." It is remarkable to observe how closely these views of the early Church parallel the prophetic interpretations of Bible teachers today.

Another early Christian writer Irenaeus wrote a book *Against Heresies* that outlined the understanding in the early Church about the rise of Antichrist in the last days. "For when he (Antichrist) is come, and of his own accord concentrates in his own person the apostasy, and accomplishes whatever he shall do according to his own will and choice, sitting also in the temple of God, so that his dupes may adore him as the Christ." Irenaeus also wrote of the early Church's expectation that Christ would come to establish His kingdom at the end of six thousand years from Adam. "For the day of the Lord is as a thousand years; and in six days created things were completed: it is evident, therefore, that they will come to an end at the sixth thousand year."

However, beginning with Augustine in the fifth century after Christ and continuing through the medieval period the Church gradually abandoned the literal method of interpreting prophecy. The idea was put forward that the Antichrist was not a real individual who would torment Israel in the last days. Rather, some writers suggested that the Antichrist was a symbol of a system opposed to God's Word and his people. During those centuries the medieval church became utterly corrupt. This included a collapse of morals in the priests together with the sale of indulgences and church offices. The inquisition tortured and killed over millions, including born again believers, during four hundred years of horrifying repression. Although few have studied the historical record there were millions of true followers of Jesus who abandoned the apostate official religion to join other believers in the underground Church. During those centuries of persecution by the medieval church almost half of the population of Europe joined this underground Church. Millions joined the Waldenses in the valleys of Italy, the Albigensians in France and the Cathari in Germany. They bravely chose to risk martyrdom to possess Bibles and worship Christ. When Martin Luther embarked on his great Reformation he openly admitted that he was following in the true doctrine that millions of other Christians had upheld for centuries against brutal persecution.

It was very natural for the true Christians living in the underground Church during this terrible period to identify their great enemy as the Antichrist and the Great Harlot of Babylon. Unfortunately, after the Protestant Reformation in 1520, the early reformers applied these prophecies about both the Antichrist and the Harlot to the Roman Papacy. They did not realize that the Antichrist could not logically be both Babylon and the Antichrist simultaneously because the Bible describes them as distinct entities with two different destinies. By the mid 1700s prophecy interpreters returned to a literal interpretation of Scriptures. The reformers recovered the view of the early Church that the Antichrist will be a literal person who will rule the earth during the last seven years leading to the Messiah's return.

Following the Reformation Christians began to study the Bible in their own language. As they poured over the precious truths for themselves millions rediscovered the prophetic truth of a literal Second Coming of Christ in the last days. The Church returned to studying the Scriptures as our only true guide to faith, conduct and truth. Many Bible teachers began to search the Bible to clearly understand the details of the last day events involving the Antichrist, the Great Tribulation and the Rapture. Writers began to sort through the Scriptures to rediscover the details and the sequence of prophetic events. As a result of their research, from 1750 A.D. on, there was a veritable explosion of books on prophecy that has continued to the present day and the book you are reading.

15

The Great Tribulation and the Wrath of God

The recent peace agreement between Israel and the PLO will create the illusion of peace in the Middle East. Eventually, despite the denials of the Israeli government, the PLO will establish a new Palestinian state in the West Bank, Gaza, with East Jerusalem as their capital. This peace agreement and the return of the strategically vital area of the Golan Heights to Syria will leave Israel with no strategic depth. At her vulnerable central populated area of Tel Aviv, Israel will be less than nine miles wide. For the first time since 1948 Israel will be unable to defend herself with conventional weapons and her valiant citizen army. Without the vital strategic depth provided by the military control of the West Bank, Gaza and the Golan, the Jewish state will have only one military option when it finds itself facing an overwhelming invasion from the vastly larger Arab armies.

Currently the Arab standing armies surrounding Israel outnumber and outmatch Israel's military forces by a ratio of eight to one. Israel possesses more than three hundred nuclear weapons that would need to be launched in the first few hours of Arab invasion, or else the Jewish population would be overwhelmed and slaughtered by their enemies. The Arabs have repeatedly threatened to murder all of the Jews and turn the Mediterranean red with their blood. An Israeli retaliatory nuclear strike would wipe out all major Arab capital cities and military bases with their armies. Obviously, at that time, Iran and the Arab allies would retaliate with the nuclear arms they possess, together with a devastating attack of chemical and biological weapons. At the present time Iran has acquired four functioning nuclear warheads from Kazakhstan together with several long range ballistic missiles.

If this nightmare scenario occurs an Arab nuclear and chemical counter strike of only a few warheads would bury Israel and its population "from Dan to Beersheba." The problem for Israel is two-fold. First, she will no longer be able to defend herself with conventional weapons; second, she would certainly be destroyed in the event of a suicidal Middle Eastern nuclear war. This deadly situation may set the stage for the seven-year treaty between the European Antichrist and Israel. The United Nations and the United States have already begun to pressure Israel to give up her nuclear weapons. Increased pressure in the future, along with the acquisition of more nuclear weapons by the Arab states, may encourage Israel to agree to a plan to denuclearize the Middle East. However, the PLO-Israeli agreement will diminish her strategic depth because of the loss of the territories. Without this strategic depth Israel will be unwilling to relinquish her nuclear shield unless a powerful superpower guarantees her borders and security. This situation may create the conditions that will force Israel to accept a seven-year security guarantee from the rising European superpower. After almost forty-five years of armed conflict, Israel's Jewish population longs for real peace with their Arab neighbors. The Antichrist will use his satanic skills to produce this peace treaty in the Middle East. Israel will be so grateful that they will treat him as a messianic figure.

DANIEL'S SEVENTIETH WEEK—A SEVEN-YEAR TREATY WITH ISRAEL

"Then he shall confirm a covenant with many for one week; but in the middle of the week He shall bring an end to sacrifice and offering. And on the wing of abominations shall be one who makes desolate, even until the consummation, which is determined, is poured out on the desolate" (Daniel 9:27).

AN AGREEMENT WITH HELL

"You have said, 'We have made a covenant with death, and with Sheol [hell] we are in agreement. When the overflowing scourge passes through, it will not come to us, for we have made lies our refuge, and under falsehood we have hidden ourselves'" (Isaiah 28:15). The prophet Isaiah warned that this treaty, that will look so promising to a war-weary Israel, will prove to be a "covenant with death." Instead of looking to their God for security the leaders of Israel will make the same mistake their ancient predecessors made before in their country's tragic history. Just as Egypt and Syria so often betrayed Jerusalem in the past, once again the Chosen People will place their faith in a piece of paper rather than in the God of Abraham.

DANIEL'S 70TH WEEK			
Antichrist Will Sign a 7 Year Treaty With Israel			
	Antichrist Signs Treaty	Antichrist Defiles Temple	Christ Destroys Antichrist
Rapture Imminent	First 3 1/2 Years	Second 3 1/2 Years	1000 Yrs.
10 Nations	Harlot Church Persecutes Saints	1260 Days The Great Tribulation	Millennium Christ's Kingdom
		Mark of the Beast	

THE GREAT TRIBULATION

"For then there will be great tribulation, such as has not been since the beginning of the world until this time, no, nor ever shall be" (Matthew 24:21). Scriptures teach that the Great Tribulation, leading up to the Battle of Armageddon, will be a time of trial for both the Gentile nations and Israel. Jeremiah called this period the "time of Jacob's trouble" but promised that God would supernaturally protect and deliver His Chosen People. In his prophecy he declared, "Alas! For that day is great, so that none is like it; and it is the time of Jacob's trouble, but he shall be saved out of it" (Jeremiah 30:7). Satan's plan for man's destruction will finally break out in all its horror and he will be revealed as the true enemy of mankind. The wrath and judgment of God will be poured out upon the rebellious sinners who kill the tribulation saints. These rebels will openly worship Satan and his Antichrist because they despise God's laws and holiness. Unrepentant sinners will give themselves up to every kind of immorality, Satan worship and brutal violence.

The Great Tribulation will occupy the last half of this seven-year treaty period and will last precisely three-and-one-half biblical years. The ancient Jews used a year of 360 days, as recorded throughout the Bible. In both Daniel and Revelation the prophets clearly refer to this 360-day biblical year. Both prophets describe the last half of the seven-year treaty period as precisely 1260 days: three years of 360 days plus the half year of 180 days. The reason for the Bible's precision in recording the precise number of days is connected with the fact that the key prophetic events will likely occur on the anniversaries of the ancient biblical festival calendar. In my book *ARMAGEDDON* I pointed out that for the last four thousand years the major historical events for Israel have fallen on the anniversaries of Passover, Pentecost, Tabernacles, et cetera. The horrors of his reign of terror will be so terrible that Christ foretold the exact duration of the Antichrist's power. Christ will defeat the Antichrist at Armageddon precisely 1260 days after the "abomination of desolation" when he violates the sanctity of the Holy of Holies of the rebuilt Temple. Christ's prophetic words were designed to encourage the tribulation saints to resist the Mark of the Beast and to hide from the Antichrist's forces as long as possible: "He who endures to the end shall be saved" (Matthew 24:13).

THE GREAT DAY OF THE LORD'S WRATH

Throughout the Old and New Testament the whole seven-year tribulation period is often referred to as the Great Day of the Lord. "For the great day of His wrath has come, and who is able to stand?" (Revelation 6:17). Warnings were given by the prophets of the terrors in that day when God will open the heavens to pour down His wrath and judgment on evil men. "The nations were angry, and Your wrath has come, and the time of the dead, that they should be judged, and that You should reward Your servants the prophets and the saints, and those who fear Your name, small and great, and should destroy those who destroy the earth" (Revelation 11:18). God's judgment will commence following the signing of the seven-year treaty between Antichrist and Israel. His righteous wrath will be poured out in a seven-fold series of wrath and judgment that will create a hell on earth for unrepentant sinners throughout this period.

For thousands of years brutal sinners have abused, tortured and killed innocent victims. To outward appearances the wicked often seem to get away with evil actions without significant punishment. Every one of us has read or heard of unspeakable crimes against innocent people and have wondered: Where is the justice? As Solomon, the wisest of men once said: "Because the sentence against an evil work is not executed speedily, therefore the heart of the sons of men is fully set in them to do evil" (Ecclesiastes 8:11). Often it seems that good is unrewarded while those who do evil live in wealth and health. However, the Bible promises that there will be a day of reckoning when all men will stand before God to account for their lives. In addition to that final judgment which will occur after death, the Bible promises that the evil deeds done during the Great Tribulation will be punished. The day of judgment is coming. Finally, the day will arrive when God will pour out His wrath on those evil ones who persecute innocent people.

THE SEVEN SEAL JUDGMENTS

The wrath of God will commence following the signing of the seven year treaty when Christ will open the seven Seal Judgments, beginning with the Four Horsemen of the Apocalypse. These four judgments include: (1) False Peace, (2) War, (3) Famine, and finally, (4) Death, the Sword, Hunger, Pestilence, and Wild Animals (see Revelation 6 and 7). These specific judgments are identified in numerous passages in the Old Testament as the definite signs of the wrath of God. As an example, consider the words recorded in Ezekiel 14:21. "For thus says the Lord God: 'How much more it shall be when I send My four severe judgments on Jerusalem; the sword and famine and wild beasts and pestilence—to cut off man and beast from it?' " In this and several parallel passages it is clear that these specific judgments, which are identical to the Four Horsemen judgments that commence the tribulation period, are identified as the wrath and judgment of God. Since 1 Thessalonians 1:10 promises the Church an escape from the wrath of God we conclude that the Church will be raptured before any part of the tribulation period. In this verse Paul promised that we are "to wait for His Son from heaven, whom He raised from the dead, even Jesus who delivers us from the wrath to come."

In confirmation of this interpretation, the fifth Seal Judgment described the martyred souls of the tribulation saints calling out for God's vengeance on their persecutors. However, the Bible forbids Christians to call for vengeance. The fact that the tribulation saints call for vengeance suggests strongly that they are not Christians living under the grace of God. Their behavior is similar to the people of the Old Testament who often called for the destruction of their enemies. This tends to confirm that the Christian saints will already be raptured to heaven by the time of the martyrdom of these tribulation saints. The seven Seal Judgments will continue throughout the whole seven year tribulation period leading to Armageddon.

THE TRUMPET JUDGMENTS

The Trumpet Judgments that will pour out the wrath of God upon the earth, the sea, the waters, and the heavens making life intolerable for the evil men who persecute the tribulation saints (Revelation 8, 9 and 11). During the fifth trumpet judgment demonic spirits will be released from the bottomless pit that will torment sinful men for five months. The seventh Trumpet Judgment, encompassing a number of events, apparently begins in the middle of the seven-year tribulation period and will also continue until Armageddon.

THE BOWL JUDGMENTS

A third series of judgments, the Bowl Judgments (Revelation 16) will occur during the final 1260 days leading up to the Battle of Armageddon. Revelation warns of the judgment of God upon Babylon the Great, the Mother of Harlots, the false world church (Revelation 17). John also tells us about the destruction of the city of Babylon in Iraq, one of the capitals of the Antichrist. Finally, the wrath of heaven will be poured out on the nations and their armies as they are gathered together for the climactic Battle of Armageddon. The Bible indicates that as many as four billion people will die during the terrible wars, pestilence, inquisitions, and judgments of the Great Tribulation. Astonishingly, Scriptures record that unrepentant sinners living in that period will still defy God. "But the rest of mankind, who were not killed by these plagues, did not repent of the works of their hands, that they should not worship demons, and idols of gold, silver, brass, stone, and wood, which can neither see nor hear nor walk; and they did not repent of their murders or their sorceries or their sexual immorality or their thefts" (Revelation 9:20,21).

War in the Heavens—Hell on Earth

"At that time Michael shall stand up, the great prince who stands watch over the sons of your people; And there shall be a time of trouble, such as never was since there was a nation, even to that time. And at that time your people shall be delivered, every one who is found written in the book" (Daniel 12:1). Satan still has access to some part of heaven as he has from the beginning. In the book of Job we are told that he appeared "with the sons of God" before the throne of God to accuse Job. Later, in the New Testament we are told that Satan accuses Christians before the throne of God. Jesus Christ, as our Advocate, defends us to our heavenly Father. The prophet Daniel revealed that Satan's freedom in the heavens is finally about to end. At the midpoint of the seven-year treaty period a war will occur in heaven that will end with Satan and his fallen angels being cast out to the earth. Michael, the Archangel, will defeat Satan's fallen angels, forcing them out of heaven.

Revelation declares that "the great dragon was cast out, that serpent of old, called the Devil and Satan, who deceives the whole world; he was cast to the earth, and his angels were cast out with him" (Revelation 12:9). However the consequences for those living on the earth at that time will be catastrophic. Revelation 12:12 warns, "Woe to the inhabitants of the earth and the sea! For the devil has come down to you, having great wrath, because he knows that he has a short time." Satan can understand prophecy as well as any human. He will be filled with wrath because he will know that his imprisonment in the bottomless pit will be only 1260 days away.

The Death and Resurrection of Antichrist

At the mid-point of the seven-year treaty, simultaneously with Satan's expulsion from heaven, the Antichrist will be killed by a sword wound to his head or neck. While some have suggested that he will fake his death and resurrection, the prophecy tells us he will die and supernaturally rise from the grave. "I saw one of his heads as if it had been mortally wounded, and his deadly wound was healed. And all the world marveled and followed the beast" (Revelation 13:3). This satanic miracle will convince many that he is the promised Messiah. He will consciously try to fulfill the ancient prophetic expectations of the Jews looking for a messiah-deliverer. The False Prophet will force men to worship a statue of the Antichrist, "telling those who dwell on the earth to make an image to the beast who was wounded by the sword and lived" (Revelation 13:14). If people refuse to worship Satan's Prince of Darkness or his statue they will be killed. The False Prophet will introduce the Mark of the Beast system after the resurrection of the Antichrist. This diabolical control system will continue for three-and-a-half years until his defeat at Armageddon. The system will be introduced initially throughout the ten-nation power base of his worldwide kingdom. It is possible that some people will be able to escape to the wilderness in other continents. Christ will judge the Gentiles at the judgment of the nations on the basis of how they treated the tribulation saints, the Jewish and Gentile victims of the Antichrist, who will flee the Mark of the Beast system. In addition they will be judged for their treatment of God's servants throughout history.

THE ENEMIES OF ANTICHRIST

While the Antichrist's power will initially be limited to the ten nations, he will bring more and more nations under his satanic power throughout the seven years. Finally, the whole world will serve him for a time. Toward the middle of the tribulation period the nations, beginning with Israel, and eventually involving almost half the planet, will start rebelling against the forces of the Antichrist. A series of enemies will rise in rebellion against the brutal power of the Antichrist. This rebellion will finally culminate in the Battle of Armageddon involving all the armies of the world.

ISRAEL

The first nation to rebel will be Israel. The Antichrist will violate the Holy of Holies at the mid-point of the seven-year tribulation period. At that point many in Israel will realize that he is not their true Messiah but an impostor. In Revelation 12:6 we are told that Israel will flee into the nations for the last three-and-a-half years. "Then the woman fled into the wilderness, where she has a place prepared by God, that they should feed her there one thousand two hundred and sixty days." God promised that He will supernaturally protect those righteous Jews who reject the satanic system of the False Prophet. Satan will try to destroy the fleeing Jews with supernatural powers but God will intervene to protect her.

THE KINGS OF THE SOUTH AND THE NORTH

As nation after nation tries to throw off the yoke of the Antichrist the entire tribulation period will be filled with war and famine that inevitably follow war. In Revelation John described the red horseman of the Apocalypse taking peace from the earth despite the false promises of peace from the Antichrist. Finally, the Prince of Darkness will establish a military base in Israel to dominate the Middle East. The kings of the North (possibly Syria) and the South (Egypt) will attack his forces in Palestine. However, the Antichrist will use his strategic brilliance and massive armies to overwhelm and defeat their armies. "At the time of the end the king of the South shall attack him; and the king of the North shall come against him like a whirlwind, with chariots, horsemen, and with many ships; and he shall enter the countries, overwhelm them, and pass through" (Daniel 11:40). The first major battles will be won by the forces of the Prince of Darkness.

The Kings of the East

However, the other nations of the East will realize that it is now or never if they want to throw off the chains of the world dictator. When the Antichrist hears of the eastern alliance mobilizing in Asia he will bring together the massive military forces of the West for the final battle to establish who will rule the world. Daniel 11:44 declares: "But news from the east and the north shall trouble him; therefore he shall go out with great fury to destroy and annihilate many." He will establish his military headquarters in Jerusalem and will prepare for the final conflict. He will continue to attack the enormous 200 million man army of the kings of the East during their march across Asia toward the Middle East. John described the buildup for the fateful battle. "And they gathered them together to the place called in Hebrew, Armageddon" (Revelation 16:16).

The book of Revelation tells us that the Euphrates River will miraculously dry up to allow the enormous army of the Kings of the East to cross into northern Israel. Throughout history the great Euphrates River has been the major military barrier between East and West. However, Turkey built the Ataturk Dam several years ago that can dam up the Euphrates River completely for the first time. "Then the sixth angel poured out his bowl on the great river Euphrates, and its water was dried up, so that the way of the kings from the east might be prepared" (Revelation 16:12). The eastern armies will fight as they march across Asia, killing one-third of humanity in their path. The final battle will center on the Valley of Jezreel "to a place called in Hebrew, Armageddon." Despite the huge military and satanic forces of the Antichrist, Daniel 11:45 declared that "he shall come to his end, and no one will help him."

The Sheep Nations

"When the Son of Man comes in His glory . . . All the nations will be gathered before Him, and He will separate them one from another, as a shepherd divides his sheep from the goats. And He will set the sheep on His right hand, but the goats on the left" (Matthew 25:31–33). This judgment of the sheep and the goats will provide rewards and punishments for nations and individuals according to their treatment of those Jews and Gentiles who flee the Antichrist during the Tribulation. Although their resistance to the Antichrist's forces may be passive, the "sheep" nations will provide a sanctuary for those escaping the Mark of the Beast system. Those who befriend them will be the "sheep" nations and will receive rewards from Christ. To those who are faithful He will say, "Come, you blessed of My Father, inherit the kingdom prepared for you from the foundation of the world" (Matthew 25:34). The "goat" nations who persecuted the saints will be cast "into everlasting fire."

THE ARMY OF JESUS CHRIST

"Then I saw heaven opened, and behold, a white horse. And He who sat on him was called Faithful and True, and in righteousness He judges and makes war . . . And the armies in heaven, clothed in fine linen, white and clean, followed Him on white horses" (Revelation 19:11,14). The last and most powerful enemy to face the Prince of Darkness will be Jesus Christ and His army of millions of saints from heaven. After his many military victories against human armies the Antichrist and his forces will be puffed up with pride. He will bring his huge armies into position to attack the 200 million army of the kings of the East and the army of Israel. However, when the battle is raging and millions are being slaughtered on every side, they will be interrupted by an invasion from heaven. "I saw the beast, the kings of the earth, and their armies, gathered together to make war against Him who sat on the horse and against His army. Then the beast was captured, and with him the False Prophet who worked signs in his presence, by which he deceived those who received the mark of the beast and those who worshiped his image. These two were cast alive into the lake of fire burning with brimstone" (Revelation 19:19,20).

The prophet Daniel described the supernatural defeat of the Prince of Darkness when he confronts Jesus Christ, the true "Prince of princes": "He shall even rise against the Prince of princes; but he shall be broken without human hand" (Daniel 8:25). The apostle Paul confirmed the vision of Daniel and declared that Christ would personally destroy the Man of Sin with His supernatural power. "And then the lawless one will be revealed, whom the Lord will consume with the breath of His mouth and destroy with the brightness of His coming" (2 Thessalonians 2:8).

An analysis of the warnings of the Old Testament prophets together with the prophecies of Matthew and Revelation suggests that as many as two-thirds of the earth's population will die during the Great Tribulation. This will be a time of unparalleled terror, war, persecution and martyrdom. In addition, the awesome wrath of God will be poured out in judgment on evil men. In mercy God has promised that the Tribulation will be limited in duration. Billions will reject God's salvation and spend eternity in hell without hope. However, millions will reject Satan's Prince and will find salvation as martyrs during that time of unparalleled suffering.

THE PROMISE OF DELIVERANCE FROM THE WRATH OF GOD

"Because you have kept My command to persevere, I also will keep you from the hour of trial which shall come upon the whole world, to test those who dwell on the earth" (Revelation 3:10). Christ's promise to His Church is that He "will keep you from the hour of trial which shall come upon the whole world." This promise to supernaturally deliver the Church from His wrath through the Rapture is confirmed by many other passages as outlined in the earlier chapter on the Church and the Antichrist. Throughout the Bible the burden of evidence is that God will remove His Church to heaven before the time of wrath during the tribulation period. In addition, the apostle Paul declared that our destiny as Christians was to escape the coming wrath of God. In 1 Thessalonians 5:9 he wrote, "For God did not appoint us to wrath, but to obtain salvation through our Lord Jesus Christ, who died for us, that whether we wake or sleep, we should live together with Him."

16

The Final Witnesses to the Coming Messiah

God promises that He will never leave this world without a witness to His truth. After the Rapture of the Church the Lord will send three different groups to witness and preach repentance during the Great Tribulation. Revelation tells us that these messengers include the two witnesses, a group of 144,000 Jewish witnesses and finally, three angelic messengers to warn men to repent of their wicked rebellion and seek the face of God.

THE TWO WITNESSES

John the Baptist preached his message as "the voice of one crying in the wilderness: 'Prepare the way of the Lord, make His paths straight' " (Matthew 3:3). Jesus, also taught this same message, "From that time Jesus began to preach and to say, 'Repent, for the kingdom of heaven is at hand' " (Matthew 4:17). This same prophetic message, a call to repentance in light of the quickly approaching judgment, will be preached throughout the world by the two witnesses. "And I will give power to my two witnesses, and they will prophesy one thousand two hundred and sixty days, clothed in sackcloth. These are the two olive trees, and the two lampstands standing before the God of the earth" (Revelation 11:3,4). This passage tells us that the Lord will give His two witnesses supernatural protection for three and a half years to preach fearlessly during the final days of this age. God's supernatural power will protect them from being killed by the forces of Antichrist and the False Prophet until their 1260-day divine mission is completed.

Jesus specifically warned His disciples about being deceived in the last days concerning the identity of the Messiah. The Antichrist will have one witness to his credentials, the false prophet, who will testify that he is the messiah. The Law of Moses established the principle that two witnesses, not one, were required for the most important matters in judgment. Deuteronomy 19:15 declared, "One witness shall not rise against a man concerning any iniquity or any sin that he commits; by the mouth of two or three witnesses the matter shall be established." This principle was of such importance that it is repeated seven times throughout the Bible. In 2 Corinthians 13:1 Paul confirms this principle, "By the mouth of two or three witnesses every word shall be established." This principle is so fundamental that God will send two witnesses to warn mankind of the coming true Messiah, Jesus the Christ.

THEIR PURPOSE

Whenever God's Word is faithfully preached there is always a response. As the prophet Isaiah declared, "So shall My word be that goes forth from My mouth; it shall not return to Me void, but it shall accomplish what I please, and it shall prosper in the thing for which I sent it" (Isaiah 55:11). Although the Rapture will remove all true believers to heaven before the tribulation period, God will not leave the earth without a witness, even in man's darkest hour. He will send His message of repentance to mankind through the words of His two witnesses: "I will give power to my two witnesses, and they will prophesy one thousand two hundred and sixty days, clothed in sackcloth" (Revelation 11:3–4). God will give supernatural power to His two witnesses to authenticate their message.

There will be a tremendous response to their message of repentance with hundreds of millions from every nation following Christ as tribulation saints. However, the cost of their belief in Christ will be instant martyrdom for any who fall into the hands of the police of the Antichrist. This unprecedented response to God is described in the Revelation 7:9: "After these things I looked, and behold, a great multitude which no one could number, of all nations, tribes, peoples, and tongues, standing before the throne and before the Lamb, clothed with white robes, with palm branches in their hands." When John asked the angel who this group of martyrs was, the reply was, "These are the ones who come out of the great tribulation, and washed their robes and made them white in the blood of the Lamb" (Revelation 7:14).

Some wonder how anyone could respond to God after the Rapture when the Holy Spirit is removed as comforter of the Church and restrainer of the Antichrist. They incorrectly suggest that the Holy Spirit will no longer be on the earth after the Rapture. However this is wrong. The Holy Spirit is God. By definition, God is omnipresent. This means He is everywhere simultaneously throughout His infinite universe at all times. Therefore, the Holy Spirit cannot remove Himself from the earth. At the time of the Rapture only His special roles as comforter of the Church and restrainer of Antichrist will end. As God, the Holy Spirit will still be here convicting sinners. Otherwise, no one could be saved during the tribulation period.

The Holy Spirit revealed Himself in His special role as comforter and strengthener of the Church on the day of Pentecost (Acts 2). However, the Holy Spirit was on the earth before that moment. John the Baptist was filled with the Holy Spirit "from his mother's womb," long before the day of Pentecost. Also, the Old Testament reveals the presence of the Holy Spirit with King David, King Saul, and many others, long before the Day of Pentecost. The Holy Spirit has always, and will always, be present on the earth. Otherwise, no man could ever respond to God's calling.

THEIR ROLE

The two witnesses will proclaim the gospel of the Kingdom of the Messiah during a period of 1260 days. The wicked men of that day will resist their testimony and seek to destroy them. Revelation 11:5 tells us that the two witnesses will destroy with fire anyone who attempts to hurt them. They will stop the rain for three-and-a-half years, producing the longest and worst drought in human history. In addition, they will have "power over waters to turn them to blood, and to strike the earth with all plagues, as often as they desire." Notice that these two witnesses do not behave as Christians. They will not "turn the other cheek" as Christians are commanded to do. Instead, the two witnesses behave exactly as Old Testament prophets. This behavior is appropriate for the tribulation period after the Rapture has taken the Christians to heaven. The Age of Grace will end with the Rapture and God's wrath will now be poured out on unrepentant sinners.

After the two witnesses complete their 1260 day mission when they "have finished their testimony," the Antichrist will kill them. John declared, "the beast that ascends out of the bottomless pit, will make war against them, overcome them, and kill them" (Revelation 11:7). Although they will be supernaturally protected for the first three-and-a-half years, the Antichrist, now possessed by Satan, will be able to kill them. When their dead bodies lie in the street of Jerusalem the unrepentant peoples of the earth will rejoice over their death. For the first time in history, through the use of international news broadcasts like CNN, we can understand how the prophecy of John could be fulfilled.

However, "after the three and a half days the breath of life from God" will resurrect the two witnesses to the astonishment and fear of those who witness the event. Then, hearing "a loud voice from heaven saying to them, 'Come up here,' " they will ascend "to heaven in a cloud" in the sight of their enemies. The whole world will be astonished at this reversal of the destruction of God's witnesses. When they see the two witnesses dead, the sinful men of earth will believe they have defeated God. Then,

Christ will reveal His power by raising them just as He raised Lazarus two thousand years ago.

THE IDENTITY OF THE WITNESSES

From the first centuries after Christ until today, most Bible commentators have taught the Revelation 11 passage points to two distinct individuals who will return from heaven for a special mission. While some believe the evidence points to Elijah and Enoch, others identify Elijah and Moses as the two witnesses. Some Bible interpreters, especially in the last century, believed that these two witnesses will not be actual men, but symbols of two entities that will witness to mankind. They proposed combinations such as the Old and New Testaments, the Bible and the Holy Spirit, or the martyrs of the Old and New Testaments. However, a close examination of the Revelation 11 passage reveals that these two witnesses must be individual human beings. They are clothed with sackcloth and they are given supernatural power to produce miraculous signs. In addition they physically destroy the enemies of God with fire. The two witnesses give testimony, torment evil men, and are finally killed by the Antichrist. Their dead bodies will lie in the street in Jerusalem and not be buried. Their corpses will be seen by wicked "peoples, tribes, tongues, and nations" who will rejoice at their apparent victory over God's messengers. Finally, the two witnesses will supernaturally rise from the dead and ascend to heaven in the sight of their enemies. To fulfill these prophecies, the two witnesses must be two individual human beings.

The prophet Malachi declared that Elijah will be one of the two witnesses. "Behold, I will send you Elijah the prophet before the coming of the great and dreadful day of the Lord" (Malachi 4:5). A fascinating parallel is that Elijah and the two witnesses both stop the rain for 1260 days. In Revelation 11:6, John said, "these have power to shut heaven, so that no rain falls in the days of their prophecy." We are told that the days of their prophecy (and the supernatural drought) will also be 1260 days (Revelation 11:3). This is exactly the same period as Elijah's drought during the days of King Ahab, as Luke records, "But I tell you truly, many widows were in Israel in the days of Elijah, when the heaven was shut up three years and six months" (Luke 4:25). Further support for Elijah being one of the two witnesses is that he appeared with Moses on the Mount of Transfiguration, witnessing to the glory of Jesus the Messiah.

Elijah is a fascinating biblical character whose career ultimately spans from the beginning of his prophetic ministry during the reign of King Ahab (850 B.C.), to his appearance on the Mount of Transfiguration with Jesus, and extends thousands of years into the future until his 1260 day ministry during the Great Tribulation. While the Bible tells us little about his background, his name "the Tishbite" may indicate that his home was the city of Tishbeh, a city to the east of the Jordan River. The Talmud also suggests that Elijah was a priest. The Jewish rabbis see a similarity between Elijah and Melchizedek, the King of Salem, in that the Bible is strangely silent about both of their fathers, mothers, ancestors, and descendants.

For thousands of years the Jews have believed Malachi's prophecy that God will send them "Elijah the prophet before the coming of the great and dreadful day of the Lord" (Malachi 4:5). Each year, at Passover, the Jews set out a wine cup as an invitation for the prophet Elijah. They leave the door or window slightly ajar to invite Elijah's entrance at their Passover seder meal in the hope that this year he will usher in the coming Messiah. As the Gospels record, priests and Sadducees asked both John the Baptist and Jesus of Nazareth, "Are you Elijah?" The Jews questioned them because they knew the biblical prophecies that Elijah's mission will precede the coming of the Messiah.

Over the centuries the Jews have developed a number of traditions about Elijah the prophet. These traditions often expressed their hopes for a coming savior, their Messiah. The Jewish sages interpreted the prophecy of Isaiah as a prediction about Elijah, "The voice of one crying in the wilderness: 'Prepare the way of the Lord; make straight in the desert a highway for our God' " (Isaiah 40:3). His appearance as the forerunner of Messiah will motivate the Jewish people to national and individual repentance. The rabbis believe that Elijah and the Messiah will usher in a time of peace and harmony for all nations. They believe that Elijah will resolve all legal questions and the discrepancies in religious law (Halachah). In addition they expect him to establish the proper rituals for the restoration of the Temple service. Curiously, they describe Elijah as a partner to Moses in God's coming kingdom, the same role that Aaron used to perform during the Exodus. The unanimous opinion of the Jewish Talmudic and the Midrashic literature is that Elijah did not taste death. The Jewish belief in this unusual "rapture" of Elijah is fundamental to their understanding of his unique future role in preparing for the return of the Messiah.

The rabbis teach that Elijah will appear at some point in time (either three days or three years) before the advent of the Messiah. They anticipate that he will appear in Palestine and utter a lament over the devastation of the Holy Land. After Michael the Archangel blows his trumpet, Elijah will introduce the Messiah to the world. The Talmud claims that several wonders will accompany the coming of Elijah and the Messiah: (1) He will bring Moses back to life. (2) He will reveal the secret location of the three holy vessels that mysteriously disappeared: the Ark of the Covenant, the Flask of Manna and the container of sacred anointing oil. (3) He will carry the royal scepter of Judah which God promised "shall not depart from Judah . . . until Shiloh comes" (Genesis 49:10). (4) He will transform the geography of the Holy Land, leveling the mountains.

They claim that the fulfillment of these predictions will lead all of Israel to believe that Elijah is truly the prophet promised by the Bible. They teach that, after these prophecies are fulfilled, Israel will believe that the Messiah has truly come. Another curious belief of the rabbis is that Elijah will be one of the eight princes that will form the cabinet of the Messiah. Additionally, they tell us that Elijah will restore the tribal identities of the Jews.

There is a Talmudic tradition that Elijah will flee from Satan into the desert with "the rest of the righteous." Then, after a stay of forty-five days, they will return with the Messiah to begin the age of redemption.

This mention of forty-five days is interesting because that is the precise time difference between the 1290 day period and the 1335 day period recorded in Daniel 12:12. The prophet states, "Blessed is he who waits, and comes to the one thousand three hundred and thirty-five days." Jewish sages such as Joseph ha-Levi and Nahmanides discuss the anointing of the Messiah by the prophet Elijah. Maimonides, the greatest Jewish teacher, wrote that Elijah will appear at some point in time before the coming of the Messiah: "Before the War of Gog and Magog, a prophet will arise to rectify Israel's conduct and prepare their hearts [for the redemption]" (Mishneh Torah, Hilchos Melachim 12:2).

Many commentators suggest that Enoch will be the second of the two witnesses. The main reason appears to be that Enoch was the only other person, besides Elijah, who was "raptured" to heaven without dying. Elijah, who is definitely one of the two witnesses, was raptured according to 2 Kings 2:11: "Suddenly a chariot of fire appeared with horses of fire, and separated the two of them; and Elijah went up by a whirlwind into heaven." They interpret Hebrews 9:27, "It is appointed for men to die once, but after this the judgment," as meaning that every single human must "die once." Since Enoch and Elijah both missed death the first time, they conclude that they must come back to earth and die. However, every Christian who is alive when Christ comes at the Rapture will never "die once." As Paul promised, "We shall not all sleep, but we shall all be changed" (1 Corinthians 15:51). The Bible also records a number of humans who died twice. These people were miraculously raised to life after dying once—Lazarus, Jairus's daughter, and the daughter of the ruler of the synagogue. Each of these was raised to life to prove the power of Christ over death, but years later they ultimately died a second time. Hebrews 9:27 is a general statement regarding the normal events for the vast majority of men, not an absolute and universal statement demanding that all men "die once." Also, since Enoch, who lived before the Flood, was not a Jew and had no connection with Israel, there is little evidence to indicate that Enoch will return as one of the two witnesses.

After many years of study, my conclusion is that Moses will almost certainly join Elijah as the second of God's two witnesses. The reasons for identifying Moses as the second witness are quite strong although we should not be dogmatic about this. Students of prophecy will differ in their conclusions on some prophetic details regarding future events. In several of these areas, only the fulfillment of the prophecy will reveal the answer. Until they are fulfilled, a humble attitude of earnest searching is appropriate. Moses was Israel's great leader and lawgiver. Therefore it is natural to think of Moses in this role as a witness to Israel and the world about the coming Messiah. Both Elijah and Moses were Old Testament prophets of judgment who exercised miraculous power from God to authenticate their message and destroy their enemies. There are many similarities between the ten plagues associated with Moses during the Exodus and the future judgments connected with the two witnesses during the Tribulation. Although Moses was not raptured to heaven like Elijah, there is a mystery concerning the fate of his body. It was never found because God, in His infinite wisdom, hid it. Deuteronomy 34:6 records, "And He buried him in a valley in the land of Moab, opposite Beth Peor; but no one knows his grave to this day." This prevented the Jews from falling into idolatry surrounding his tomb. Satan was very interested in Moses' body and fought to capture it, "Yet Michael the archangel, in contending with the devil, when he disputed about the body of Moses, dared not bring against him a reviling accusation, but said, 'The Lord rebuke you!' " (Jude 9). There is a mystery about this matter that we will not fully understand until Christ returns.

The method which both the archangel Michael and Jesus Christ dealt with Satan provides specific warning on how we should respond to attacks from the devil. Sometimes we hear speakers mock Satan and speak casually about this deadly enemy of our soul. Satan remains powerful although he is a fallen archangel. The Bible warns us to treat Satan in the same prudent manner Christ used in His confrontation with him. "Then Jesus said unto them, 'Away with you, Satan! For it is written, "You shall worship the Lord your God, and Him only you shall serve" ' " (Matthew 4:10). If our Lord Jesus Christ quoted Scripture to Satan rather than mock him, we should follow His example.

One of the strongest proofs supporting Moses as one of the two witnesses lies in his appearance with Elijah on the Mount of Transfiguration testifying to Jesus as the Messiah. Only six days before, Christ prophesied to his disciples, "Assuredly, I say to you, there are some standing here who shall not taste death till they see the Son of Man coming in His kingdom" (Matthew 16:28). A few days later Christ's words were fulfilled when He took three of those same disciples up to a mountain where he "was transfigured before them. His face shone like the sun, and His clothes became as white as the light. And behold, Moses and Elijah appeared to them, talking with Him" (Matthew 17:2,3). Moses, representing the Law, and Elijah, representing the Prophets, appeared on the Mount of Transfiguration, attesting to Jesus as the Messiah and to His glorious kingdom. As Christ's face shone with the revealed glory of His divine nature, the Law and the Prophets both witnessed to the majesty of Jesus Christ. Moses and Elijah witnessed about Jesus as the coming King during His first advent. It is appropriate that these same two witnesses will again witness to men about His second advent at the end of this age.

"Remember the Law of Moses, My servant, which I commanded him in Horeb for all Israel, with the statutes and judgments. Behold, I will send you Elijah the prophet before the coming of the great and dreadful day of the Lord" (Malachi 4:4,5). This well known prophecy of Malachi not only foretells that Elijah will appear "before the coming of the great and dreadful day of the Lord," it also mentions God's other great leader of Israel, "Moses, My servant." Why would God mention both Elijah and Moses together in this context? Malachi specifically tells them to "Remember the Law of Moses, My servant" connecting Moses with the prophecy of Elijah's return.

Luke 24:4 records that "two men" in "shining garments" appeared to the disciples following the resurrection of Jesus to attest to the fact of His miraculous rising from the dead. Is it possible that these "two men" were actually Moses and Elijah testifying and witnessing about

Jesus? The physician Luke, who wrote his Gospel and the book of Acts, possibly intended to convey that both appearances involved the same two individuals. "And while they looked steadfastly toward heaven as He went up, behold, two men stood by them in white apparel, who also said, 'Men of Galilee, why do you stand gazing up into heaven? This same Jesus, who was taken up from you into heaven, will so come in like manner as you saw Him go into heaven' " (Acts 1:10). Since Luke calls these witnesses "men" some scholars believe that he may be referring to Elijah and Moses, rather than two angels.

One of the Ten Commandments is to, "Honor your father and your mother, that your days may be long upon the land which the Lord your God is giving you" (Exodus 20:12). Malachi prophesied that Elijah will reconcile the hearts of the fathers to their children, saving the earth from God's curse: "Behold, I will send you Elijah the prophet . . . And he will turn the hearts of the fathers to the children, and the hearts of the children to their fathers, lest I come and strike the earth with a curse" (Malachi 4:6). The rabbis interpreted this prophecy to teach that he will reconcile families in preparation for the coming Messianic Era.

Another interpretation of this Malachi passage has to do with the restoration of identities to the Jews. Ezekiel 48:1–29 tells us that, in the Millennium, God will divide the land of Israel into twelve allotments (as outlined in my earlier book MESSIAH). When the Roman army of Titus burned the Temple on that disastrous ninth day of Av, A.D. 70, along with God's sanctuary they destroyed the voluminous Temple archives and the genealogical records of Jewish tribes and families. In the decades from the Resurrection until that infamous day in A.D. 70, Christians pointed to these genealogical records as proof that Jesus of Nazareth was the legitimate successor to the throne of King David, as Matthew and Mark both recorded. Since that day two thousand years ago, only the tribe of Levi, those Jews whose names are Levi or Cohen, can prove their correct tribal lineage. The Kohanim, "the sons of Aaron," are Levites descended from Aaron, Moses' brother, who were given special duties in Temple worship services. How will the land be divided into tribal allotments if the Jews do not know their tribal lineage? Jewish rabbis interpret Malachi's declaration that Elijah "will turn the hearts of the fathers to the children, and the hearts of the children to their fathers," as meaning that Elijah will restore the tribal identities as part of his prophetic mission to prepare Israel for their coming Messiah.

When the Jews returned to Israel after seventy years of captivity in Babylon in 536 B.C. the genealogical records were incomplete. This presented a severe problem because the leaders could not affirm the identity of some of the returning captives who claimed they were from priestly families. These exiled priests "sought their listing among those who were registered by genealogy, but they were not found; therefore they were excluded from the priesthood as defiled. And the governor said to them that they should not eat of the most holy things till a priest could consult with the Urim and with Thummin" (Ezra 2:62,63). This inspired declaration in the book of Ezra predicts that the complete restoration of the Levitical and priestly sacrifice system will not occur "till a priest could consult with the Urim and with Thummin."

This prophecy may relate to the future role of Elijah and the miraculous identification of the tribes through the divine use of the restored "Urim and Thummin." The Urim and Thummin was used in the Old Testament by the High Priest to supernaturally reveal the will of God. "He shall stand before Eleazar the priest, who shall inquire before the Lord for him by the judgment of the Urim" (Numbers 27:21). The Talmud speculates that the mysterious Urim and Thummin formed a part of the breastplate of the High Priest. They claim the twelve stones of the breastplate represented the twelve tribes and somehow signaled the answers to questions presented by the High Priest. Some suggest that one of the twelve stones miraculously glowed, indicating God's answer to the question posed by the High Priest.

John's reference in Revelation 11 to the two witnesses being clothed in sackcloth is significant. As a sign that they had renounced the pleasures and comforts of this world, both Elijah and John the Baptist wore sackcloth (a garment made of course material, also worn during mourning). Revelation tells us that the two witnesses of the tribulation period will also be "clothed in sackcloth" as they "prophesy" the coming Kingdom of Christ for 1260 days. Two earlier prophets, Malachi and Zechariah, spoke about these latter-day witnesses. Malachi prophesied that God would send "Elijah the prophet before the coming of the great and dreadful day of the Lord" (4:5). Zechariah described the two end-time witnesses as "two olive trees." The angel showing him the vision explained that these "olive trees" were "the two anointed ones, who stand beside the Lord of the whole earth" (4:3,11,14), referring to the practice of anointing with olive oil those who were separated for service to God. The prophet John identified the two witnesses of his vision as the ones which Zechariah spoke of some five hundred years earlier, "These are the two olive trees . . . standing before the God of the earth" (Revelation 11:4).

THE 144,000 JEWISH WITNESSES

In addition to the two witnesses, God will select 144,000 Jewish witnesses from the twelve tribes of Israel to reach the world with His call to repentance from sin. "And I heard the number of those who were sealed. One hundred and forty four thousand of all the tribes of the children of Israel were sealed: of the tribe of Judah twelve thousand were sealed; of the tribe of Reuben twelve thousand were sealed; of the tribe of Gad twelve thousand were sealed; of the tribe of Asher twelve thousand were sealed; of the tribe of Naphtali twelve thousand were sealed; of the tribe of Manasseh twelve thousand were sealed; of the tribe of Simeon twelve thousand were sealed; of the tribe of Levi twelve thousand were sealed; of the tribe of Issachar twelve thousand were sealed; of the tribe of Zebulon twelve thousand were sealed; of the tribe of Joseph twelve thousand were sealed; of the tribe of Benjamin twelve thousand were sealed" (Revelation 7:4–8).

These 144,000 Jewish witnesses will be supernaturally "sealed" by the angels to protect them against the coming judgments of God upon the earth and the sea. "Then I saw another angel ascending from the east, having the seal of the living God. And he cried with a loud

voice to the four angels to whom it was granted to harm
the earth and the sea, saying, 'Do not harm the earth, the
sea, or the trees till we have sealed the servants of our
God on their foreheads' " (Revelation 7:2–3). Throughout
the Bible we see that God always differentiates between
the righteous and the unrighteous in terms of His wrath
and judgment. The Lord never pours out His wrath upon
the righteous. To prove His righteous judgment, God will
hold back the angels that are prepared to pour out the
judgments to "harm" the earth and sea until they place
the divine protection of the seal of God on the foreheads
of these 144,000 Jewish witnesses, supernaturally protecting them during this terrible persecution.

In Numbers 31 we read about a similar example of
God's divine protection of Israel. God chose one thousand
Israelites from each of the twelve tribes to fight against
the fierce army of the Midianites. "So there were recruited from the divisions of Israel one thousand from
each tribe, twelve thousand armed for war" (Numbers
31:5). These twelve thousand Jewish soldiers won an astonishing victory due to God's supernatural protection. At
the end of the battle the officers counted the Israelite survivors and discovered that every single warrior had returned alive. "They said to Moses, 'Your servants have
taken a count of the men of war who are under our command, and not a man of us is missing' " (Numbers
31:49).

As we have already shown, God will not use the
Church to witness during the Tribulation because the
Christians will already be raptured at this point in time.
However, God will never leave the world in spiritual
darkness. So after the Church is gone, God will call
twelve thousand from each of the twelve tribes of Israel to
witness to the nations about their coming King. God had
originally given His Chosen People the command to be a
"light to the Gentiles." Jewish rabbis were famous in that
period for seeking Gentile proselytes who would reject paganism and join themselves to the Jewish synagogue. Jesus
referred to the successful missionary efforts of the Phari-
sees during the first century of this era, "for you travel
land and sea to win one proselyte" (Matthew 23:15). The
New Testament record refers to numerous Gentiles

throughout the Roman Empire who abandoned paganism and, like Cornelius, joined the Jewish synagogue. There was a Court of the Gentiles in the Jewish Temple because God had commanded Israel to be "a light unto the Gentiles." Tragically, Israel became spiritually isolationist and generally failed in that great mission. A great number of the early converts to Christianity came from this Gentile group in the synagogues. After Israel's rejection of Jesus as their Messiah the Lord created a Gentile and Jewish Christian Church to reach the world with the "good news," the gospel of Jesus Christ.

The great Jewish scholar Moses Maimonides declared that the tribal identity of each Jew will be revealed during the era of the Messiah. "During the Era of the King Mashiach . . . the entire line of descent will be established on the basis of his words . . . He will define the lineage of the Israelites according to their tribe alone; i.e., he will make known each person's tribal origin, stating that "This one is from one tribe" and "This one is from another tribe" (*Hilchos Melachim* 12:3).

THE MISSING TRIBE OF DAN

Bible scholars have long noticed that the listing of the twelve tribes making up Israel's 144,000 witnesses in Revelation 7:1–8 does not include the tribe of Dan. This tribe will not be divinely protected or used as a witness during the Great Tribulation. In order to make up the full list of twelve tribes as recorded in Revelation 7, the Lord included the priestly tribe of Levi. The tribe of Levi is normally not listed with the other tribes because the Levites had special priestly duties and rewards. What would cause the Lord to drop the tribe of Dan from the list of twelve tribes to witness to the world? Although the Bible does not specifically tell us the reason, there are several possibilities. The most likely reason is that the tribe of Dan allowed itself to become a center of idolatry in ancient times. Jereboam made two calves of gold and placed one in Dan and the other in Bethel following the division of the nation into Judah and Israel (1 Kings 12:26–30). The people of Dan worshiped these idols. Since God hates idol worship, possibly He will not allow the tribe of Dan to participate in witnessing with the other tribes as a specific judgment for its ancient sin. Another less likely possibility is that the Antichrist or the false prophet will come from the tribe of Dan. God may judge the tribe of Dan because of this. However, the tribe of Dan will finally be restored to God's favor in the Millennium. Ezekiel 47 and 48 provides a prophetic vision of the future division of the land of Israel during the Millennium. Ezekiel's vision reveals that the first and most northerly portion of land will be allotted to the tribe of Dan.

THE WITNESSES IN HEAVEN

"Then I looked, and behold, a Lamb standing on Mt. Zion, and with Him one hundred and forty-four thousand, having His Father's name written on their foreheads. . . . and they sang, as it were a new song before the throne, before the four living creatures, and the elders; and no one could learn that song except the one hundred and forty-four thousand who were redeemed from the earth. These are the ones who are not defiled with women, for they are virgins. These are the ones who follow the Lamb wherever He goes. These were redeemed from among men, being first fruits to God and to the Lamb. And in their mouth was found no guile, for they are without fault before the throne of God" (Revelation 14:1,3–5).

After witnessing the 144,000 Jewish witnesses being sealed by God to protect them on the earth during the Tribulation, John reveals that the 144,000 will be taken to the throne of heaven to worship the Lord. Some writers suggest that these are two separate groups of people. However, the whole tenor of the book of Revelation strongly suggests that John is describing the same 144,000 Jewish witnesses. The first vision (chapter 7) describes them in their role on earth. John's second vision (chapter 14) describes these same witnesses after they have been supernaturally "raptured" to heaven. The fact that the specific number 144,000 is used for both groups provides the strongest indication that the same people are involved in both visions. John's phrase explaining that they "were redeemed from the earth" and "redeemed from among men" confirms that these 144,000 are the same men we read about in Revelation 7.

In Revelation 14 the 144,000 in heaven are described as "not defiled with women, for they are virgins." This phrase could legitimately refer to righteous Jewish men from the twelve tribes that have been specially chosen by God to witness to the nations. The phrase "virgins" and "undefiled" does not necessarily demand that these 144,000 be unmarried men. The sense of the passage is that they are morally and sexually pure of sinful relations with women. Since "the marriage bed is undefiled" it is possible that these are faithful, married Jewish followers of the Messiah.

THE THREE ANGELIC MESSENGERS

"Then I saw another angel flying in the midst of heaven, having the everlasting gospel to preach to those who dwell on the earth —to every nation, tribe, tongue, and people—saying with a loud voice, 'Fear God and give glory to Him, for the hour of His judgment has come; and worship Him who made heaven and earth, the sea and springs of water.' And another angel followed, saying, 'Babylon is fallen, is fallen, that great city, because she has made all nations drink of the wine of the wrath of her fornication.' Then a third angel followed them, saying with a loud voice, 'If anyone worships the beast and his image, and receives his mark on his forehead or on his hand, he himself shall also drink of the wine of the wrath of God, which is poured out full strength into the cup of His indignation. And he shall be tormented with fire and brimstone in the presence of the holy angels and in the presence of the Lamb' " (Revelation 14:6–10).

In addition to the two witnesses and the 144,000 Jewish witnesses, Revelation declares that God will send three angels during the Great Tribulation to warn men to repent and turn from their sinful rebellion. Over the centuries many saints have wondered why God didn't simply send His angels to proclaim His Holiness by miraculously appearing in the sky to proclaim the words of God. During the terrors of the Tribulation, God will finally declare His message through angelic messengers that cannot be ignored by sinful men.

The first angel will fly "in the midst of heaven, having the everlasting gospel to preach to those who dwell on the earth—to every nation, tribe, tongue, and people" (Revelation 14:6). The phrase "in the midst of heaven" indicates the second heaven, the atmosphere close to the earth. Flying close enough to the earth to be visible to mankind, this first angel will preach the same gospel of the kingdom to mankind that will be preached by the two witnesses and the 144,000. The supernatural messenger will proclaim in "a loud voice" that men must "fear God and give glory to Him, for the hour of His judgment has come." While the Church calls men to forgiveness of sins, this angel, knowing there is little time left, will preach that the "hour of His judgment has come."

The second angel will follow proclaiming, "Babylon is fallen, is fallen, that great city, because she has made all nations drink of the wine of the wrath of her fornication" (verse 8). Flying in the midst of the heavens, this angel will proclaim the final destruction of the literal city of Babylon. The city will become a towering inferno of fire and smoke when the seventh vial judgment is poured out from heaven. Babylon, which is being rebuilt by Saddam Hussein and the Iraqi government today, will become one of the three capitals of the Prince of Darkness during the Tribulation. From the earliest history of man recorded in Genesis, Babylon has been the center of opposition to God. As the center of witchcraft and Satan worship during the reign of Antichrist, God will utterly destroy it during the Great Day of the Lord.

The third angel will follow the other two angels and cry out with a loud voice to warn those living in the kingdom of Antichrist against receiving the Mark of the Beast. The angel warns, "If anyone worships the beast and his image, and receives his mark on his forehead, or on his hand, he himself shall also drink of the wrath of God" (Revelation 14:9–10). The Lord's declaration about the fate of those who reject His command is final. The third angel declares, "He shall be tormented with fire and brimstone in the presence of the holy angels, and in the presence of the Lamb. And the smoke of their torment ascends up forever and ever" (Revelation 14:10,11).

Many theologians have searched the Scriptures in an attempt to discover verses that would support their views that those who reject God's mercy might be either annihilated or placed in hell for a limited period of time. However, the clear and consistent teaching of the Bible, as we read in the above passage, Revelation 14:10,11, is that the punishment of sinners who refuse God's salvation is an eternity in hell. Jesus Christ spoke about the horrors of hell far more than He spoke about the glories of heaven. Jesus paid the awesome price of His crucifixion on the Cross because He knows that the destiny of unrepentant men and women will be an eternity in hell.

The Great Multitude

"After these things I looked, and behold, a great multitude which no one could number, of all nations, tribes, peoples, and tongues, standing before the throne and before the Lamb, clothed with white robes, with palm branches in their hands, and, . . . 'these are the ones that come out of the great tribulation, and washed their robes and made them white in the blood of the Lamb' " (Revelation 7:9,14).

Israel, after the Rapture, will be given a final opportunity to become "a light to the Gentiles" and their fellow Jews with their faithful witness to their coming King. Revelation 7:9 tells us about the tremendous spiritual response throughout the world to the message of these 144,000 witnesses, the two witnesses and the three angelic witnesses. John saw a "great multitude which no one could number, of all nations, tribes, peoples, and tongues." The angel told him that these came "out of the great tribulation," indicating that this huge group of future saints are the Gentile and Jewish tribulation saints who responded to the gospel of the Kingdom proclaimed during the Great Tribulation: "Repent, the Kingdom of God is at hand." This fascinating verse in Revelation 7:9 affirms that believers will retain our individual and group identities in heaven. John describes them as coming from "all nations, tribes, peoples, and tongues."

"And those of the people who understand shall instruct many; yet for many days they shall fall by sword and flame, by captivity and plundering" (Daniel 11:33). Daniel's fascinating prophecy reveals that, even in the horrors of the Great Tribulation, there will be men of God who will understand the prophecies being fulfilled around them. They will "instruct many" because one of the major purposes of end time prophecy is to evangelize and uphold the faith of those tribulation saints who "will endure till the end."

17

The False Prophet and the Prince of Darkness

The prophet John, in describing his symbolic vision recorded in Revelation 13, talks about two terrible "beasts." John watched as the first beast rose from the sea. It had seven heads and ten horns, with crowns on each horn. Inscribed on his head was a blasphemous name. The first beast is the Antichrist, the Prince of Darkness. Then John describes a second beast, this one "coming up out of the earth, and he had two horns like a lamb" but "spoke like a dragon." This second beast "exercises all the authority of the first beast in his presence, and causes the earth and those who dwell in it to worship the first beast, whose deadly wound was healed" (Revelation 13:11–12). The Bible calls the second beast the False Prophet (Revelation 16:13; 19:20; 20:10).

THE IDENTITY OF THE FALSE PROPHET

The False Prophet is one of the most mysterious of all the personages encountered in Bible prophecy. The Scriptures tell us little about his origin, his country, his parents, or his career up to the point when he joins forces with the

Prince of Darkness, the Antichrist. John reveals that this second beast will support the Antichrist in his rise to world political supremacy. Some commentators have suggested that the False Prophet may not be an actual person but a symbol for evil religious power. However, a close examination of Revelation 13:11 reveals that John uses the Greek term *allos theerion*, which means "another beast" of the same kind and nature as the first beast which came out of the sea. The first beast is specifically called a man in Revelation 13:18, "Calculate the number of the beast, for it is the number of a man: His number is 666." Since the first beast is called a "man" the second beast must also be a living man. In addition, personal pronouns are used by John to describe both individuals.

HE WILL BE LIKE ELIJAH

Malachi, the last prophetic book in the Old Testament, reveals that God will send a special "messenger of the covenant" who will "prepare the way before Me" (Malachi 3:1). The prophet explains that God will send "Elijah the prophet" before the Messiah comes (4:5). As a result of this prophecy the Jewish people have anticipated Elijah's appearance as the major sign of Messiah's approach. This explains why the Jews asked both John the Baptist and Jesus if they were the prophet Elijah. This expectation regarding Elijah is reflected in the Jewish legends found in the Talmud concerning the miracles and supernatural deeds of Elijah that will usher in the messianic era.

These questions revealed that the Jews in the first century clearly expected the appearance of Elijah the Prophet to precede the coming of their promised Messiah. It is fascinating to compare the Jewish expectations of Elijah with the prophecy in Revelation about the False Prophet's activities. "Then I saw another beast coming up out of the earth, and he had two horns like a lamb and spoke like a dragon. And he exercises all the authority of the first beast in his presence, and causes the earth and those who dwell in it to worship the first beast, whose deadly wound was healed. He performs great signs, so that he even makes fire come down from heaven on the earth in the sight of men. And he deceives those who dwell on the earth by those signs which he was granted to do in the sight of the beast, telling those who dwell on the earth to make an image to the beast who was wounded by the sword and lived" (Revelation 13:11–14). This will be the most successful propaganda and disinformation campaign in history.

Tragically the vast majority of people on earth after the Rapture will be deceived by the False Prophet and the Antichrist. These people will believe their lies and, ultimately, lose their eternal souls. Our Lord warned of the incredibly deceptive efforts of the Antichrist and said, "For false christs and false prophets will arise and show great signs and wonders, so as to deceive, if possible, even the elect" (Matthew 24:24). Notice that Jesus said, "if possible." The elect (the tribulation believers, Jews and Gentiles) will not be deceived, but Christ forewarned us of Satan's powerful deception.

John's description of the second beast coming "up out of the earth" leads many scholars to believe that this refers to his Jewish origin in the Holy Land, ancient Palestine. The False Prophet must be a Jew to be accepted by the Jewish people as the prophet Elijah. No Jewish rabbi or layman would accept a Gentile as the prophet Elijah. This phrase about "coming up out of the earth" does not indicate that the False Prophet is a reincarnated man, as some suggest. Revelation describes these two evil individuals as normal men who will surrender themselves entirely to the power of Satan. After living a sinful and wicked life, the Antichrist and False Prophet will sell their souls in return for Satan's promise to give them the kingdoms of this world. These wicked men will be destroyed at the hands of Jesus Christ at His triumphant victory at Armageddon. The apostle Paul tells us, "Then the lawless one will be revealed, whom the Lord will consume with the breath of His mouth and destroy with the brightness of His coming" (2 Thessalonians 2:8).

He Is a Deceiver

The False Prophet, the second person in the satanic trinity that will arise in the last days, will imitate the role of the Holy Spirit. He will force men to worship the Prince of Darkness just as the Holy Spirit directs our worship to Jesus Christ, the Kings of kings. Just as God the Father gives power to the Son and to the Holy Spirit, Satan will seek to imitate the Most High God by giving power to the Antichrist and his False Prophet. The title of "False Prophet" reminds us of the warning Christ gave His disciples during His extended prophecy on the Mount of Olives about the signs of His return. "Jesus answered and said unto them, 'Take heed that no one deceive you. For many will come in My name, saying, I am the Christ, and will deceive many. . . . Then many false prophets will rise up and deceive many'" (Matthew 24:4,5,11). The first prophetic warning sign of the end of the age will be the appearance of many false Christs and false prophets. Warnings are given throughout the Old and New Testaments to beware of false prophets who would seek to deceive men by claiming, "Thus says the Lord," but they are imposters. Christ warned us to test the spirits in these last days to see if they truly are from God.

John described the False Prophet as having "two horns like a lamb, yet he spoke like a dragon," describing the spiritual deception that will characterize this man. He will attempt to deceive men by appearing to be gentle as a lamb. His true purpose will be the destruction of mankind. The power of the False Prophet will be derived directly from Satan who will totally possess this man, as John revealed in Revelation 13:11: "He . . . spoke as a dragon [Satan]." He will "exercise all the power of the first beast," the Antichrist, and will deceive billions of people through his satanic power. He "causes the earth and those who dwell in it to worship the first beast, whose deadly wound was healed."

HE WILL PERFORM SIGNS AND
MIRACLES

The False Prophet "deceives those who dwell on the earth
by those signs which he was granted to do in the sight of
the beast." It is fascinating to compare the Jewish expectations of Elijah with the description in Revelation about
activities of the False Prophet. John wrote that "he performs great signs, so that he even makes fire come down
from heaven on the earth in the sight of men" (Revelation
13:13). This unique miracle was performed by Elijah the
prophet. Second Kings 1:10 records that when King Ahab
sent his military officers to arrest the prophet, "Elijah answered and said to the captain of fifty, 'If I am a man of
God, then let fire come down from heaven and consume
you and your fifty men.' And fire came down from
heaven and consumed him and his fifty." The satanic
counterfeit of Elijah's miracle by the False Prophet will deceive many Jews into believing that he is truly Elijah the
prophet. Satan will use the Jewish expectation of Elijah to
encourage many to accept the false messianic claims of the
Antichrist. The False Prophet's satanic miracles will lend
credibility to his diabolical claims that the Antichrist is
their long-awaited Messiah. The true Elijah will direct the
worship of men towards the real Messiah, Jesus Christ.
Similarly, the False Prophet will not accept worship himself, but will direct men to worship the Antichrist, the first
beast.

Jesus warned that the last days will produce an evil
and adulterous generation that will seek miracles and
signs as proof of the identity of the Messiah. He uses the
word "adulterous" to characterize both their immorality
and their spiritual unfaithfulness to God. Despite fulfillment of hundreds of specific Old Testament messianic
prophecies the vast majority of the Jews and Gentiles still
rejected His claims. However, Jesus warned that this final
evil generation will be deceived through its dependence on
"signs" and its willingness to follow the satanic miracles
of the False Prophet. There is a growing tendency for
many in the Church today to seek after "experiences"
rather than rely on the great truths of God's Word. This
phenomenon is an indication that our world will be easily

deceived by the "signs and wonders" of the Antichrist. The Bible wisely warns, "Beloved, do not believe every spirit, but test the spirits, whether they are of God; because many false prophets have gone out into the world" (1 John 4:1). While Christians rejoice in true miracles that glorify God, Christ warned of counterfeit "signs and wonders," in the last days, especially those that glorify someone other than God. We should remember God's words, "I am the Lord, that is My name; and My glory I will not give to another, not My praise to graven images" (Isaiah 42:8). When you evaluate a ministry, ask yourself this question—who is receiving glory—this man, or Christ?

THE ROLE OF THE FALSE PROPHET

The False Prophet will become a world leader in religious affairs. He will arise suddenly to prepare the way for his partner, the Prince of Darkness, to appear publicly. John the Baptist appeared in public to prepare the way for Jesus to minister publicly. Unlike John, the False Prophet will perform miracles. However, the False Prophet's miraculous power will be limited to whenever he is in the direct line of sight of the Antichrist. Although Satan is a powerful fallen angel, he is still quite limited in power compared to the overwhelming power of Jesus Christ. Satan is not omnipresent like God. He is only a created and powerful cherubim, a fallen angel of God. After the Antichrist is killed and rises from death through Satan's power, the False Prophet will demand that all men worship the Prince of Darkness as god. When Satan is cast out of heaven to the earth at the mid-point of the seven year treaty period, he will totally possess the souls and bodies of the Antichrist and his False Prophet. This will produce an enormous increase in their demonic supernatural power to persecute those who resist them. The False Prophet will not accept mens' worship himself, but he will demand that people worship his leader, the Antichrist. His power will come directly from Satan, who also possesses the soul of Antichrist.

THE IMAGE OF THE BEAST

The False Prophet will tell "those who dwell on the earth to make an image to the beast who was wounded by the sword and lived" (Revelation 13:14). The resurrection of the Antichrist marks a major change in the careers of these evil individuals. From this point on they become totally possessed by Satan as no men have ever been possessed. The Second Beast "was granted power to give breath to the image of the beast, that the image of the beast should both speak and cause as many as would not worship the image of the beast to be killed" (Revelation 13:15). There is something mysterious, evil, and supernatural connected to the creation of this "image." It cannot be a normal computer or robot. Otherwise men would not be overwhelmed by it. Satan will give the False Prophet the supernatural ability to animate this statue or image. Men will be forced to worship this "image of the beast" as "god" or they will lose their lives. In some supernatural manner, this "image" will both speak and cause the destruction of men who refuse to worship the image. Thousands of years of idolatry and idol worship will culminate in this diabolical creation of Satan, the "image of the beast." The idolatry that has afflicted mankind throughout his history will return in the last days. Idolatry will be the central feature of the worship system of the Antichrist. In this regard, the startling and pervasive growth of the worldwide New Age movement in our generation is very significant. The New Age, in all its guises, with its obvious idolatry, aims at the establishment of Oriental and Hindu worship symbols. New Age rituals and philosophy are based on pantheistic worship of ourselves and the earth itself while encompassing ancient pagan worship rituals.

The False Prophet will be the head of the satanic religion of the Great Tribulation. He will force people to join in the worship of Satan in the person of the Antichrist. The wealth of the world in gold, silver, and precious stones will be committed to buildings and rituals honoring Satan and his earthly agent, the Antichrist. "He shall regard neither the God of his fathers nor the desire of women, nor regard any god; for he shall magnify himself above them all. But in their place he shall honor a god of fortresses; and a god which his fathers did not know he shall honor with gold and silver, with precious stones and pleasant things" (Daniel 11:37–38).

The closing days of this age will witness an unparalleled revival of idol worship and satanic rituals involving demons. Only two decades ago such a statement would have seemed absurd. However, the rise of open worship of Satan and a growing fascination with the occult characterize our generation. The prophet John warned that men would persist in idolatry and Satan worship despite the wrath of God being poured out on unrepentant sinners. "But the rest of mankind, who were not killed by these plagues, did not repent of the works of their hands, that they should not worship demons, and idols of gold, silver, brass, stone, and wood, which can neither see nor hear nor walk; and they did not repent of their murders or their sorceries or their sexual immorality of their thefts" (Revelation 9:20–21).

THE FALSE PROPHET AND THE MARK OF THE BEAST

"And he causes all, both small and great, rich and poor, free and slave, to receive a mark on their right hand or on their foreheads, and that no one may buy or sell except one who has the mark or the name of the beast, or the number of his name" (Revelation 13:16,17). Religious persecution will be relentless throughout the last seven years leading up to Armageddon. The false church, the Mother of Harlots, Babylon, will persecute the tribulation saints during the first three-and-a-half years of the seven-year treaty period. However, following the Antichrist's death and resurrection, the False Prophet will introduce the Mark of the Beast forcing all citizens to worship the Antichrist if they want to "buy or sell." The diabolical Mark of the Beast system will be introduced to enforce the satanic worship of the Antichrist. The Bible warns that anyone who accepts the satanic Mark of the Beast will "drink the wine of the wrath of God." Throughout history men and women of God have paid with their lives when they resisted spiritual tyranny and the evil madness of men who claimed to be "god." Christ promises those who reject the worship of the Antichrist and his Mark that they will receive eternal glory and honor from God. "And I saw thrones, and they sat on them, and judgment was committed to them. And I saw the souls of those who had been beheaded for their witness to Jesus and for the word of God, who had not worshiped the beast or his image, and had not received his mark on their foreheads or on their hands. And they lived and reigned with Christ for a thousand years" (Revelation 20:4). In the next chapter of this book we will explore the Mark of the Beast system in great detail.

He Will Persecute Those Who Resist

During the last 1260 days of the satanic power of the Antichrist, the False Prophet will persecute all who resist the worship of Satan. The Antichrist will plot to "make war with the saints and to overcome them" (Revelation 13:7). Blasphemy against the true God in heaven will characterize the speeches of Antichrist because he hates God and His true followers. The Antichrist will "magnify himself above them all" in his overwhelming and sinful pride. John tells us that the second beast will "cause as many as would not worship the image of the beast to be killed" (Revelation 13:15). The forces of the Antichrist will "shed the blood of saints and prophets" (Revelation 16:6). The religious terror of the Tribulation will exceed the horrors of Roman paganism or the Spanish Inquisition. Those saints who reject being marked will be tortured and beheaded for their faith in God. "And I saw the souls of those who had been beheaded for their witness to Jesus and for the word of God, who had not worshiped the beast or his image, and had not received his mark on their foreheads or on their hands" (Revelation 20:4). Despite the horrors of the persecution, millions of people will choose martyrdom by rejecting the Mark of the Beast. John described "a great multitude that no man could number" who "came out of great tribulation"

(Revelation 7:9). They will be washed in the blood of the Lamb of God and will "come out" by the thousands daily as they are martyred to heaven for their faith in Christ.

The Antichrist will organize the religious persecution of those who reject this Mark. Daniel prophesied that the Antichrist, "was making war against the saints, and prevailing against them, until the Ancient of Days came, and a judgment was made in favor of the saints of the most High, and the time came for the saints to possess the kingdom" (Daniel 7:21,22). The duration of this satanic warfare against these tribulation saints will be limited to 1260 days. "He shall speak pompous words against the Most High, shall persecute the saints of the Most High, and shall intend to change times and law. Then the saints shall be given into his hand for a time and times and half a time" (Daniel 7:25). Throughout this terrible persecution the tribulation saints will rely on the unbreakable promises of God. Finally, the persecution will end when Jesus Christ defeats the Antichrist and False Prophet at the Battle of Armageddon. Despite the horrors of the coming religious persecution, the promise of God is that the Antichrist's power over the tribulation saints will be utterly destroyed at the return of Christ.

HE WILL SEND THE WORLD TO WAR

"And I saw three unclean spirits . . . spirits of demons, . . . which go out to the kings of the earth and of the whole world, to gather them to the battle of that great day of God Almighty" (Revelation 16:13,14). Toward the end of the 1260 days of the Great Tribulation three "spirits of demons, performing signs" will supernaturally call the kings of the earth to "gather them to the battle of the great day of the God Almighty." The prophet Joel declared, "Let the nations be wakened, and come up to the Valley of Jehoshaphat; for there I will sit to judge all the surrounding nations" (Joel 3:12). The nations will be called by God to their appointed destiny at the final battle at Armageddon.

The Final Destruction of the False Prophet

After years of persecuting the tribulation saints, the unholy trinity—the Antichrist, the False Prophet, and Satan—have an appointment with destiny to meet their Creator and Judge, the Lord Jesus Christ. Satan's career of sinful rebellion extends back through the mists of time to that day when "iniquity was found in you" (Ezekiel 28:15). The Antichrist and False Prophet will be willing allies of Satan in his final battle for this planet earth and the destruction of the souls of man. Some writers have pointed to an apparent contradiction in the biblical prophecies describing the defeat of the Antichrist and the False Prophet. One passage indicates that these two enemies of God are killed, "I watched till the beast was slain, and its body destroyed, and given to the burning flame" (Daniel 7:11). Another passage declares that they will be "cast alive" into the lake of fire: "The beast was captured, and with him the false prophet who worked signs in his presence, by which he deceived those who received the mark of the beast and those who worshiped his image. These two were cast alive into a lake of fire burning with brimstone" (Revelation 19:20).

How can these apparently contradictory prophecies in Daniel and Revelation be reconciled? The resolution will be found in carefully examining the precise wording of these passages, as the Berean Christians of the first century who "received the word with all readiness, and searched the Scriptures daily to find out whether these things were so" (Acts 17:11). The bodies of the Antichrist and the False Prophet will definitely be killed by the supernatural power of Jesus during the Battle of Armageddon. However, the spirits of these two enemies of God will be consciously alive when they are "cast alive" into the lake of fire. The final destruction of these two terrible enemies of the saints of God will usher in the Kingdom of God as Jesus Christ establishes His Millennial Kingdom.

18

The Technology of the Mark of the Beast

For two thousand years the number 666 has held a special terror because the prophet John predicted that it would be used by the dreaded Antichrist during the Great Tribulation. This number 666 has formed the basis of numerous speculations about its meaning and connection to the mysterious man who will become the Prince of Darkness. In this chapter we will explore the Bible's prophecies about the Mark of the Beast and its use by the False Prophet to enforce the worship of the Antichrist. The False Prophet will control mankind through a system using the Mark of the Beast, the name of the beast, or the number of his name. The book of Revelation declares that these marks will be used to identify the worshipers of the Antichrist from those who reject his claims to be god. "And he causes all, both small and great, rich and poor, free and slave, to receive a mark on their right hand or on their foreheads, and that no one may buy or sell except one who has the mark or the name of the beast, or the number of his name. Here is wisdom. Let him who has understanding calculate the number of the beast, for it is the number of a man: His number is 666" (Revelation 13:16–18).

The term "Mark of the Beast" has held a unique fascination in the minds of men for many centuries. What kind of a mark will it be? It will be a physical mark, probably visible, that the False Prophet will force every man and woman to receive on his right hand or forehead. The mark will be related to both the "name of the beast" as well as the "number of his name"—666. Possession of the mark will indicate that you willingly worship the "beast," the satanic Prince of Darkness. If you do not possess the mark of the Beast, his name, or his number 666, you will be unable to buy or sell during the Great Tribulation. This system was technically impossible until the introduction during the last decade of laser scans, computer chips beneath the skin and computerized financial systems. The diabolical Mark of the Beast system will hold mankind in an invisible economic prison with little hope of escape. The worldwide economic, religious and political system of the last days will be under the direct control of the False Prophet using this Mark of the Beast system. In the past, no matter how horrible the totalitarian control, it was possible for an escaping refugee to bribe a border guard with gold or to buy some food with silver coins. However, the Mark of the Beast system will eliminate money, forcing men to buy and sell through a computerized system requiring each person to possess an individual Mark. The true horror of the coming New World Order is that its global and all-encompassing secret police state will be equipped with the most advanced technology making escape virtually impossible.

THE NUMBER 666

"Let him who has understanding calculate the number of the beast, for it is the number of a man: His number is 666" (Revelation 13:18). The prophet tells the reader to "calculate the number of the beast." In light of this encouragement past students of the Bible can be forgiven for some of the excesses they have committed over the centuries in their attempts to "calculate the number" and discern its true meaning. What did John mean when he said that "it is the number of a man: His number is 666"?

The book of Revelation was written in the Greek language, the common language of the Roman world in the days of Christ. Although the Romans spoke Latin, most educated people, even in Rome, wrote and discussed intellectual matters in the Greek language. The conquest of the known world by Alexander the Great in 320 B.C. established Greek culture and language throughout the ancient civilized world. Centuries later, most educated men still wrote in Greek. One of the curious features of the Greek and Hebrew language is that they do not use the Arabic numerals—1,2,3 et cetera. They express numbers by using the appropriate letter from their alphabet. Each letter of the Greek and Hebrew alphabet serves a dual purpose of both a letter and a number. For example, the letter X stands for the number 600; the letter ξ stands for 60 and the letter ς for 6. Thus, when John recorded "the number of the beast" in Revelation 13:18 in his original manuscript he used these three Greek letters X ξ ς which in Revelation 13:18 are translated as 666.

As a result of this Greek and Hebrew numeric-language system, every single word in these languages is composed of individual letters that also represent numbers. If you add up the numeric value of the six letters that compose the name Jesus in the Greek tongue, the total number equals 888. The value of the letters in the Greek word "Christos" is equal to 1480. Each variation of the name of Jesus: Christos, Savior, Lord, Emmanuel, and Messiah contain letters whose numeric total is a number divisible by eight. The number eight is associated with resurrection as eight souls survived on Noah's Ark and Christ rose on the eighth day. This fascinating phenomenon suggests that God designed these specific names to demonstrate a pattern. This mathematical pattern of cycles and "wheels within wheels" is discussed in more detail in my books *ARMAGEDDON* and *MESSIAH*.

The number 666 indicates that the letters in the Greek form of the name of the Antichrist will add up to 666. There is a slim possibility that his name will equal 666 in the Hebrew language since the Antichrist will be Jewish. The numeric system does not work in English or in languages other than Greek or Hebrew, so it is useless to calculate the values of names in these modern languages. When this wicked man is possessed by Satan he will be revealed as the long prophesied Antichrist.

THE PURPOSE OF THE 666 WARNING

What is God's purpose in prophesying that the future Antichrist will possess a name whose numeric value will be equal to 666? The Lord was providing a warning to the future Jewish and Gentile tribulation saints, giving them a means to identify the Antichrist. Remember that he will present himself to the world as the messiah with "signs and wonders," supernatural powers and satanic deception. The False Prophet will identify the Antichrist as the messiah. Without a warning about the "666" identification of the Antichrist's name, the tribulation saints would be deceived into worshiping this messianic impostor. Jesus warned, "Take heed that no one deceives you. For many will come in My name, saying, 'I am the Christ,' and will deceive many" (Matthew 24:4,5).

THE MARK OF THE BEAST CONTROL SYSTEM

After the Antichrist rises from the dead, the False Prophet "exercises all the authority of the first beast [Antichrist] in his presence, and causes the earth and those who dwell in it to worship the first beast, whose deadly wound was healed" (Revelation 13:12). The resurrection of the Antichrist will usher in the time of terror, the Great Tribulation. He will sit "as God in the temple of God, showing himself that he is God" (2 Thessalonians 2:4). Many Jews and Gentiles will resist his claims of divinity because they will remember the biblical prophecies of the coming Antichrist. But the False Prophet will force the worship of the Antichrist through an ingenious global police control technology that Stalin and Hitler would have envied.

The Bible tells us this 666 system will be forced on all men "rich and poor, bond and free." Automatic teller machines and laser scanning technology such as we see in stores illustrates how easily such a control system could be implemented. Optical scanning devices, including high speed and long distance optical readers, are now regularly used on the highways, toll booths, government buildings, industrial plants, and custom border posts to read your auto license plate. Until the last few decades of technological advances it was difficult to understand how the prophecy of Revelation 13:17 could be fulfilled. Today, advanced computer technology, laser scanning devices and widespread electronic surveillance have made the fulfillment of the 666 Mark of the Beast control system possible for the first time in history. The prophet John declared that "authority was given him over every tribe, tongue, and nation" (Revelation 13:7) indicating that his totalitarian authority will extend throughout the world for at least part of his seven year rule.

This "mark" is not identical with the name or the number 666 because Revelation 13:18 mentions the three as separate items. It will be applied to the right hand or forehead of the individual. The mark may be a physical brand on the skin using the name of the Antichrist or his number 666. Possibly it will be implanted beneath the skin of the right hand or forehead as an invisible bar code or a miniature computer chip. A powerful electronic scanner could detect the implanted chip and read the data unobtrusively. While such a mark will be visible to the scanner, the mark may be invisible to the human eye.

THE NAME OF THE BEAST

The identity of the Antichrist is hidden from us and will only be revealed during the tribulation period. The Mark of the Beast does not directly concern the Church because the prophecies tell us the Rapture will translate the Christians to heaven before the wrath of God is poured out on the sinful rebels who worship the Antichrist. At the midpoint of Daniel's seventieth week the Antichrist will be killed and rise from the dead. He will receive satanic power to oppress the tribulation saints and kill the two witnesses. The Antichrist may change his birth name at that time to a new name, the "name of the beast." In the Old Testament God changed many names of bible characters at moments of crisis to reflect their new spiritual condition: Abram=Abraham, Jacob=Israel, Saul=Paul. In light of the Bible's silence regarding his name, it is worthless and vain speculation to attempt to name the Antichrist before he appears. Where God had drawn a veil, it is presumptuous for a prophecy student to attempt to pull back the veil. The tribulation saints who live through the Great Tribulation will recognize the Antichrist based on his fulfillment of the Bible's prophecies. The final proof will be the correspondence between the numeric value of his name in Greek or Hebrew with the number 666. This revelation was given as God's final warning to the believers of that day to refuse the Mark of the Beast even at the cost of their lives.

Many Greek or Hebrew names correspond to the numeric value 666. In my library of some four thousand books on prophecy and theology I have compiled a list of over 85 different individuals that have been identified as the Antichrist over the centuries. Some writers believe the Antichrist will be some reincarnated leader from the past. Their suggestions include: Nimrod, King Ahab, Judas Iscariot, Julius Caesar, Nero, Vespasian, Titus, and Emperor Hadrian. In recent centuries prophetic speculations have also suggested candidates including: Napoleon, various Popes, Kaiser Wilhelm, Hitler, Mussolini, Kissinger, Gorbachev, King Juan Carlos, Otto von Hapsburg, Saddam Hussein, and David Rockefeller. Obviously, these speculations are as useless and futile as trying to name the date for the Rapture. The 666 identification will only be relevant to the saints living during the Great Tribulation. The value of studying these prophecies lies in the understanding we achieve of the times we live in and how they relate to the rapidly unfolding prophecies of the coming Messiah. In ancient Israel there was a tribe called "the children of Issachar who had understanding of the times, to know what Israel ought to do" (1 Chronicles 12:32). We need to be like the children of Issachar "to understand our times and to know what to do." Today it is vital that Christians understand the prophecies that indicate how close we are to the return of Christ. This knowledge should motivate us to walk in holiness and witness to a generation that is facing an eternity without God.

THE TECHNOLOGY OF THE MARK SYSTEM

As discussed in another chapter a new identification system for animals uses a tiny implantable computer chip the size of a grain of rice. It contains a passive electronic coil that activates a computer chip with 45 billion bits of information. They have successfully implanted tens of thousands of these chips in dogs and cats throughout North America. An electronic scanner triggers the chip to reveal the complete medical information together with the identification of the animal and owner. Obviously this system could be modified in the future for human use by implanting the chip beneath the skin of the right hand or forehead of a human. There are many good arguments for introducing such a system. It would provide fail-safe identification in the case of missing children or adults. Instead of people worrying about losing or forgetting their Personal Identification Number (PIN), the credit card and banking data can be permanently implanted beneath the skin. The government will argue that this system will make our financial systems very efficient and improve personal security.

THE CONSEQUENCES OF WORSHIPING THE ANTICHRIST

The Lord hates the Mark of the Beast because it represents a soul sold out to Satan. When every believer gets to heaven God will place His seal on their forehead signifying His unbreakable convenant with those who accept Christ as the Lord of their lives. If a person accepts the Mark of the Beast his soul will be lost forever. During the Great Tribulation horrible skin infections will afflict those who accept the Mark and worship the Beast. "A foul and loathsome sore came upon the men who had the mark of the beast and those who worshiped his image" (Revelation

16:2). Possibly these sores will be a physical reaction to the implant or brand placed on their forehead or right hand.

In addition to the terrible earthly consequences of accepting the Mark the Bible warns that the worst punishment will come after death for those who worship Satan. The whole "wrath of God" will be poured out on those who reject Christ and choose to worship Satan and his Antichrist as "god." "Then a third angel followed them, saying with a loud voice, 'If anyone worships the beast and his image, and receives his mark on his forehead or on his hand, he himself shall also drink of the wine of the wrath of God, which is poured out full strength into the cup of His indignation. And he shall be tormented with fire and brimstone in the presence of the holy angels and in the presence of the Lamb. And the smoke of their torment ascends forever and ever; and they have no rest day or night, who worship the beast and his image, and whoever receives the mark of his name' " (Revelation 14:9–11).

THE VICTORY OF THE MARTYRS

The tribulation saints who reject the Antichrist's Mark of the Beast will rule the earth and receive the rewards of heaven. "And I saw the souls of those who had been beheaded for their witness to Jesus and for the word of God, who had not worshiped the beast or his image, and had not received his mark on their foreheads or on their hands. And they lived and reigned with Christ for a thousand years" (Revelation 20:4). It will take tremendous courage for the tribulation saints to reject the mark knowing it will mean their death by beheading. However, their choice is the same choice as that faced by all Christian martyrs for the last two thousand years. Christ commanded, "Do not fear those who kill the body but cannot kill the soul. But rather fear Him who is able to destroy both soul and body in hell" (Matthew 10:28). Jesus warned believers, "But whoever denies Me before men, him I will also deny before My Father who is in heaven" (Matthew 10:33). These brave tribulation martyrs are promised a special position in God's millennial government as "they lived and reigned with Christ for a thousand years."

19

The Coming Inquisition

A man-made theocracy is the most dangerous and the worst of all possible governments. If a nation must suffer under a tyrant, it is preferable to endure a money hungry dictator than a religious inquisitor that wants to force all men to worship in a particular way. Eventually the greedy dictator may satisfy his greed. He may even realize at some level that he is in the wrong. However, the tortures inflicted by an inquisitor know no bounds because he is convinced he is absolutely right in his attempts to force his victims to change their religious beliefs. During the Middle Ages a religious tyranny, called the Inquisition, brought about the torture and murder of approximately forty million innocent men, women, and children for the crime of believing that the Papacy was in religious error. Many of those victims were born-again Christians who believed in their right to have the Bible in their own hands. These martyrs rejected the doctrinal errors and practices of the medieval church and tried to live a simple and pure spiritual life based on the Gospels.

The last seven years of this age will witness a new inquisition. After the Rapture, hundreds of millions of tribulation saints will respond to the "gospel of the kingdom." However, they will pay the supreme price of martyrdom for their new faith in God and their rejection of the Antichrist. During the first half of the seven-year treaty, the false church will launch a relentless inquisition against those men and women who choose to follow God.

John describes these martyrs: "When He opened the fifth seal, I saw under the altar the souls of those who had been slain for the word of God and for the testimony which they held" (Revelation 6:9).

THE RISE OF THE FALSE CHURCH

Massive changes in political and social structures are leading mankind to a new synthesis of political/religious power known as the New World Order. The new ecumenical world church, which is forming behind the scenes today is one of the major supporting structures of the coming global government. Their ambition is to absorb all other religious groups into the lowest common denominator religious philosophy. Ultimately this trend will produce a religious empire that will tolerate no interference.

The prophet John described the rise and fall of this religious apostasy as Babylon the Great, the Mother of Harlots. Unlike the true Church, the Bride of Christ, the false church of the tribulation period will be spiritually unfaithful to God and is thus termed the "Mother of Harlots." In ancient times the city of Babylon was the center of false religion based on the rebellious concept that "man is god." This false church is symbolized as a prostitute representing the false religion of the last days. "I saw a woman sitting on a scarlet beast which was full of names of blasphemy, having seven heads and ten horns. . . . And on her forehead a name was written: MYSTERY, BABYLON THE GREAT, THE MOTHER OF HARLOTS AND OF THE ABOMINATIONS OF THE EARTH" (Revelation 17:3,5). John described the false church as being allied with the Antichrist and his ten kingdoms. He warned of an apostate church dedicated to an inquisition against those who resist her false teaching. "I saw the woman, drunk with the blood of the saints and with the blood of the martyrs of Jesus" (Revelation 17:6). During the first half of the seven-year treaty between the Antichrist and Israel, the world church will support the Antichrist in his globalist plans to achieve a New World Order.

THE REVIVAL OF THE BABYLONIAN RELIGIOUS SYSTEM

The reason for identifying the false church with Babylon is that the first organized religious rebellion against God began in ancient Babylon under the rule of Nimrod. Since Nimrod's rebellion, the Tower of Babel, and centuries of spiritual rebellion, Babylon has been a key center for satanic religion. Virtually all of the perversions, heresies, false cults, and New Age religions can trace their roots back to the "mystery religion" of Babylon. When the city was destroyed after Alexander the Great conquered it, the pagan priests and the mystery schools moved westward to establish their satanic rituals in Greece, Egypt, and Rome. The religious title "Pontifex Maximus" was borrowed by the Roman emperors from the pagan religious leaders of Babylon. These mystery schools developed similar satanic initiation rituals and meditation trances whose purpose was to allow a student to "transcend" his human limitations and "become a god." Just as Lucifer sought to "be like the Most High" (Isaiah 14:14), his devoted followers continue to seek a Satanic path to transcendence through mysticism and drug induced trances.

A TALE OF TWO CITIES—TWO BABYLONS IN PROPHECY

Some writers confuse the two Babylons in the book of Revelation. The first Babylon, described in Revelation 17, Mystery Babylon the Great, the Mother of Harlots, represents the apostate church of the last days which will be based in Rome. The second Babylon, referred to in Revelation 18 and Isaiah 13, represents the rebuilt city of Babylon in Iraq. The city of Babylon will become a center of demonic religion and a great commercial power during the tribulation period. Revelation 18 lists thirty different commercial products in the city, proving that John saw an economic power in a great city. Although both entities are called Babylon, they have very different destinies in the events of the last days. Additional proof that these are different entities lies in the prophecies about the destruction of the two Babylons. In Revelation 17:16 John revealed that the apostate Babylonian church will be destroyed by the Antichrist's ten kings at the mid-point of the seven-year-treaty period. "The ten horns which you saw on the beast, these will hate the harlot, make her desolate and naked, eat her flesh and burn her with fire" (Revelation 17:16). On the other hand, the city of Babylon will be destroyed by God during the Great Day of the Lord (Isaiah 13) using fire from heaven just as in the destruction of Sodom and Gomorrah. This annihilation of the city of Babylon will occur 1260 days after the Antichrist destroys the false church.

Today the world is sinking in a cesspool of occult and satanic religious activity. Police forces across the world are faced with baffling torture and mutilation murder cases. They are finding satanic books and paraphernalia at the scenes of many of these violent crimes. Many children claim they were abducted and forced to participate in disgusting satanic rituals involving sexual abuse, cannibalism, and murder. Bookstores sell staggering amounts of New Age, occult, and satanic books in addition to Tarot cards and other methods of fortune telling. Americans spend billions of dollars annually on satanic and occult material. It's time to wake up from our comfortable pews and realize that the final countdown to Armageddon has begun.

THE REBUILDING OF THE CITY OF BABYLON

Saddam Hussein has begun to rebuild the ancient city of Babylon. He and the Iraqi government have spent more than $800 million in rebuilding Nebuchadnezzar's Palace and Temples to the pagan sun god. In my book MESSIAH I pointed out that Saddam, though outwardly a Moslem, is actually a satanist who has sold his soul to the devil. Despite more than fifty known assassination attempts by individual Iraqis who hate him for killing their friends and families, Saddam enjoys satanic protection. Although it is a violation of Islamic law, Saddam has allowed satanic rituals to be performed in Babylon. Every summer he holds a Babylonian Festival to honor the ancient pagan gods. Babylon will become one of the Antichrist's capital cities during the tribulation period. The other two will be Rome and Jerusalem.

THE GREAT ECUMENICAL CHURCH

After the Rapture millions of people left on the earth will join in this huge ecumenical church that will encompass all the great religions and multitudes of cults. The disappearance of millions of born-again Christians in the Rapture will eliminate the only real opponents of the apostate ecumenical church. The World Council of Churches and the National Council of Churches are just two of the ecumenical groups working to break down the divisions between religions. In all the ecumenical discussions of church unity there has always been an underlying agreement that the Church of Rome and its leader, the pope, will be the de facto leader of this emerging worldwide church. This church will have its headquarters in Rome, the capital city of the revived Roman Empire of the Antichrist. "Here is the mind which has wisdom: The seven heads are seven mountains on which the woman sits" (Revelation 17:9). It is significant that all of the ecumenical discussions of the last few decades were based on the assumption that Rome and the papacy will be the formal leader of this new worldwide church.

Four hundred and seventy years after the Reformation many of the formerly Protestant churches are planning to reconcile with Rome and rejoin the church our ancestors "protested" against. Several years ago, Archbishop Runcie, the head of the Church of England, told *Time* magazine that he had given a ring to Pope John Paul II as "an engagement ring" in view of the coming marriage between he Roman Catholic Church and the Church of England. The Church of Rome has not renounced any of the fundamental doctrinal errors that provoked the Protestant Reformation in A.D. 1520. This ecumenical union is being made on the basis of theological compromise by the non-catholic members of the union. Even Catholic theologians admit that John Paul II is the most traditional pope of this last century and the strongest advocate of worship of Mary as the "co-redemtrix" along with Jesus Christ. A process of intense ecumenical dialogue has proceeded quietly during the last twelve years. The church leaders are very close to healing the schism between the Greek and Russian Orthodox Churches and the Church of Rome. Pope John Paul II has met with Buddhist, Muslim, and Jewish religious leaders from around the world. For the first time in history the Vatican has sought to establish ties with these other churches. The pope has engaged in ecumenical religious rituals and services with other religions that would have been unimaginable for any previous pope.

Revelation teaches clearly that the apostate Babylonian church will become an active ally of the Antichrist in his meteoric rise to rule the planet. The collapse of the inefficient communist economic system in Eastern Europe and the former Soviet Union has opened up a tremendous opportunity for John Paul II to seize control of the political and religious agenda of these countries. Their citizens reject both the communist philosophy and the shallow, materialistic goals of popular western culture. Western media and businessmen are flooding these countries with materialistic images and products in an attempt to seduce them into our consumer society. The pope intends to become the guiding spiritual force leading these countries into a new system that is neither communistic nor capitalistic. After growing up under the Nazis and, then, the Marxist communism of the Polish government, Pope John Paul has never favored western capitalism. His goal is to produce a world of Catholic socialism "with a human face."

Mikhail Gorbachev, since leaving his post as president of the USSR, has become an international speaker, writer, and statesman. As the newly appointed chairman of the International Green Cross his popularity ratings are higher than ever. Gorbachev recently admitted in an editorial article in American newspapers that he has carried on an extensive communication with John Paul II for the last decade. They collaborated together secretly on the creation of "this new world civilization." Gorbachev declared, "Now it can be said that everything which took place in

Eastern Europe in recent years would have been impossible without the pope's efforts and the enormous role, including the political role, which he played in the world arena ... Pope John Paul II will play an enormous political role now that profound changes have occurred in European history." Other sources reveal that the pope continues to communicate weekly with other Western political leaders and plays a surprisingly active role behind the scenes in international politics.

Pope John Paul II is making a very conscious bid for the hearts and minds of the workers emerging from decades of stifling communist government in Eastern Europe and Russia. He is asking the people to consider another alternative to the communism they rejected and the capitalism they yearned for. Recently the pope claimed: "The crisis of Marxism does not rid the world of injustices on which it thrived. Capitalism is not the only economic alternative" (*The European*, May 10, 1992). He is looking for a middle way between the opposing ideologies, a Catholic socialist system. Behind the scenes John Paul II is doing everything he can to maximize the role of the Catholic Church throughout Europe and Russia. In Poland the Church is playing a major role in the government of the country. In Hungary the Catholic Church is taking over public schools from the former Marxist government and establishing their own religious teaching programs. He is considered the most conservative pope in this century. He would like to return to the medieval days when Europe was ruled by an unhealthy alliance between the secular authorities and the Catholic Church.

A friend of mine held a fascinating interview in November 1991 with the Catholic writer Malachi Martin, the author of *The Keys of This Blood*. His book explored what he called "the three-way race between Gorbachev, Bush and John Paul II to lead the New World Order." Martin admitted that, since the collapse of the former communist government, John Paul II is working to achieve a theocracy in Poland. Speaking of the former USSR president, Martin said, "Gorbachev is very comfortable. He has his think-tank in Moscow financed by [Chancellor] Kohl of Germany and assured of funds for the future. He has a refuge across the border in Finland

and he has no restraints. The Yeltsin regime will not last ... Gorbachev is sitting pretty. He will surely come back."

Martin, as a long time observer of the Vatican, points out that Catholicism in Europe is moving away from traditional beliefs and embracing a great deal of New Age theology. Speaking about the emerging European super state Martin said, "It will include all the lands occupied by the ancient Romans, but the religion will not be Christianity or Catholicism, Buddhism, Islam, Hinduism or any religion known today. It already has its own religion, if we want to call it that. It is called the New Age ... The environment will be almost deified and sanctified ... The New Age movement is at this moment influencing our present policies. If you listen to Prince Edward or Prince Charles of England, it is very obvious that they speak from a New Age background, and it bodes a lot of trouble for traditional Christianity." The Bible describes the worldwide apostate church of the last days as a tremendously oppressive religious power that will form an unholy alliance with the Antichrist to obtain world power. Many of the major churches today are totally committed to a New Age agenda that includes a plan to achieve religious unity as part of the New World Order.

THE DESTINY OF THE FALSE CHURCH

The seventeenth chapter of Revelation foretells the terrifying destiny of this satanic apostate church of the last days. "And the ten horns which you saw on the beast, these will hate the harlot, make her desolate and naked, eat her flesh and burn her with fire. For God has put it into their hearts to fulfill His purpose, to be of one mind, and to give their kingdom to the beast, until the words of God are fulfilled" (Revelation 17:16,17).

After using the false church as an ally in his rapid rise to world domination the Antichrist will be totally possessed by Satan at the mid-point of the seven-year period. The Antichrist will order the ten nations to utterly destroy this false church. Satan will not share the worship of men with anyone, not even his ally, the final apostate church.

The detailed description of the final destruction of the Mother of Harlots by the Antichrist and his allies, the ten nations, proves that the False Prophet is not the leader of the Babylonian church of the Tribulation. If the False Prophet created and led this religious body, he would not turn and destroy his own organization. In other words, the pope cannot be the Antichrist or the False Prophet. Most tyrants, after they achieve total power, betray the allies that helped them in their rise to power. Adolph Hitler and Joseph Stalin both turned on their political allies and destroyed them. The motive is simple. Their former allies knew their inner secrets, strengths, and weaknesses. Therefore, they represent the only real alternative to the dictatorial rule of the tyrant.

This end-time ecumenical church will sell its soul to Satan and the Antichrist for power and riches. Just as the medieval church attached itself to the corrupt royal governments of Europe for financial and political gain, this apostate ecumenical church will do the same. It will persecute all those who reject its claims to religious supremacy. Later the prophet saw "a great multitude which no one could number, of all nations, tribes, peoples, and tongues, standing before the throne and before the Lamb, clothed with white robes, with palm branches in their hands" (Revelation 7:9). When John asked the angel to identify these saints the Scriptures record his answer, "These are the ones who come out of the great tribulation, and washed their robes and made them white in the blood of the Lamb" (Revelation 7:14). The greatest harvest of souls in the history of Christianity will occur during the Tribulation. Tragically, it will be a harvest of blood, the Inquisition of the tribulation.

20

Antichrist in the
Temple of God

The holy Temple in Jerusalem was the most beautiful and richly ornamented building in the ancient world. It stood on the Temple Mount, one of the highest points around Jerusalem, so that those approaching the city to participate in the great festivals could catch glimpses of its golden roof reflecting the sun. Israel's greatest and most skilled craftsmen created the elaborate decorations in the Holy Place and covered the walls of the Holy of Holies with intricate designs worked in gold and silver. Scholars estimate that Solomon's temple and the second temple that replaced it would cost more than $6 billion in today's dollars. The High Priest and his officials wore beautiful and costly garments as they performed the elaborate worship and sacrifice rituals laid down by Moses, their great lawgiver. The Temple, the center of Israel's religious and national life, was a physical symbol of the soul of the nation.

The defenses of the city and the Temple were truly awesome. The walls were five stories high and very thick. The Roman general Titus declared that Rome could not conquer the city unless God delivered Jerusalem into his hands. The walls of the Temple itself were an astonishing thirty stories high. The historian Flavius Josephus revealed that the defenders of Jerusalem had access to unlimited water supplies and abundant grain reserves within the city. Several months ago my wife Kaye and I explored some newly discovered chambers in the incredible subterranean tunnel system beneath the Temple Mount. In the course of our investigations our Israeli friend showed us some of the elaborate treasuries, grain storage rooms, and cisterns. He confirmed that archeologists had calculated that these storerooms contained enough grain to feed the city for over twelve years. The sins of the people and their leaders had increased year after year. The prophets of Israel repeatedly called on the people to abandon their outward rituals and return to God with a "sacrifice of obedience." The historian Josephus, the writers of the New Testament, and the rabbinic writers all agree that Israel continued in its sinful rebellion, provoking God to remove His protecting presence from His city and sanctuary. Despite Jerusalem's elaborate defenses Jesus prophesied that "not one stone will be left upon another."

Tragically, only thirty-eight years after Jesus' prophecy, the city and Temple were burned to the ground on the ninth day of Av, A.D. 70. Amazingly, this was the very same day of the year that the Babylonians had burned Solomon's Temple some 656 years earlier. Josephus declared that this remarkable "coincidence" proved the hand of God allowed this terrible destruction. Over 1,250,000 Jews died in the fall of Jerusalem, the greatest disaster in history till that time. The Tenth Roman Legion was ordered to literally plow the beautiful city and its Temple into the ground. Only three huge towers and the subterranean foundations of the Temple were left standing by Titus to show the implacable wrath of Rome against any who would dare to rebel against the Empire.

Heartbroken Jewish captives were led in chains out of the burning ruins of their beloved city to face slavery and exile in distant lands. However, through the centuries of captivity that followed, the Jewish exiles never forgot the promise of God that they would someday return to rebuild Jerusalem and its beautiful Temple. This hope of national redemption sustained them through the long centuries of banishment from their beloved Promised Land. Each year at Passover they would console each other with these words of hope, "Next year in Jerusalem."

ISRAEL'S REBIRTH AND THE THIRD TEMPLE

Both Old and New Testament prophets foretold that the Jews will rebuild the Temple in the last days. Micah echoed Isaiah's prophecy that the Temple would stand again in "the latter days." "Now it shall come to pass in the latter days that the mountain of the Lord's house shall be established on the top of the mountains, and shall be exalted above the hills; and all nations shall flow to it" (Isaiah 2:2, Micah 4:1). Throughout centuries of bitter exile in the "valley of dry bones" the Jews prayed for their return to Jerusalem and their glorious Temple. Every year the prayer on the lips of righteous Jews was: "May the Temple be built speedily in our days!" After two thousand years of exile the flag of David flew once more as the symbol of an independent Israel. On May 14, 1948, the chief rabbi fulfilled the dream of fifty generations of Jews when he ordered the shofar (ram's horn) blown in recognition that the hour of redemption was at hand. He stated that the reestablishment of the Jewish state and the return of the exiles meant that "the age of redemption had begun." Precisely as Jesus Christ had foretold in Matthew 24:32–34, Israel, symbolized by "the fig tree," became a nation. According to His prophecy the generation that saw Israel become a nation will still be alive to see the return of Christ in glory.

The Arab nations, however, responded to the creation of Israel by immediately invading the Jewish state. Following the 1948 War of Independence, the old city and the Temple Mount remained under Jordanian control until 1967. During those two decades the Jordanians prevented the Jews from worshiping at the western wall of their ancient Temple. In June 1967, Syrian and Egyptian armies mobilized their armed forces in preparation for an attack on Israel. Israel responded with a devastating preemptive air attack on their enemies' air bases and fighter aircraft. As King Hussein of Jordan joined his Arab allies and invaded Israel, the Israeli army counter-attacked and drove the Jordanian army out of the West Bank. However, Israel's most significant conquest was east Jerusalem with the Temple Mount. After two days of fighting the Israeli army captured the old city and the Temple Mount. The feeling was electric throughout the Jewish community as Jews came pouring into their old Jewish quarter and approached the sacred western wall.

PREPARING THE LEVITES

In my book *MESSIAH* I outlined Israel's current plans to rebuild the Temple. During the last decade orthodox Jewish groups trained five hundred young Levites for their role as priests in preparation for the resumption of Temple worship. The Jerusalem Temple Institute has constructed more than seventy of the Temple vessels and objects that are needed to resume Israel's ancient form of worship. On October 16, 1989, the two chief rabbis of Israel told *Time* magazine that the Third Temple could not be built until they could complete the Sacrifice of the Ashes of the Red Heifer. This is essential because the blood of the soldiers who died there over the centuries has defiled the entire Temple Mount, including the foundation stones. These religious leaders authorized a team to locate and raise a breed of pure red cattle similar to the ancient Egyptian breed used by Moses. Once they choose a pure red heifer without blemishes, a young priest will kill it, burning it with scarlet, cedar wood, and hyssop on the Mount of Olives opposite the Eastern Gate. The ashes from this burned sacrifice will be mixed with water in a cistern under the Temple. This water of purification will be sprinkled on the defiled stones of the Temple Mount, the priests, the worship vessels, et cetera.

In November 1990 government representatives, architects, engineers, rabbis, lawyers, and archeologists met to discuss solutions to the practical problems connected with rebuilding the Temple. Researchers estimate the basic Temple structure could be built in one to two years. Naturally, the elaborate decoration work will take many years to complete. The priests and the foundation stones will be cleansed with the waters of purification, just as they were when the exiles returned from Babylon. An altar for daily morning and evening sacrifices will be built in the area to the west of the planned Temple. Once the priests resume the daily sacrifice, the construction of the Temple itself will begin.

For the first time since A.D. 70 serious people are considering the practical steps required to build the Third Temple. Naturally, a majority of Jewish laymen and rabbis do not favor this project. However, a growing number believe they must rebuild the Temple to show the world that the Jews will remain in Jerusalem forever. Even non-religious Jews are dropping their previous opposition to this project. While only a minority want the Temple rebuilt, the prophecies will be fulfilled at the appointed time when God puts this in the heart of the Chosen People. God's command has never been rescinded: "And let them make Me a sanctuary, that I may dwell among them" (Exodus 25:8).

LOCATING THE BUILDING SITE

Archeologists are quietly exploring the elaborate honeycomb of subterranean tunnels, cisterns, and secret passages beneath the Temple Mount. Their discoveries have convinced many of us that the original Temple was located in an area some fifty yards to the north of the Dome of the Rock. Documentary evidence from the *Mishneh Torah's* censored sections on the rebuilding of the Temple tell us the Temple was directly opposite the Eastern Gate. The dimensions of the Temple would place the Holy of Holies over the small structure called the Dome of the Tablets over fifty yards to the north of the Dome of the Rock. Evidence suggests that the original Ark of the Covenant rested on the *Even Shetiyah*, the foundation stone at the base of the Dome of the Tablets. This research, if correct, indicates the Third Temple can be rebuilt without disturbing the Muslim Dome of the Rock. Ezekiel prophesied that the Jews will worship God in their beloved Temple once again. The Lord promised, "I will set My sanctuary in their midst forevermore. My tabernacle also shall be with them; indeed I will be their God, and they shall be My people" (Ezekiel 37:27).

At the appointed time, the Third Temple will be built in fulfillment of the Bible's prophecies; possibly following the miraculous victory over the Russian-Arab army. After describing the War of Gog and Magog Ezekiel prophesied, "I will set My glory among the nations; all the nations shall see My judgment which I have executed, and My hand which I have laid on them" (Ezekiel 39:21). The prophet's statement "I will set My glory" may refer to the return of the missing Ark of the Covenant to the Temple. It will represent God's presence and unbreakable covenant. A curious prophecy of Jeremiah suggests that the Ark of the Covenant will return to the Temple before Christ sets up His millennial kingdom. " 'Then it shall come to pass, when you are multiplied and increased in the land in those days,' says the Lord, that they will say no more, 'The ark of the covenant of the Lord.' It shall not come to mind, nor shall they remember it, nor shall they visit it, nor shall it be made anymore' " (Jeremiah 3:16). The prophet declared that, once the Messiah returns, the Ark will no longer "come to mind," nor will "they visit it." Since Israel has not possessed the Ark for almost three thousand years, this prophecy suggests that the Jews will "visit" and "talk" about the Ark just before the return of Christ. However, once the Messiah comes, their worship and attention will turn to Christ.

THE ARK OF THE COVENANT AND THE THIRD TEMPLE

The Ark of the Covenant disappeared from biblical history three thousand years ago during the reign of King Solomon. In my book *Armageddon—Appointment With Destiny*, I related significant historical and biblical evidence about the possible location of the Ark. Evidence suggests that it was taken to Ethiopia by Prince Menelik, the son of King Solomon and the Queen of Sheba, following Solomon's apostasy from God. If a perfect replica of the Ark was created in the days of Solomon, as Ethiopian tradition and the Jerusalem Talmud claims, the replica may have been hidden under the Temple. The replica of the Ark left in the Temple would have been treated as genuine by the priests in Jerusalem. Either this replica or the true Ark may have been secretly hidden underneath the Temple Mount along with other Temple treasures to protect them from invading Babylonian and Roman armies. Jewish archeologists have secretly explored the subterranean structures beneath the thirty-five acre Temple Mount for the last twenty-five years under the direction of former Chief Rabbi Schlomo Goren and Rabbi Getz, chief rabbi of the Western Wall. One of their goals was to locate the treasures of the Temple, including the lost Ark.

On May 15, 1992, CBS broadcast a unique two-hour television special called *Ancient Secrets of the Bible*. It was the first positive examination of biblical history by a secular television network and won the highest ratings with forty million viewers. The location of the lost Ark of the Covenant was one of the topics. The narrator reported that Rabbi Getz claimed that they have discovered the Ark of the Covenant in the tunnels. However, my Israeli sources report that they were unable to examine the object. Although they could only see it with flashlights for a few minutes in a darkened tunnel from fifty feet away, Rabbi Getz and Rabbi Goren concluded they had found the Ark. Unfortunately, the Arabs heard them and broke into the tunnel from the sub-structures beneath the Dome of the Rock. A terrible fight took place which prevented the rabbis from actually examining the object. Within hours the Arabs sealed the gate with concrete preventing Jewish archeologists from exploring this tunnel area. At this point we cannot be certain if it was the Ark or another object.

The CBS producers asked me to share my research and film of the Temple tunnels as well as the evidence suggesting that the Ark may have been taken to Ethiopia in the days of Solomon. Our videos of the secret tunnel system beneath the Temple Mount were shown to illustrate the ongoing exploration effort. During the program I explained the history of the Ark and the evidence indicating that it was guarded in an underground Temple in Aksum, Ethiopia, for thousands of years. In the last few years three secular books were written about the possibility that the Ark was in Ethiopia. In a fascinating article in the *Biblical Archeological Review* in 1993 the reviewer wrote that there is some credible evidence that the Ethiopians may have possessed the Ark during the last three thousand years.

I received reports from three sources, Canadian, Ethiopian and Israeli, that claimed the Ark was secretly returned to Israel during the violent closing days of the Ethiopian Civil War some thirty months ago. As the Israeli Mossad agents prepared to fly thousands of Ethiopian Jews home to Israel they were forced to bribe the Ethiopian officials to allow them to free their Jewish brothers. As the victorious northern army closed in on the capital, the evil communist officials of the defeated government demanded millions in bribes from Israel before they fled to wealthy exile Switzerland. As the last twenty thousand black Jews of Ethiopia began to fly to Jerusalem, the Israeli cargo planes landed every few minutes in Addis Ababa to pick up another load of Ethiopian Jewish refugees.

Three credible sources independently told me the same fascinating story. For years, since the rebirth of Israel, the Mossad and Jewish religious authorities tried to negotiate the return of some priceless Jewish relics from the underground Temple in Aksum, Ethiopia, including the Ark of the Covenant. Apparently, the corrupt Ethiopian officials demanded a secret bribe of an additional $42 million from Israel to permit them to take the Ark of the Covenant home. The reports claim a special team of trained Levites carried the Ark with the staves in the prescribed manner into an unmarked cargo plane. They said the Levites carried the Ark on their shoulders while supported with leg braces during the long flight because they would not set the Ark down. My sources claim the $42 million paid to the crooked officials turned out to be counterfeit money. Israel took $42 million in real currency and gave it to the incoming democratic government of Ethiopia. Since the outgoing dictatorship left the treasury without a penny, this $42 million was the only money the new government had to begin its operations. My sources told me the Ark is now held in a secret location in Israel waiting for the rebuilding of the Temple. Is this credible?

I can only tell you that my sources are credible, one of them a Christian former Canadian diplomat. However, their reports are based on information given to them by others. Only time and the final appearance of the Ark of the Covenant in the Third Temple will reveal the truth.

THE SIGNIFICANCE OF THE ARK OF THE COVENANT

The Ark of the Covenant is the outward symbol of God's holy covenant with Israel. The Ten Commandments, written by the finger of God, are stored within the holy Ark and represent God's covenant relationship with His Chosen People. The Ark was the only object in the Temple that pointed clearly to the second coming of the Messiah. The rediscovery of the Ark would provide the strongest probable motivation for Israel to rebuild the Temple. It would also be a rallying cry for the Jews in other countries to return to the Holy Land. The Ark is a profound symbol and guarantee of God's unbreakable covenant with Israel. The Antichrist would find the Ark a tremendous temptation to capture and use for his own political and religious goals. The Prince of Darkness will hate the Jews and their holy Ark of the Covenant because it represents God's eternal relationship with Israel.

THE PRINCE OF DARKNESS WILL DEFILE THE TEMPLE

"Then he shall confirm a covenant with many for one week; but in the middle of the week He shall bring an end to sacrifice and offering" (Daniel 9:27). The Antichrist will violate his seven-year-treaty with Israel, stop daily sacrifices, and enter the Holy of Holies. The apostle Paul warned about the son of perdition "who opposes and exalts himself above all that is called God or that is worshiped, so that he sits as God in the temple of God, showing himself that he is God" (2 Thessalonians 2:4). The fulfillment of Paul's prophecy may occur when he defiles the restored Ark of the Covenant by touching or sitting on the Mercy Seat. This would surely qualify as the "abomination of desolation" spoken of by Christ in Matthew 24:15. This would allow Satan to present the Antichrist as "god in the Temple." An abomination is something religiously defiling. There is something so terrible about the Antichrist's action in the Temple that the prophet Daniel could barely speak of it. The act of Satan's Prince of Darkness is so abominable that God will pour out His wrath from heaven when the Antichrist defiles the Holy of Holies.

Jesus warned His disciples, "Therefore when you see the 'abomination of desolation,' spoken of by Daniel the prophet, standing in the holy place' (whoever reads, let him understand), 'then let those who are in Judea flee to the mountains. Let him who is on the housetop not come down to take anything out of his house' " (Matthew 24:15–17). Christ warned the Jews to literally flee to the hills when this abomination occurs. The wrath of God will be unleashed on earth at that very moment. This crisis will commence the Great Tribulation. In the words of Christ: "For then there will be great tribulation, such as has not been since the beginning of the world until this time, no, nor ever shall be" (Matthew 24:21).

THE BATTLE FOR THE TEMPLE

When the Prince of Darkness defiles the Temple many Jews will recognize that he is actually the false messiah. As the Jews rebel against his claims to be "god," Satan will supernaturally empower his prince to fight against the "holy people." He will use Satan's power in his attempt to destroy Israel as the Jewish remnant flees into the wilderness. The Temple will probably be the initial battleground as the righteous priests battle to the death against the supporters of the Antichrist. Revelation 12:17 warns that "the dragon was enraged with the woman, and he went to make war with the rest of her offspring, who keep the commandments of God and have the testimony of Jesus Christ."

THE ASSASSINATION OF THE ANTICHRIST

As mentioned in an earlier chapter, someone will kill the Antichrist with a sword after he stops the daily sacrifice. Some Jewish believer may break through his security and stab him in the head or neck. There are several verses that describe his assassination. Revelation 13:3 says: "I saw one of his heads as if it had been mortally wounded, and his deadly wound was healed. And all the world marveled and followed the beast." After his satanic resurrection, the False Prophet will use this incredible event, possibly watched by billions on CNN, to convince the world that the Antichrist is the long awaited messiah. Once the Antichrist consolidates his control of Jerusalem and the Middle East the False Prophet will force the people under the jurisdiction of his world government to worship the Antichrist. From that point until Armageddon, 1260 days later, the world will be convulsed with spiritual and physical warfare between the forces of Antichrist and those Jews and Gentiles who will resist them. In the next chapter we will examine the evidence that indicates this is the generation when our Lord will return.

21

Is This the Generation
of Christ's Return?

"Now as He sat on the Mount of Olives, the disciples came to Him privately, saying, 'Tell us, when will these things be? And what will be the sign of Your coming, and of the end of the age?' " (Matthew 24:3).

For thousands of years men have studied the Bible's ancient prophecies and wondered if they would live to witness the return of Christ to redeem the earth. Many today long for the coming of Christ. However, sceptics remind us that past generations of believers also believed they would see the Second Coming but died with the promise unfulfilled. They ask: Why should our generation be different? After thirty years of study I believe the evidence is overwhelming that Christ will return in our lifetime. Jesus and the other prophets described a number of prophecies that would occur in the generation when He would return. Is this the generation? The answer to this question has profound implications for our daily walk with the Lord, our witnessing and the priorities of our life.

THIRTY-EIGHT PROPHECIES
FULFILLED IN OUR GENERATION

In this chapter we will examine thirty-eight significant prophecies that have been fulfilled in our generation that point to the Lord's return at any moment. Almost two thousand years have passed from the time of Christ until our generation. At its simplest level we can ask: What are the odds that these thirty-eight specific prophecies could occur by chance during our generation rather than in fulfillment of God's divine plan? In the Bible, a generation is usually defined as forty years, as indicated in the reigns of Gideon, King David, King Solomon, et cetera. During the last two thousand years since the days of Christ, fifty such forty-year generations have passed. Therefore, the odds are one chance in fifty of any one of these specific prophecies happening by chance in our generation rather than some other generation. Take the prophecy of the rebirth of Israel, as prophesied by Matthew 24:32, as an example. There was only one chance in fifty that Israel would become a nation in our lifetime rather than in some other generation such as A.D. 350 or A.D. 1600.

According to the laws of combined probability the chance that two or more events will occur in a given time period is equal to the chance that one event will occur multiplied by the chance that the second event would occur. If the odds are fifty to one against Israel being reborn in our lifetime and the odds are fifty to one against the revival of the Roman Empire in our generation; then the combined probability is fifty times fifty which equals one chance in twenty-five hundred. To chart this thought:

What are the Odds That These 38 Prophecies Occurred by Chance?
There are 40 years to a Generation.
There are 50 Generations from Christ till today.
Therefore:
The Odds are 1 in 50 of any of these prophecies occurring in our lifetime

The Odds of 1 event	=	1 chance in 50
	=	1 in 50
The Odds of 2 events	=	50 x 50
	=	1 in 2500
The Odds of 3 events	=	50 X 50 X 50
	=	1 in 125,000
The Odds of 4 events	=	50 X 50 X 50 X 50
	=	1 in 6.25 Million
The Odds of 5 events	=	50 X 50 X 50 X 50 X 50
	=	1 in 312.5 Million
The Odds of 6 events	=	50 X 50 X 50 X 50 X 50 X 50
	=	1 in 15.6 Billion

The Odds of 38 events occurring by chance in one generation are simply staggering.

In this book we have covered details of these thirty-eight prophecies in connection with the rise and fall of the Antichrist. In this chapter I will simply list the specific prophecy and the biblical reference where the original prophecy was given. Each of these prophecies is a unique event that has never been fulfilled in any other generation. By their very nature many of the predictions could not be fulfilled again.

The Prophecy:	The Reference:
1. The rebirth of Israel, the "fig tree" buds	Matthew 24:32–34
2. The Hebrew language recovered	Zephaniah 3:9
3. The Ethiopian Jews return to Israel	Zephaniah 3:10
4. The Exiles returning to Israel	Ezekiel 37:21
5. Israel becomes fertile and blossoms	Isaiah 27:6
6. Israel's rainfall increases dramatically	Joel 2:23
7. The Roman Empire will revive	Daniel 2:40–44
8. Russia Rises as a Military Power	Ezekiel 38:1–12

9. The City of Babylon is rebuilt	Isaiah 13:1,6,19
10. Iraq is defeated in War in the Gulf	Jeremiah 50:1,9; 51:27
11. Preparations for a One-World Government	Daniel 7:14; Rev. 13:7
12. Financial Systems depending on numbers not cash	Revelation 13:17,18
13. Intra-dermal computer ID chips	Revelation 13:15–18
14. A Global arms race	Matthew 24:6,7; Joel 3:9
15. Worldwide television communications	Revelation 11:9,10
16. Israel surrounded by enemy Arab nations	Psalms 83:4–8
17. Worldwide famine destroying	Revelation 6:5,6; Matthew 24:7
18. Deadly Pestilence kills one-fourth of Earth	Revelation 6:8; Matthew 24:7
19. Increasing Earthquakes in strange places	Revelation 6:12–15; Matthew 24:7
20. An Increase in False Messiahs	Matthew 24:4,5
21. Explosion of false prophets and heresies	Matthew 24:24
22. The rise of anti-Semitism worldwide	Matthew 24:9,10
23. Men's Hearts Failing Them in Fear	Luke 21:26
24. Asia developing 200-million-man army	Revelation 9:14–16
25. The Euphrates River can be dried up	Revelation 16:12–14
26. A Military Highway Across Asia	Revelation 9:14,15; 16:12–14
27. Society accepts perversion and evil as normal	2 Timothy 3:1–3; Revelation 9:20,21

28. Ecological devastation of the planet	Revelation 11:18
29. Doomsday weapons threaten earth	Matt. 24:21,22; Joel 2:3
30. Plans to Rebuild the Temple	Isaiah 2:2,3; Micah 4:1,2
31. Levites and priests train for Temple service	Ezekiel 43:14,15
32. Temple vessels are prepared	Ezekiel 43:14–19
33. Preparations for the Sacrifice of the Red Heifer	Numbers 19; Ezekiel 36:25
34. Jerusalem rebuilt in 9 specific directions	Jeremiah 31:38–40
35. Massive increases in wealth and possessions	James 5:3
36. Formation of worldwide apostate church	Revelation 17
37. Israel Dwelling Without Walls or Gates	Ezekiel 38:11
38. The Powers of uranium shaken; elements melt	Luke 21:26; 2 Peter 3:10–12

This chapter demonstrates that a truly incredible number of specific prophecies have been fulfilled in our generation. What are the odds against these thirty-eight prophecies occurring by chance? The odds are 50 X 50 X 50 X 50 . . . (38 times)! This number is so large that there is no name for it. However, to illustrate the odds; consider this. The odds are equal to the estimated number of grains of sand in all the oceans, rivers, and lakes of the earth. Imagine that we were to take a single grain of sand and paint it gold. We take it into orbit and drop it out of the space shuttle over one of the world's seven oceans. Then we blindfold you and let you search the planet for as long as you wish. When you think you are in the right ocean, the right square mile, the right square inch, pick up a random grain of sand. If you picked up by chance the one grain of sand painted gold you would have equaled the odds against these thirty-eight prophecies being fulfilled by chance in our generation. Frankly, I don't think you would find the grain of sand. I believe it is virtually impossible that these prophecies were fulfilled by chance. Our Lord Jesus Christ warned us, "Now when these things begin to happen, look up and lift up your heads, because your redemption draws near" (Luke 21:28). It will be worthwhile to examine a few of these amazing predictions in detail to illustrate the tremendous precision of biblical prophecies.

THE GLOBAL ARMS RACE

"Proclaim this among the nations: 'Prepare for war!' " (Joel 3:9).

The Bible warns that the world will never know true peace until the Prince of Peace comes. Although men desperately seek peace, the Antichrist, will only bring the world false peace. While there have always been "wars and rumors of war" the worst arms race in history rages while our leaders talk of peace. Despite the talk of "peace in our time," the nations are still arming for Armageddon. The armament factories of Russia, China, and the West are producing deadly weaponry at an awesome rate. China is fueling a massive arms race in the Middle East with huge sales of high-tech ballistic missile systems to Arab regimes opposed to Israel and the West. Iraq, Iran, and Libya now possess missiles capable of destroying Paris or London. For the first time since the year A.D. 800, Europe faces a military threat from the Muslim Arab world. China is negotiating with Syria and Pakistan to deliver nuclear-capable intermediate range ballistic missiles capable of destroying cities in Europe or Israel.

Chemical and biological weapons proliferation has proceeded to the point where it is impossible to put the genie back in the bottle. Syria, Iraq, Egypt, and Iran are rapidly developing advanced biological and chemical weapons. Libya recently built two massive advanced biological and chemical weapons complexes deep in the desert. Saddam Hussein used chemical weapons to kill thousands of Kurds and Iranian soldiers in the Iran-Iraq War. When U.S. soldiers occupied southern Iraq they discovered sixty-five thousand Iraqi chemical artillery shells ready for use. For centuries the winds have blown from Iraq south into Kuwait and Saudi Arabia. Captured Iraqi soldiers confirmed Saddam's plans to use chemical weapons, including deadly Sarin nerve gas, expecting the southerly wind to carry the deadly gas south into the American troops. However, on the night before the allied attack, as millions of Christians prayed for our troops, the wind changed direction for the first time in hundreds of years. As the wind reversed direction to blow north into Iraqi army positions, Hussein's generals were forced to abandon their plan to use chemical weapons lest the wind blow the gas into Iraqi lines. Despite the 1925 Geneva Convention against such weapons, many countries have stockpiled huge quantities of these doomsday weapons in case they are needed in a future conflict. Many unstable nations now possess artillery and missiles with chemical and biological warheads. Only a hopeless optimist believes these dreadful weapons will never be used.

Experts believe fifteen third world countries will join the nuclear club by A.D. 2000, complete with nuclear warheads and ballistic missiles. There are still forty-five thousand nuclear warheads in the former Soviet Union. In addition to North Korea's nuclear threat to American and South Korean forces, it is selling its nuclear technology to Iraq, Iran, Syria, and Libya. Military strategists have abandoned the hope that these Arab nations will remain non-nuclear. From the beginning of history every major arms race has ultimately ended in war. The international arms buildup is setting the stage for the final battle of Armageddon that will drench the world in blood.

DEADLY PESTILENCE

The Bible describes terrible pestilences and horrible sores occurring throughout the world's population as one of the horrors of the Great Tribulation. The plague and pestilence that will destroy hundreds of millions in the last days may include the effects of biological and chemical weapons.

THE AIDS PESTILENCE

"So I looked, and behold an ashy pale horse, . . . and its rider's name was Death, and Hades . . . followed him closely; and they were given authority and power over a fourth part of the earth, to kill with the sword and with famine and with plague (pestilence, disease) and with wild beasts of the earth" (Revelation 6:8, *Amplified Bible*).

The prophecy of the Four Horsemen of the Apocalypse warned that a quarter of humanity will be killed by plague and pestilence symbolized by the fourth horseman. Until this decade it was almost impossible to understand how this prophecy could be fulfilled literally. Tragically, the AIDS epidemic in Africa, South America and Asia is demonstrating how this prophecy may be fulfilled exactly as the Bible warned. The AIDS plague is now poised to destroy a large portion of mankind in the worst epidemic in history. Although the Black Plague killed one-third of the population of Europe in 1348–50, a majority of those infected survived the disease. Thus far no one has survived AIDS for more than twelve years.

In North America and Europe the AIDS virus is still primarily found within the homosexual community and those who share illegal drugs through needles. However, in the Third World the situation is quite different. Massive numbers of heterosexuals in Africa, South America, and Asia are infected with AIDS. High levels of unprotected promiscuous sexual activity between males and females facilitates the rapid transmission of the AIDS virus throughout the sexually active population in the Third World. Many in these countries have fifty or more sexual partners every year. An absence of sanitation, minimal AIDS education, and a lack of antibiotics has accelerated an epidemic of sexually transmitted diseases, including AIDS. The only solution to the AIDS crisis is to return to God's laws regarding a faithful marriage relationship. This is the only true "safe sex" that exists.

In the fall of 1991 the Central Intelligence Agency produced a report on the AIDS epidemic in Africa that was staggering in its conclusions. The evidence pointed to the greatest epidemic and loss of life in human history. The CIA gathered evidence from the World Health Organization, the Center for Disease Control, and many doctors in Africa. Their report concluded that up to 75 percent of the population of Africa south of the Sahara may become infected with AIDS over the next eight years. This will mean the death by AIDS of over 300 million people in Africa alone. We are witnessing the death of a whole continent. The mind can scarcely imagine death on this massive scale. The *South African Medical Journal* in July 1991 reported that a staggering 47 percent of black male and female blood donors tested positive for AIDS during 1989. The prognosis for Asia and parts of South America is tragically similar. They are about six years behind Africa in terms of the spread of the epidemic. There is a staggering rise in cholera and typhoid epidemics around the world.

WORLDWIDE FAMINE

In Revelation 6:5 John described his vision of the horrible famine in the last days. "And I looked, and behold, a black horse, and he who sat on it had a pair of scales in his hand." The scales represent famine, and the prophet explains that a day's wages will only buy enough wheat or barley to feed the workman, not his family. The United Nations claims that over thirty million in Africa are at risk of dying from the most devastating famine in this century. Despite the great advances in food production and storage techniques more people are starving today than any other time in history. The UN estimates that one billion people are in danger of starvation while another billion lack proper nutrition. North American food reserves (grain and corn) are at the lowest level in sixteen years. Wheat reserves are at a forty-five-year low as our government sends food to Russia, Bosnia, and Somalia. With the massive changes in world weather patterns we may witness famine in the future in countries that felt themselves immune to hunger.

A WORLD TURNING TO DUST

Since World War II, we have destroyed four and a half billion acres of the earth's topsoil. This is an area larger than China and India combined. So far, 11 percent of the globe's topsoil has been eroded destroying the hopes for food self-sufficiency in the Third World. The problems are over-grazing, deforestation, and poor farming methods. Recently the World Resources Institute released a devastating study of the world's soil conditions. One of the hardest hit areas is the center of the prairies of Canada and the Midwest American states. This small area, while only 5.3 percent of our agricultural land, has literally been the "world's breadbasket" for decades. The study details the continued erosion of our best topsoil, with over 235 million acres now considered "degraded." Over 20 percent of the agricultural soils of Europe, Asia, Africa, and Central America have been "degraded." The Sahara Desert is expanding southward relentlessly, destroying the topsoil and the agriculture of millions of Africans. The Amazon Rain Forest produces great quantities of the essential oxygen we breathe. However, every day thousands of acres of these precious forests are burned. Each year they burn an area the size of the United Kingdom. These actions are destroying one of the earth's great irreplaceable resources.

THE RISE IN MAJOR "KILLER" EARTHQUAKES

Jesus prophesied that the last generation would witness the greatest earthquakes in history. Also, Ezekiel, Zechariah, Haggai, and Revelation predicted awesome earthquakes preceding the Messiah's appearance. Jesus declared that these earthquakes will occur in "various places." Huge earthquakes are now occurring in places that have never previously experienced this activity. Enormous forces are accumulating deep beneath the massive tectonic plates supporting the continents. As I am finishing the final editing of this chapter on January 17, 1994, Los Angeles was shaken by a devastating earthquake destroying billions in property and collapsing many buildings and highways. Scientists warn that this series of major earthquakes in California are only a foretaste of the "Big One," the most massive earthquake in human history.

Major "killer" quakes (7.2 or greater on the Richter Scale) occurred only once per decade throughout history until our century. However, since A.D. 1900, the growth in major earthquakes has been relentless. From 1900 to 1949 it averaged three major quakes per decade. From 1949 the increase became awesome with 9 killer quakes in the 1950s; 13 in the 60s; 56 in the 1970s and an amazing 74 major quakes in the 1980s. Finally, in the 1990s, as the present rate, we will experience 125 major killer quakes in this decade (Source: U.S. Geological Survey Earthquake Report, Boulder, Colorado). As the prophets warned, the planet is being shaken as never before. This rising quake activity will culminate in a series of enormous earthquakes throughout the Great Tribulation. The judgment of God will finally unleash the greatest earthquake in history. "There were noises and thunderings and lightnings; and there was a great earthquake, such a mighty and great earthquake as had not occurred since men were on the earth" (Revelation 16:18).

PERVERSION AND EVIL

"And because lawlessness will abound, the love of many will grow cold" (Matthew 24:12). The natural love of men and women is being attacked by satanic forces as never before. More than 2.7 million children are abused each year in the U.S.A. according to an article in *U.S.A. Today* on April 23, 1992. These tragic figures represent the precious lives of children who will bear these terrible emotional wounds for years. How can someone harm a defenseless child or woman? Surely this rising tide of violence is occurring because a spirit of lawlessness prevails throughout the world.

As a horrifying evidence of satanic influence today, Red China, according to the Chinese University in Hong Kong, is selling expensive kidneys, hearts, and other organs of executed prisoners for organ transplants to the wealthy. In Brazil a judge reported that young homeless children are kidnapped and taken to clinics where they are killed. Their organs are then implanted in wealthy foreign clients who refuse to wait for a normal donor organ. These stories sound like something out of a late night horror movie but they are tragically true. The love of many people is becoming cold as ice as the basic love and respect for God's laws disappears.

THE RISE OF VIOLENCE

The average American now watches television more than six hours a day. That amounts to thirty hours per week, almost one third of our waking hours. A February 1992 study by the American Psychological Association reveals that high school students will witness 16,000 violent murders and 200,000 other acts of violence by graduation. Television is now the main source of information for 65 percent of Americans. More than 50 percent of cartoons teach violence and antisocial behavior as the norm. A Yale study on cartoon violence reported an 88 percent increase in children's violence, including choking and hurting animals after they watched television cartoons. Every hour a viewer will witness nineteen acts of violence. This exposure to non-stop video brutality is desensitizing viewers to the horrors of violence.

In the wake of the tragic Los Angeles race riots we have seen how close we are to the total breakdown of law and order. Over 150,000 gang members belong to a thousand gangs in Los Angeles County. Each year gangs use greater violence as they acquire Uzi machine guns and assault rifles. No city in America would be safe if the power failed for a few hours.

The Scriptures teach that a single generation will witness the rebirth of Israel and the coming of the promised

Messiah. The evidence presented in this chapter proves that our generation will witness the triumphant victory of Jesus the Messiah. In the next chapter we will examine the climactic events of the coming Battle of Armageddon. The words of Jesus speak to our generation, "Now when these things begin to happen, look up and lift up your heads, because your redemption draws near" (Luke 21:28).

22

The Battle of Armageddon

The prophet Joel declared, "Proclaim this among the nations: 'Prepare for war! Wake up the mighty men, let all the men of war draw near, let them come up. Beat your plowshares into swords and your pruninghooks into spears' " (Joel 3:9–10). The final years of the Great Tribulation will be marked by a series of ferocious wars as many nations rebel against the Antichrist. After his victory over the Babylonian church the armies of the Antichrist will be concentrated in Europe and the Middle East. "I saw three unclean spirits like frogs coming out of the mouth of the dragon, out of the mouth of the beast, and out of the mouth of the false prophet. For they are spirits of demons, performing signs, which go out to the kings of the earth and of the whole world, to gather them to the battle of that great day of God Almighty. And they gathered them together to the place called in Hebrew, Armageddon" (Revelation 16:13,14,16). These "unclean spirits" will call the "kings of the earth" to gather their armies to Israel for the final conflict of the age. First, the King of the South (Egypt and her allies) will attack the Antichrist's forces in Israel. Then the King of the North (Russia, Syria) will join the invasion by bringing his forces down from the north in a lightening attack. "At the time of the end the king of the South shall attack him; and the king of the North shall come against him like a whirlwind, with chariots, horsemen, and with many ships" (Daniel 11:40). The Antichrist will swiftly counterattack and totally annihilate them. Daniel prophesied that, "He shall enter the countries, overwhelm them, and pass through." The forces of Satan's prince will decisively win the first round of the war against his tyranny.

THE ARMIES OF ANTICHRIST

The Antichrist will command the support of most western nations led by his inner circle of ten European and Mediterranean nations. He will consolidate his military forces in Israel knowing that the final war will be fought in the Promised Land. "He shall also enter the Glorious Land, and many countries shall be overthrown; but these shall escape from his hand: Edom, Moab, and the prominent people of Ammon. He shall stretch out his hand against the countries, and the land of Egypt shall not escape" (Daniel 11:41,42). The armies of the Antichrist will conquer Israel and Egypt. Daniel tells us that Edom, Moab and Ammon in present-day Jordan will escape. Possibly, they are willing allies of Satan's prince. The Antichrist will conquer Libya and Ethiopia as his armies consolidate his control over North Africa.

THE ARMY OF THE KINGS OF THE EAST

"But news from the east and the north shall trouble him; therefore he shall go out with great fury to destroy and annihilate many. And he shall plant the tents of his palace between the seas and the glorious holy mountain; yet he shall come to his end, and no one will help him" (Daniel 11:44,45). At the moment of his triumph over these rebellious nations the Antichrist will receive intelligence reports that an enormous army is mobilizing far to the east and north. These reports will greatly disturb him because the army of "the kings of the East" will contain two hundred million soldiers.

While the world talks of peace the Chinese government continues to arm for war. The nations of Asia will combine forces to produce the 200 million man army of the Kings of the East. China already has over 100 million men in its military reserves. The growing alliance between Japan, China and the rapidly developing nations of Asia could produce the armaments and men for such an enormous army. The western world will face its greatest danger when the technology and engineering of Japan is joined to the huge manpower and natural resources of China. On May 22, 1992 China exploded one of the largest nuclear bombs in history, over 70 times the size of the bomb that devastated Hiroshima. China is expanding its awesome nuclear arsenal while building a dangerous military alliance with Iran, Pakistan, Saudi Arabia and Algeria. She is providing sophisticated intermediate ballistic missiles and access to her nuclear facilities despite international criticism.

THE DOOMSDAY SUPERWEAPONS

The weapons used in the battle of Armageddon will be the most destructive in history. Jesus warned that no one would survive the horrors of the Great Tribulation if He did not return from heaven to end the battle. The truly advanced weapons that will be unleashed in the cataclysmic wars at the end of this age will stagger men with their awesome destructiveness. The weapons in the secret armories of the nations will produce devastating casualties in a future war. America, Britain, Russia, China, and Israel are designing advanced neutron atomic bombs that kill everyone in a city block without damaging any buildings.

During the Gulf War special satellite cameras transmitted instantaneous pictures of the live battle back home to the War Room in Washington. Special Russian killer satellites are now equipped with lasers capable of destroying vital American surveillance satellites that allow our military commanders to observe military operations. In response America has produced a series of back-up satellites orbiting in deep space that will be activated when our first set of satellites are destroyed. The replacement satellites will fire their rockets and descend into the proper orbit to observe the conflict. Israel has recently developed several new high energy plasma physics weapons that will revolutionize the nature of warfare. The Israelis did not use these advanced weapons in the War in the Gulf because they knew that the danger from Iraq was limited to a few SCUD's.

Despite denials, the Russians have spent billions on the development of Particle Beam Weapons that can vaporize a target at great distances. In a future war targets will be destroyed at great distances through new high energy weapons. A single particle beam weapon can be aimed at hundreds of targets per minute destroying them at the speed of light with the destructive power of a tactical nuclear weapon. As we approach the final conflict, the total manpower of the standing armies and reserves of the nations exceed 500 million soldiers. Over 85,000 nuclear weapons and huge stockpiles of dangerous biological and chemical weapons are in the armories of the nations. The military establishments are constantly developing new armaments to replace our obsolete armaments. Our ten-year old weapons are sold to countries like Egypt who then sell their twenty-year old equipment to Yemen. The arms race of the last five decades has turned the world into an armed camp. There are now enough arms in the world to supply every human on the planet with a military weapon. There is something obscene in the nations spending a trillion dollars a year for armaments while we cannot find the money to feed the hungry or house our homeless.

THE CROSSING OF THE EUPHRATES RIVER

For thousands of years the Euphrates River has stood as a great military barrier between the East and West. It runs for over a thousand miles from its headwaters in the mountains of Turkey until it flows into the Persian Gulf.

Its width varies from a few hundred feet to over a mile. The prophets foretold that this great river will someday dry up to allow the army of the Kings of the East to cross it on their march toward northern Israel. John prophesied "Then the sixth angel poured out his bowl on the great river Euphrates, and its water was dried up, so that the way of the kings from the east might be prepared" (Revelation 16:12). Two years ago the massive Ataturk Dam was completed in Turkey. As the President of Turkey pressed a button the dam closed and the great Euphrates River dropped 75%. For the first time in history the Euphrates River can be blocked to allow the fulfillment of this prophecy from the book of Revelation.

The Lord prophesied about the final preparations for the last battle of this age. "Release the four angels who are bound at the great river Euphrates. So the four angels, who had been prepared for the hour and day and month and year, were released to kill a third of mankind. Now the number of the army of the horsemen was two hundred million, and I heard the number of them" (Revelation 9:14–16). This incredible 200 million man eastern army will fight its way across Asia as its moves toward the great valley of Jezreel in northern Israel. This final battle between the Kings of the East and the western armies of the Antichrist will determine who will rule the world for the next millennium.

The Last World War

The final battle will be focused on the plain called Armageddon in northern Israel. Although the final stages of the battle will occur there, the war will engulf Asia, North Africa, Europe and the Middle East. Hundreds of millions will die in bloody warfare as the advanced doomsday weapons are finally taken out of the armories to slaughter the nations. Nothing will be held back as the nations unleash total destruction on their enemy's armies and cities. A full scale nuclear, biological and chemical war could destroy over 90% of the population in the countries attacked. The devastation will be so overwhelming the survivors may envy the dead.

The prophet John described the final phase of the battle of Armageddon as the huge armies engage in pitched battle against each other and Israel. To the consternation of the leaders of this titanic battle Jesus Christ and the armies of heaven will intervene supernaturally against both evil forces. "I saw the beast, the kings of the earth, and their armies, gathered together to make war against Him who sat on the horse and against His army" (Revelation 19:19). The enormous military forces of the entire planet will attack the armies of heaven led by Jesus Christ. Despite their staggering military forces, the armies of the Antichrist and the Kings of the East will be utterly destroyed by the power of Christ. The resurrected Christians will return from heaven with their Messiah to join in His incredible victory over the armies attempting to destroy Israel. John promised, "the armies in heaven, clothed in fine linen, white and clean, followed Him on white horses" (Revelation 19:14).

Both the Old and New Testament foretold the return of the hundreds of millions of the "saints" on the day the Messiah will establish His Kingdom. The first prophet in the Bible, Enoch, predicted that the Lord will bring His saints with Him on the Great Day of the Lord. "Behold, the Lord comes with ten thousands of His saints" (Jude 1:14). The expression "ten thousands" means "ten thousand times ten thousand" which equals one hundred million. Moses also described the Lord and His heavenly army coming from Sinai to take vengeance against Satan's forces. "The Lord came from Sinai, and dawned on them from Seir; He shone forth from Mount Paran, and He came with ten thousands of saints; from His right hand came a fiery law for them" (Deuteronomy 33:2).

THE DEFEAT OF THE ANTICHRIST AND THE FALSE PROPHET

"Then the beast was captured, and with him the false prophet who worked signs in his presence, by which he deceived those who received the mark of the beast and those who worshiped his image. These two were cast alive into the lake of fire burning with brimstone. And the rest were killed with the sword which proceeded from the mouth of Him who sat on the horse. And all the birds were filled with their flesh" (Revelation 19:20,21).

The Battle of Armageddon may end quite quickly once the armies of heaven intervene or it may rage on for several days. Regardless of the duration, the ultimate victory of Christ's armies is assured. The Apostle Paul prophesied, "Then the lawless one will be revealed, whom the Lord will consume with the breath of His mouth and destroy with the brightness of His coming" (2 Thessalonians 2:8). Daniel also referred to the supernatural defeat of the Antichrist in Daniel 8:25: "He shall even rise against the Prince of princes; but he shall be broken without human hand." When Christ was betrayed He indicated the vast power available to Him as the Son of God. "Or do you think that I cannot now pray to My father, and He will provide Me with more than twelve legions of angels?" (Matthew 26:53). When the final day of reckoning comes Christ will call on His innumerable legions of angels as well as the saints of the Church to join in His triumphant return to establish His millennial kingdom.

The Final Destiny of the Antichrist and False Prophet

The Antichrist and False Prophet will be captured and killed at the Battle of Armageddon while leading their forces against the armies of Christ. Despite Satan's supernatural power, their bodies will be destroyed by the miraculous power of Jesus. "I beheld even till the beast was slain, and his body destroyed, and given to the burning flame" (Daniel 7:11). However, as mentioned in the chapter on the False Prophet, the spirits of these two will be conscious as they are "cast alive" into the burning Lake of Fire. As John prophesied "These both were cast alive into a lake of fire burning with brimstone" (Revelation 19:20).

The Triumphant Return of Christ

"And then the sign of the Son of Man will appear in heaven, and then all the tribes of the earth will mourn, and they will see the Son of Man coming on the clouds of heaven with power and great glory" (Matthew 24:30). Jesus promised His return will appear, "as the lightning comes from the east and flashes to the west." Incredible signs in the heavens will announce that the return of the Messiah is at hand. When Christ returns He will appear in all His glory as Almighty God "the King of Kings and Lord of Hosts." This title, the "Lord of Hosts," indicates that the Lord is the "commander" of the military forces of heaven.

The Last Siege of Jerusalem

"It shall be in that day that I will seek to destroy all the nations that come against Jerusalem" (Zechariah 12:9). During the Great Tribulation the Antichrist will attempt to destroy the Jews who reject his claims to be the Messiah. The armies of the Antichrist and the Kings of the East will attack each other in the Middle East in their attempt to dominate the planet. The prophet Zechariah (12:2) warned that God "will make Jerusalem a cup of drunkenness to all the surrounding peoples, when they lay siege against Judah and Jerusalem." After two thousand years of exile, persecution and the Holocaust, Satan will lead the sinful nations in one last attempt to destroy God's Chosen People. The armies of the world will besiege Jerusalem as the prophet Zechariah (12:3) foretold, "it shall happen in that day that I will make Jerusalem a very heavy stone for all peoples; all who would heave it away will surely be cut in pieces, though all nations of the earth are gathered against it." He indicated that the armies would still pursue their attack on Jerusalem even though their forces were defeated by Christ at Armageddon. Several days (possibly ten days) after the battle, the armies of the Antichrist will break through the city's defenses. "For I will gather all the nations to battle against

Jerusalem; the city shall be taken, the houses rifled, and the women ravished. Half of the city shall go into captivity, but the remnant of the people shall not be cut off from the city" (Zechariah 14:2).

Tragically, the city of Jerusalem, conquered twenty-seven times in the past, will fall to its enemies one final time. The enemy soldiers will attack the women and place half the population in captivity. They will loot the riches of the city as the "spoil will be divided in your midst" (Zechariah 14:1). At the moment when all seems lost the Messiah will appear on the Mount of Olives to save the Jewish people. "Then the Lord will go forth and fight against those nations, as He fights in the day of battle. And in that day His feet will stand on the Mount of Olives, which faces Jerusalem on the east" (Zechariah 14:3,4). During centuries of bitter exile the Jews have longed for the day when their Messiah would appear in His glory to defeat their oppressors. Finally, the days of waiting will end. The Mount of Olives will split in two as Jesus Christ descends with supernatural power to deliver His people. The Jews of Jerusalem will flee for protection into this supernaturally created valley between the two halves of the mountain. They will be protected against the plague and pestilence unleashed by the wrath of God.

Christ will destroy the armies attacking Jerusalem with a terrible plague. The Lord will afflict their soldiers with madness causing soldiers to fight the men in their own units. "This shall be the plague with which the Lord will strike all the people who fought against Jerusalem: Their flesh shall dissolve while they stand on their feet, their eyes shall dissolve in their sockets, and their tongues shall dissolve in their mouths" (Zechariah 14:12). Those who have come to loot, rape and kill the Jewish citizens of Jerusalem will perish under the righteous wrath of God. During the battle the Jewish soldiers will be given supernatural power to defeat their enemies. "In that day the Lord will defend the inhabitants of Jerusalem; the one who is feeble among them in that day shall be like David, and the house of David shall be like God, like the Angel of the Lord before them" (Zechariah 12:8).

THE JEWS AND THEIR COMING MESSIAH

"And it shall come to pass that whoever calls on the name of the Lord shall be saved. For in Mount Zion and in Jerusalem there shall be deliverance, as the Lord has said, among the remnant whom the Lord calls" (Joel 2:32). A tremendous spiritual transformation will occur among the Jews in their moment of greatest danger. As the enemy armies conquer the Holy City Jesus Christ and His saints will return to save His Chosen People. The Jews who recognize and call on their true Messiah will be saved. "Whoever calls on the name of the Lord shall be saved." The Apostle Paul warned the Church against thinking they had replaced Israel in God's sovereign plan. Both Israel and the Church have vital but separate roles to play in God's plan to redeem mankind. Although Paul prophesied about "Israel's blindness in part," the Lord promised that "when the fullness of the Gentiles is finished, all Israel shall be saved" (Romans 11:25). God is not through with Israel. After the Rapture, Israel will play a tremendous role in the evangelization of the world during the Great Tribulation. The salvation of the Jews will produce tremendous spiritual blessings for Israel and the nations during the Millennium and in the "world to come."

During the battle of Jerusalem Israel will undergo an extraordinary spiritual transformation. Centuries of spiritual blindness will end as God lifts the veil from the eyes of His Chosen People enabling them to clearly see their Messiah for the first time. God promised that He will finally reconcile Himself to His people. "I will pour on the house of David and on the inhabitants of Jerusalem the Spirit of grace and supplication; then they will look on Me whom they have pierced; they will mourn for Him as one mourns for his only son, and grieve for Him as one grieves for a firstborn" (Zechariah 12:10). Israel will finally see their Messiah-King, their deliverer, whose hands still bear the scars of His crucifixion. They will realize that Jesus is the Messiah they have longed for over the centuries. Zechariah tells us that there will be "mourning in Jerusalem" as they recognize their Messiah was waiting for them all this time. The people will weep for the incredible losses in the battle but they will rejoice in their Messiah's deliverance.

The ancient sages of Israel mourned in remembrance of the day God turned away from His people, Jerusalem and His Temple. When Israel refused to repent of their personal and national sins, the Holy Temple was burned to the ground and they were sent into captivity among the nations. As the prophet Hosea warned: "Then God said: 'Call his name Lo-Ammi, for you are not My people, and I will not be your God'" (Hosea 1:9). Thankfully God is ever merciful to any who will turn from their sin and repent. Hosea also foretold: "it shall come to pass in the place where it was said to them, 'You are not My people,' there it shall be said to them, 'You are the sons of the living God'" (Hosea 1:10). Israel's spiritual exile and captivity will finally end. Their final reconciliation with God will set the stage for the establishment of Christ's throne in Jerusalem as the capital of the world.

"David My servant shall be king over them, and they shall all have one shepherd; they shall also walk in My judgments and observe My statutes, and do them. Moreover I will make a covenant of peace with them, and it shall be an everlasting covenant with them; I will establish them and multiply them, and I will set My sanctuary in their midst forevermore" (Ezekiel 37:24,26).

23

The Ultimate Victory of the Messiah

THE MESSIAH AND THE EASTERN GATE

When Christ descends on the Mount of Olives to defeat the armies of Satan, He will enter the rebuilt Temple through the sealed Eastern Gate. This gate, often called the Golden Gate, guards the entrance to the Temple on the eastern wall of the Temple Mount. Jesus will cross the Kidron Valley past His beloved Garden of Gethsemane to approach the sealed Eastern Gate. Ezekiel 43:1–5 foretold the coming of the Messiah to His Temple: "Behold, the glory of the God of Israel came from the way of the east. His voice was like the sound of many waters; and the earth shone with His glory. And the glory of the Lord came into the temple by way of the gate which faces toward the east" (Ezekiel 43:2,4). No sealed gate will hinder the Messiah, the Son of God, from entering through this gate to usher in His Millennial Kingdom.

THE JUDGMENT OF THE NATIONS

When the Messiah returns, Israel and the nations will finally participate fully in the coming Kingdom of God. His righteous government will commence with the judgment of the nations in the Valley of Jehoshaphat, the "valley where Jehovah judges." In the valley of Kidron between the Mount of Olives and the Temple Mount, Christ will judge the Gentile nations on the basis of their treatment of the Jews and His Gentile followers. Some will be punished while others will be blessed and rewarded in the Millennium (Matthew 25).

THE KINGDOM OF THE MESSIAH

Napoleon Bonaparte conquered most of Europe in his ruthless ambition to rule the world. Yet he realized that Jesus Christ was ultimately the real conqueror, not only of the world, but of men's souls. "Alexander, Caesar, Charlemagne and myself founded great empires; but upon what did the creations of our genius depend? Upon force. Jesus alone founded His empire upon love, and to this very day millions would die for Him." Since man left Paradise in Eden he has searched for righteous government with justice, equity and security for all people. The nations will finally see God's justice and mercy when Jesus the Messiah rules from the Throne of David. Isaiah the prophet received a vision of the coming Kingdom of God. "The government will be upon His shoulder. And His name will be called Wonderful, Counsellor, Mighty God, Everlasting Father, Prince of Peace. Of the increase of His government and peace there will be no end, upon the throne of David and over His kingdom, to order it and establish it with judgment and justice from that time forward, even forever. The zeal of the Lord of hosts will perform this" (Isaiah 9:6,7).

THE GUNS WILL BE SILENT

After the horrors of seven years of war during the Tribulation the guns will finally be silenced. When Christ reigns, there will be no need for hospitals, prisons, locks or fear. Man will experience true peace for the first time in history. Sons and husbands will never leave their homes to die in distant lands again. We will enjoy the incredibly beautiful earth that God created for us. Nature will be transformed by Christ as the prophet Isaiah foresaw:

"The wolf also shall dwell with the lamb, the leopard shall lie down with the young goat, the calf and the young lion and the fatling together; and a little child shall lead them" (Isaiah 11:6).

SATAN WILL BE IMPRISONED FOR A THOUSAND YEARS

The Great Tribulation will end with the destruction of the Antichrist and the False Prophet. Christ will bind Satan in the bottomless pit for one thousand years. "Then I saw an angel coming down from heaven, having the key to the bottomless pit and a great chain in his hand. He laid hold of the dragon, that serpent of old, who is the Devil and Satan, and bound him for a thousand years" (Revelation 20:1). Satan has tempted men to spiritual destruction for thousands of years. Finally, after Armageddon, he will be imprisoned throughout the duration of the Millennial Kingdom. Though defeated, Lucifer will not be cast into hell until God allows one final spiritual test for mankind. During the Millennium man will be free of the temptation of Satan as Adam was in the beginning of the Garden of Eden. Though there will be some sin, it will be minimal without the continual temptation from Satan. Jesus will reign as Messiah with a "rod of iron." Any open sin or crime will be judged immediately by the Messiah. Man will know true peace, security and justice for the first time since the Garden of Eden.

CHRISTIANS IN THE MILLENNIAL KINGDOM

During the Millennium Christians will live in mansions in the New Jerusalem in heaven. However, the Scriptures describe the saints "ruling and reigning" on the earth. In Jesus' parables He taught that those who are faithful will receive the privilege of administering several cities. Jesus and the resurrected Old Testament saints (Matthew 27:52) appeared to men, walked, talked and ate food. The resurrected Christian saints will have access to the earth to carry out God's plan to rule His kingdom. The Scriptures teach that the saints will be teaching, preaching and administering the nations during the Millennium and beyond as examined in *Heaven - The Last Frontier*. Resurrected Christians will teach those on earth about their need for personal salvation. Throughout the Millennium billions of Gentiles and Jews, born to those who survived the Great Tribulation, will respond to the preaching of the Gospel by the resurrected saints. John was given a vision of the rewards for the martyred saints who paid the supreme price for their faith. "I saw thrones, and they sat on them, and judgment was committed to them ... And they lived and reigned with Christ for a thousand years" (Revelation 20:4).

SATAN'S LAST REBELLION

At the end of the thousand years the Lord will release the Devil to tempt the men and women born during the Millennium. John warned that many will be deceived and join in Satan's final rebellion. "Now when the thousand years have expired, Satan will be released from his prison and will go out to deceive the nations which are in the four corners of the earth, Gog and Magog, to gather them together to battle, whose number is as the sand of the sea" (Revelation 20:7,8). Incredibly, many citizens of the Millennium will join in this final rebellion against the Messiah. Despite the fact that Jesus will visibly rule from Jerusalem billions will rebel against God when Satan is released from the bottomless pit "for a season." Perhaps God will test the billions of souls born during the Millennium to prove that, even in a Paradise of peace and justice, without personal salvation and the grace of God, man, when tempted, will always choose sinful rebellion.

SATAN'S FINAL DESTINY

God will destroy Satan's armies with fire from heaven when they attack the "beloved city." This will be Satan's final battle. One thousand years after Armageddon, Satan will be cast into hell to join his two evil partners. "The devil, who deceived them, was cast into the lake of fire and brimstone where the beast and the false prophet are. And they will be tormented day and night forever and ever" (Revelation 20:10). Satan will never rise again to tempt men to sin against God. Evil will never again be a part of the universe. Hell was created for Satan and his fallen angels as Christ described, "the everlasting fire prepared for the devil and his angels" (Matthew 25:41). God never wanted a single human to go to an eternity in hell. However, if a person insists on rejecting God's mercy by insisting on being their own "god," they will have chosen hell as their eternal home.

WHO DO YOU SAY THAT I AM?

Jesus asked His disciples this vital question, "Who do you say that I am? Simon Peter answered and said, 'You are the Christ, the Son of the living God' " (Matthew 16:15,16). Our answer to that question will determine our eternal destiny. Ultimately, each of us must answer this question for ourselves. We cannot evade it. If we refuse to answer, we have already rejected Christ's claims as the Son of God. According to God's Word, the choices we make in this life have eternal consequences in the next.

If you have never responded to the call of God on your life, I urge you to carefully consider the consequences of your choice. After years of studying the precision of fulfilled prophecy I am convinced the Bible is the inspired Word of God. Therefore, when I read the words of Jesus Christ, I am forced to believe them. Jesus said, "I am the way, the truth, and the life. No one comes to the Father except through Me" (John 14:6). God declares that there is no other road to salvation than the "way, the truth and the life" of Jesus Christ. The prophecies speak of a spiritual battle for the souls of men. Whether or not you realize it, a battle is raging between Christ and Satan for your soul. The Devil tempts us to turn from God in our sinful pride and say, "I'll be the god of my life." Yet, in each of us, a still small voice calls us to turn from our sin and ask God for forgiveness. As long as we have life,

God encourages us to ask for forgiveness and be reconciled to Christ.

The Scriptures warn that we have all sinned against God. Every sinner is on a road that is taking him directly to an eternity without God. The Apostle Paul reminded us that "all have sinned and fall short of the glory of God" (Romans 3:23). Even if we could stop sinning today, which we can't, our previous sins and our rebellious nature would make it impossible for us to enter the presence of a holy God and His heaven. The only way we can ever be reconciled to God is by accepting the salvation that Christ purchased for us when He died in our place on the Cross. "For the wages of sin is death, but the gift of God is eternal life in Christ Jesus our Lord" (Romans 6:23). The invitation is still open. If you are tired of your sinful, purposeless life, Jesus Christ stands waiting to take the burden of sin from your life and leave it at the Cross where He paid the price of our forgiveness.

Jesus used the phrase "born again" to describe the total spiritual transformation in the soul of a person who accepts Him as their Savior. When a "religious" man named Nicodemus came to ask Jesus about salvation, "Jesus answered and said to him, 'Most assuredly, I say to you, unless one is born again, he cannot see the kingdom of God' " (John 3:3). It isn't simply a matter of intellectually accepting the facts about Christ and salvation. To be "born again" you must sincerely repent of your sinful life and ask Him to forgive you. You must wholeheartedly trust in Christ for the rest of your life. This commitment will transform you life forever. God will give you a new purpose and meaning to life. The Lord promises those who follow Him will receive eternal life in heaven: "this is the will of Him who sent Me, that everyone who sees the Son and believes in Him may have everlasting life; and I will raise him up at the last day" (John 6:40). The moment you commit your life to Christ, you will receive eternal life. Though our body may die, our spirit will live forever with Christ.

For those who have already accepted Christ, He calls us to be "witnesses" of His prophetic message to our world. The Scriptures declare that man's only hope lies in abandoning his sinful rebellion and returning to a loving relationship with God. Our role as a witness demands an active, not passive, involvement in the life of our brothers and sisters. It requires a willingness to pay the price of a personal commitment to Jesus. Our belief in the imminent coming of Christ should motivate each of us to a renewed love of the Lord and a willingness to witness to our brothers about His salvation. The hope of Christ's return will purify our daily walk as John said, "And everyone who has this hope in Him purifies himself, just as He is pure" (1 John 3:3).

FINAL CHOICES - FINAL DESTINY

The Bible warns that an eternity in hell awaits all who choose Satan over God. Some writers who reject the reality of hell have argued that those who reject Christ will be annihilated or, after serving their punishment in hell, will be allowed to enter heaven. However, the clear teaching of the Bible warns that the consequences of our earthly choices about faith in Christ will be eternal. The book of Revelation confirms that those who reject the salvation of Jesus Christ will spend eternity in the torments of hell. "He shall be tormented with fire and brimstone in the presence of the holy angels and in the presence of the Lamb. And the smoke of their torment ascends forever and ever" (Revelation 14:9–11). The clarity of the Bible's language allows no escape from the conclusion that hell will last forever.

Naturally, few people have spent much time considering the nature of life in hell. Even for religious people, the mind recoils from that grim reality. However, since our choice of an eternal destiny in heaven or hell is the most important decision we will ever make, it is worthwhile to consider what the Bible reveals about hell. The horror of hell will consist of an eternity without God, without love or beauty or hope. The Bible calls it the "lake of fire" referring to its physical torment and suffering. Those who go to hell will receive resurrection bodies that can feel pain but cannot die. "And I saw the dead, small and great, standing before God, and books were opened" (Revelation 20:12). In Mark 9:43 Christ warned that the body of sinners would never die: One of the worst horrors of hell will be the unrepentant sinners that will share that terrible experience. Most people have never considered who their companions will be in hell if they choose to reject God's mercy. Sinners sometimes joke that they will meet their friends in hell for a re-union. Those poor souls who have been sentenced to a penitentiary will tell you that unspeakable horrors were inflicted on new prisoners by the hardened criminals who had no hope of getting out. In hell every unrepentant killer, torturer, violent and hateful person in history will share that prison with those average people whose sinful pride prevented them from accepting God's salvation. There will be no guards, bars or laws to protect one prisoner from another. Those violent predators who enjoy tormenting others will have no reason to restrain their evil impulses. And it will never end.

Jesus Christ died on the Cross to save us from the horrors of hell. He gave His life to save those who will repent because He knows that hell is real and it will last forever. The Apostle Paul preached the Gospel despite imprisonment, torture and repeated stonings because he understood the horror of hell. "Knowing, therefore, the terror of the Lord, we persuade men" (2 Corinthians 5:11).

Many people picture Jesus only as "the gentle Savior." Jesus is a merciful Savior to all who repent and accept Him as their Lord. But Jesus is also the holy "King of Kings" who cannot allow sin and evil to enter heaven. The Scriptures promise that "As I live, says the Lord, every knee shall bow to Me, and every tongue shall confess to God" (Romans 14:11). It isn't a question of whether you or I will acknowledge Jesus Christ as God. The Scriptures declare that every one of us will someday acknowledge God's sovereignty. This is the question each of us must answer: Will we accept Christ's pardon today or will we reject His mercy in our rebellious attempt to be the 'god' of our own life? On the Day of Judgment even sinners will finally acknowledge Christ as Almighty God but it will be too late for them. Unrepentant sinners will be sentenced to hell because their sinful pride refused to accept God's mercy while it was available. For those who confessed they are sinners, asked for forgiveness and accepted Christ as their Savior, they received the promise of eternal life in heaven with their Lord.

Time is running out for our generation. A measure of time was set aside for mankind to turn from their sinful rebellion and return to God. After centuries of prophetic warning, our time is almost up. The world is rushing to its final judgment in the "valley of decision" at Armageddon. However, every one of us has a personal appointment with Christ in our own "valley of decision." In these last days the nations will choose to stand with Christ or Satan. You and I must choose as well. Who will you put your faith in? The final choice is yours.

Each day we receive letters from those who have seen loved ones come to know Jesus through reading our prophecy books. There is a natural curiosity in the heart of man about the future. That is why many people read horriscopes and New Age books. This growing fascination with prophecy is opening the door to the greatest opportunity to witness in our lifetime. I trust my books and tapes will prove worthwhile to your personal study and witnessing. In these last days we are called to live in a dynamic spiritual tension. On one hand we need to walk in purity and witness to others because Christ may return at any moment. Yet, we are also commanded to "occupy till He comes." Therefore we must plan and work as though we have a generation till our Lord returns. This is the spiritual balance that is required for Christians living in the last days.

Occupy Till I Come

On May 19, 1780 the sky across the United States was illuminated with meteor showers unlike those ever seen before. By 10:00 A.M. the next morning the sky became black as night and the moon turned blood red. In the State Legislature of Massachusetts panic set in among the distressed representatives. Some fearful members called for a motion to adjourn the hearings in the light of the possible return of the Lord. However, one of the wiser Christian legislators replied, "Gentlemen, bring candles. If it is not the Day of Judgment we should continue our deliberations. However, if it is the Day of Judgment we should be found at our post. Gentlemen . . . To business!"

After analyzing the prophecies relating to Satan's Prince of Darkness and the destiny of this generation we can rest in the knowledge that God is in full control. Despite the apparent anarchy of events in our world, everything is proceeding according to God's plan as detailed by His ancient prophets. The world is moving relentlessly toward its final crisis. The nations are rushing to surrender their sovereignty and freedom for a seat at the council table of the New World Order. While the darkest hour lies ahead for the nations, those who place their faith in Christ know this crisis will culminate in the return of Jesus the Messiah. The prophecies point to the rise of Satan's Prince of Darkness. This means the Rapture of the Church is even closer. The early Christians also lived in a time of great trial. They greeted each other with these inspiring words of hope, "MARANATHA" - "THE LORD RETURNETH!"

Selected Bibliography

Anderson, Robert. *The Coming Prince*. London: Hodder & Stroughton, 1894.

Auerbach, Leo. *The Babylonian Talmud*. New York: Philosophical Library, 1994.

Bradley, John. *World War 111 - Strategies, Tactics and Weapons*. New York: Crescent Books, 1982.

Bresler, Fenton. *Interpol*. Toronto: Penguin Books, 1992.

Bullinger, E.W. *The Apocalypse*. London: Eyre & Spottiswoode, 1909.

Calder, Nigel. *Unless Peach Comes*. Victoria: Penguin Books, 1968.

Elliott, E.E. *Horœ Apocalyptic*. London: Seeley, Burnside, & Seeley, 1846.

Fruchtenbaum, Arnold G. *The Footsteps of the Messiah*. Tustin: Ariel Press, 1982.

Gill, Stephen. *American Hegemony and the Trilateral Commission*. Cambridge: 1990.

Gorbachev, Mikhail. *Perestroika*. New York: Harper & Row, Publishers, 1987.

Hindson, Ed. *The New World Order*. Wheaton: Victor Books, 1991.

Josephus, Flavius. *Wars of the Jews*. Kingston: N.G. Ellis, 1844.

Kidron, Michael and Smith, Dan. *The War Atlas*. London: Pan Books Ltd., 1983.

LaHaye, Tim. *No Fear Of The Storm*. Sisters: Multnomah Press Books, 1992.

Larkin, Clarence. *The Book of Daniel*. Philadelphia: Clarence Larkin, 1929.

Lowth, William. *A Commentary Upon the Prophet Ezekiel*. London: W. Mears, 1773.

McAlvany, Donald, S. *Toward A New World Order*. Oklahoma City: Hearthstone Publishing, 1990.

Malachi, Martin. *The Keys of This Blood*. New York: Simon and Schuster, 1990.

Mesorah Publications. *Daniel*. Brooklyn: Mesorah Publications, Ltd., 1980.

Newton, Bishop Thomas. *Dissertations on the Prophecies*. London: Gilbert, 1817.

Pacepa, Ion. *Red Horizons*. Washington: Regnery Gateway, 1987.

Pentecost, Dwight. *Things to Come*. Grand Rapids: Dunham, 1958.

Peters, George. *The Theocratic Kingdom*. Grand Rapids: Kregel Publications, 1957.

Schell, Johnathan. *The Fate Of The Earth*. New York: Avon Books, 1982.

Seiss, Joseph. *The Apocalypse*. Philadelphia: Approved Books, 1865.

Sklar, Holly. *Trilateralism*. Montreal: Black Rose Books, 1980.

Suborov, Victor. *Inside The Soviet Army*. London: Granada Publishing Ltd., 1984.

The Ante-Nicene Fathers. 10 Volumes. Grand Rapids: Eerdmans Publishing Co., 1986.

Tinbergen, Jan. *Reshaping The International Order - A Report To The Club Of Rome*. Scarborough: The New American Library Of Canada, 1976.

About the Author

Grant Jeffrey is internationally recognized as an outstanding prophecy teacher. Over a million readers enjoyed his four bestselling prophecy books inspiring them to look for the soon return of Christ.

Speaking Engagements
or
Teaching Seminars

Grant R. Jeffrey is available for seminars and speaking engagements throughout the year for churches, conferences and colleges.

Please Contact:
**Grant Jeffrey Ministries
Box 129, Station "U"
Toronto, Ontario, M8Z 5M4
Canada**

Discover how the prophecies of the Bible are coming true in our lifetime . . .

GRANT R. JEFFREY *details his extraordinary discoveries*

ARMAGEDDON: APPOINTMENT WITH DESTINY

___28537-8 $5.50/$6.99 in Canada • The recovery of the long-lost ark of the covenant • The arrival of the Antichrist and the Second Coming of Jesus Christ • The climactic Battle of Armageddon

HEAVEN: THE LAST FRONTIER

___29286-2 $5.50/$6.99 in Canada • What your resurrected body will look like • The new Heaven and Earth God will create after the New Millennium • Revelations on the Ezekiel Tablets

MESSIAH: WAR IN THE MIDDLE EAST AND THE ROAD TO ARMAGEDDON

___29958-1 $5.99/$7.99 in Canada • Astonishing biblical evidence reveals the rapid approach of world upheaval and the Second Coming of the Messiah . . .

APOCALYPSE: THE COMING JUDGMENT OF THE NATIONS

___56530-3 $5.99/$7.99 in Canada • The violent breakup of the Soviet Union • A false peace in the Middle East • The threat of worldwide famine, plague, civil war, and nuclear terrorism